La Cosecha

La Cosecha

Harvesting Contemporary United States Hispanic Theology (1972–1998)

Eduardo C. Fernández, S.J.

Foreword by
Ada María Isasi-Díaz

A Michael Glazier Book
THE LITURGICAL PRESS
Collegeville, Minnesota

A Michael Glazier Book published by The Liturgical Press.

Cover design by David Manahan, O.S.B. Illustration: "Año del Barrio" by Magda García and Alex Rodríguez.

1   2   3   4   5   6   7   8   9

Library of Congress Cataloging-in-Publication Data

Fernández, Eduardo C.
  La cosecha : harvesting contemporary United States Hispanic theology (1972–1998) / Eduardo C. Fernández ; foreword by Ada María Isasi-Díaz.
     p.   cm.
  Includes bibliographical references and index.
  ISBN 0-8146-5896-2 (alk. paper)
  1. Hispanic American theology—History—20th century. I. Title: Cosecha. II. Title.

BT83.575 .F47 2000
230'.089'68073—dc21

                                        99-059256

A mi querida familia, con todo cariño y agradecimiento

Contents

Foreword

At the beginning of the twenty-first century one can look back and see a bountiful harvest that has been planted throughout the ages by grassroots Christians whose religious beliefs sustain their daily struggle to survive and to make justice flourish. They are admirably capable of explaining their own beliefs and religious practices, and committed academic theologians have found in the religious understandings of the people a rich source for our theological work and a blessing for our lives. Hispanic/Latino theology and theologians witness to this.

This century also starts with the assertive clamor of those who have been marginalized and impoverished, a cry that insists, "This time we shall not be erased from history." The people's movements of the 1960s raised this cry, which made explicit the violence and oppression of governments, economic structures, and societal institutions and organizations. Latinas and Latinos, most of us economically poor and all of us socially and politically marginalized, have inherited this legacy of struggle, and our cry echoes that of our ancestors as we insist on the validity and value of our perception of reality. Hispanic/Latino theology makes explicit our relationship with the divine and insists on our own way of doing theology, which is committed to voicing the religious understandings and practices of our people, practices that are at the service of liberation struggles.

Hispanic/Latino theologians continue to maintain that during the last two decades we have firmly established our theological enterprise, an accomplishment that Eduardo Fernández masterfully examines in this book. Yet the fact is that so-called mainline theologians and the churches seem to pay little attention to us. Often we feel as if we are talking to ourselves, and it is only when we see how important our work is for our own people that we realize its value. Hispanic/Latino theology's accomplishment in the academic and church worlds may be limited, but we believe it certainly has contributed to the creation of a matrix of resistance and solidarity and a liberating vision.

Fernández shows in this book that Hispanic/Latino theology is not a monolithic enterprise but one rich with different perspectives, all of them rooted in the lives and struggles of our people. Fernández indicates, even when it may be thought to undermine his work, that we resist all attempts to be classified as this or that kind of theology. In our dialogue with him those of us whose work he examines have insisted on the fact that our work does not fit into any one model, and we are most grateful to him for his respect of our self-understanding. Our theological enterprise is as *mestizo/mulato* as we are, as hybrid as our culture, our language, our daily living.

Eduardo Fernández' work in this book is highly valuable, for it shows the many theological strands Hispanic/Latino theologians have inherited and use. His careful analysis of our work shows that Hispanic/Latino theology is firmly entrenched in our *mestizo/mulato* culture, which has taught us not to claim any kind of uniqueness but rather adamantly to insist on our own specificity. Of course Hispanic/Latino theology is a contextual theology. But so are *all* other theologies, traditional theologies as well as contemporary theologies, official Church theologies as well as liberation theologies! His work is also valuable because it is a valid comparative effort that gives us, Hispanic/Latino theologians, much to consider about one another's work.

Fernández's book remains important to the last pages, where he takes a valuable look into the future. His list of what Hispanic/Latino theology needs to do in the immediate future is most constructive. I believe that Eduardo Fernández and other Hispanic/Latino theologians "younger" than those of us whose work he examines in this book have to take the initiative in some of these areas. They have to heed Fernández's call for the need to include our youth and their cultures in our theological enterprise.

Two other areas of Fernández's wish list seem important to me. One has to do with the criticism that Hispanic/Latino theology lacks theoretical depth. I look at this point in a different way. I think Hispanic/Latino theology has been on the cutting edge of the work being done to reformulate the meaning of theoretical work. We have insisted that theoretical work is not the exclusive prerogative of academicians and that grass-roots people are also intellectuals. We have insisted on the importance and usefulness of *lo cotidiano* (the everyday) and the lived experience of our people for relating different aspects of life and understandings. We believe these categories are as useful as (or perhaps more important and useful than) speculative knowledge when it comes to accomplishing the main task of theory. Hispanic/Latino theology's insistence on the importance of our people's lived experience and *lo cotidiano* is not indicative of any lack of theoretical depth but rather contributes to the reformulation of what constitutes a theory. This insistence is central to an epistemology of accountability: one knows reality if one accepts responsibility for it and for changing it in order to create societies where no one is excluded.

Finally, Fernández points out the need to pay attention to Hispanic women. Some of us have done theology from the perspective of Latinas. However, only a few of our male colleagues have taken our work seriously. Only a few of them understand that their work is from a Hispanic/Latino male perspective. Because they have not paid sufficient attention to Hispanic women, when they talk about Hispanic/Latinos, they are in reality referring mainly to Hispanic/Latino men. Latinas are more than 50 percent of Hispanics in the U.S.A., and we are often more than 75 percent of churchgoers. As the main transmitters and sustainers of religious practices and understandings, Hispanic women play the major role in religion in our culture. *Mujerista* theology and other theological work done by Latinas is not a sideline. They have to be embraced as an intrinsic part of Hispanic/Latino theology. We agree with Fernández that cultural *machismo* has to be addressed head-on by our theological work, and we believe that until our male colleagues do this they will not be able to understand the importance of theological work done from Hispanic women's perspective.

I thank Eduardo Fernández for his work. I thank him for his willingness to listen to those of us whose work he analyzes. I thank him for his willingness to point out areas in which we have fallen short and areas that need immediate attention. I think theologians, students, and Christian believers at large will profit enormously from carefully reading this book and entering into the spirit in which it was written.

ADA MARÍA ISASI-DÍAZ

Preface

Having grown up in El Paso, Texas, a city only minutes away from Mexico, I experienced great cultural diversity early on in life. Among the great gifts of such an environment is the realization that there is always more than one way of speaking, thinking, or acting. What was appropriate in one context could very well be quite inappropriate in another. Of my four grandparents, three were born in Mexico. All died in the United States. My parents grew up in a very bicultural world. Those of us who now make up the second and third generations of Hispanics in the United States are confronted with two very different socioeconomic realities and histories. How to reconcile the two?

My family taught me to embrace both aspects of my person. Both Spanish and English were spoken in our home. My Father played Mexican songs on the guitar, and my Mother passed on the folk wisdom she had received from her parents, a couple whose love had overcome national barriers. My ten sisters and brothers provided ample opportunities for learning to live in *comunidad!* In school we were graced with the presence of teachers, many of them women religious who served under the name of Sisters of Charity of the Incarnate Word. They came from Mexico, Ireland, and the United States. I was taught by Sr. Mildred Warminski and Sr. Josetta Eveler, both masterful educators. I owe my high school education to the Christian Brothers, especially to Bro. Amedy Long, and to their lay collaborators, particularly Harry Kelleher. Our parish was staffed by Jesuits of the Mexican Povince. The Mexican American pastor, Rev. P. J. Martínez, as well as the Mexican parochial school principal, Sr. Ana Luisa Luna, did much to foment a cultural pride in us. Indeed, they assured us that we were blessed for being born into such cultural diversification.

The years have convinced me that they were right. Further studies and travel, especially in the Jesuit Order, broadened my horizons immensely. At Loyola University in New Orleans I encountered professors, especially Joseph H. Fichter, S.J., Clement J. McNaspy, S.J., Jerry and Sally Seaman, Edward Arroyo, S.J., and Lydia Voight, who challenged me to embrace my heritage and work for a greater appreciation of cultural pluralism. The people I encountered in Puerto Rico, Peru, Mexico, California, and Rome taught me a great deal about how cultural diversity can be a great gift and therefore a unique context for doing theology.

In recent years I have had the opportunity of meeting most of the Latino theologians I am writing about. In the case of those who previewed my writing, I was happy to see that they agreed with my description of their work. I am grateful for the care with which they previewed my manuscript as well as their constant encouragement to publish my findings. While some were not in favor of my using Stephen Bevans' models for contextualizing their theological method, all have been extremely supportive and helpful.[1] I feel that I have been invited into a conversation that will yield great fruit. If I can give the reader a sense of the substance and direction of this engaging colloquy, my efforts will not have been wasted.

This work has been quite an exercise in *teología de conjunto.* I am indebted to Allan Figueroa Deck and Arij Roest Crollius, my Jesuit mentors in California and Rome. They convinced me that to do good theology you have to be open to the Spirit's many manifestations, especially those experienced through God's holy people. Among my many other interlocutors are Stephen Bevans, S.V.D., who patiently helped me to understand his models, David Hayes-Bautista, whose sociological expertise proved to be a valuable resource, and James Nickoloff, who read the entire manuscript twice and provided many discriminating suggestions. My students and colleagues at Berkeley, the Mexican American Cultural Center, Oblate School of Theology, and El Paso enhanced my thought in more ways than they will ever know. Virgilio Elizondo kept encouraging me to publish, while David Batstone, Timothy Matovina, and Roberto Goizueta, Jr., guided me through its intricacies. Javier Reyes and Michael Pastizzo, S.J., generously provided literary and technical assistance. Catholic campus ministry at the University of Texas at El Paso, under the direction of Sister Ann Francis

---

1. Expressed was a desire to see comparisons made among different writings of U.S. Hispanic theologians, thus preserving the genuineness of their contribution, not a forced categorization into models developed by a non-Hispanic. My reasons for choosing Bevans' models are that he engages many theologians outside the U.S. milieu, such as Asian and Latino writers, and that my venture by its very nature is intercultural. That is, several cultural strands are in dialogue here. Moreover, such an important contribution to contextual theology cannot afford to remain apart from wider theological discourse. That is why I have chosen to interface these various Hispanic and non-Hispanic theologians.

Monedero, O.S.F., could not have done more to support me spiritually. The prayers and kind words of the people of the Diocese of El Paso, especially the parishioners of Sagrado Corazón, were never distant. Without the prayers and emotional support of such persons as the pastor, Rafael García, S.J., Mary Trujillo, Bertha Belmontes, Sylvia Sanchez, Arturo Perez, Lionel Baeza, Kim Mallet, Rosa Guerrero (whose inspirational dance opens Chapter 2), and Ponchie Vasquez, O.F.M., I would never have been able to complete this massive project. Similarly, my Jesuit brothers never failed to encourage my research and facilitate the means. My gratitude also goes to Pew Charitable Trusts, whose support of the Hispanic Theological Initiative is already bearing much fruit and to whom I am indebted for the postdoctoral grant that helped me finish this book. I thank Justo González and Daisy Machado, the pioneering directors of this initiative, who taught me a great deal about how you work toward a richer ecumenism. My indebtedness extends to Ada María Isasi-Díaz who wrote the foreword, someone who honors me with her willingness to dialogue. On more than one occasion she challenged me to think beyond my categories. I also wish to thank Magda García and Alex Rodríguez whose striking artwork graces the cover as well as Elizabeth Montgomery who patiently edited my work. Thanks are in order, similarly, to Anthony Vinciguerra, my research assistant, who meticulously produced the index.

Finally, my gratitude to *Diosito,* a God who has always been faithful. Whether in terms of giving me a father whose love now extends beyond this life, a simple man who taught me that *Dios es muy grande,* to giving me a mother whose patience surpasses that of Job, this God has never been outdone in generosity. *Bendito sea su santo nombre!*

Introduction

Most people do not suspect that the United States ranks fifth among the world's Spanish-speaking countries. Only Mexico, Spain, Argentina, and Colombia have more Spanish speakers. According to the March 1997 population survey of the U.S. Census Bureau, the number of Hispanics in the United States had reached 29.7 million people, 11.1 percent of the total population.[1] Observers have noted, however, that this figure does not include many undocumented workers and their families. The majority of these Hispanics are Catholic. Their presence, today and throughout history, has caught the attention of both the U.S. Church and the rest of the country. In their pastoral letter entitled *The Hispanic Presence: Challenge and Commitment*, which they issued in 1983, the U.S. bishops noted:

> No other European culture has been in this country longer than the Hispanic. Spaniards and their descendants were already in the Southeast and the Southwest by the late sixteenth century. In other regions of our country a steady influx of Hispanic immigrants has increased their visibility in more recent times. Plainly the Hispanic population will loom larger in the future of both the wider society and the Church in the United States.[2]

Despite the fact that this presence goes back to a time even before the founding of the United States, it is only recently, during the last thirty years or so, that these Hispanic voices have started to be heard in the area of academic theology. These pioneers, who have begun to write

1. U.S. Department of Commerce, "The Hispanic Population in the United States: March 1997 (Update)." See www.census.gov.
2. National Conference of Catholic Bishops, *Hispanic Presence* (1984) section 1, paragraph 6.

theology from a Hispanic perspective, are paving the way for the generations who will follow them.

The Object of Study

This work is a descriptive and analytic study of the writings of particular Hispanic theologians as seen within the general trend in the Church toward more contextual theologies. A major theme in this work is that these authors are coming from and directing their concerns toward the present reality of Hispanics in the United States. Given the contextualization of their theology, they represent a distinctive current within a pluralistic Church.

Latino? Hispanic? What's Behind a Name?

Much ink has been spilt over the appropriate word to use for referring to this community, or, more correctly stated, the various communities who trace at least part of their culture back to the Iberian peninsula. The U.S. Census Bureau, in allowing individuals to determine whether they are "Hispanic" or not, uses this category to lump together a wide range of persons irrespective of vast differences. For example, people often refer to a recently arrived person from a Latin American country, or Spain for that matter, in the same way they would a person with a Spanish surname who was born in the United States and whose ancestors lived centuries ago in what is now U.S. territory but at the time was part of Spain or Mexico. On the other hand, Hispanics tend to refer to themselves in terms of their national roots, for example, as being "Cuban" or "Mexican." Another common self-designation is that of the "hyphenated American," for example, "Cuban-American" or "Mexican-American."

Aside from the ambiguity of the term "Hispanic," another problem with the term is that some members of that supposed group do not accept this designation. Some see it as just another label that a dominant group has given a dominated one.[3] For that reason some prefer to use the term "Latino," which is becoming, at least politically, more accept-

---

3. In a talk at a Jesuit-sponsored conference on the Hispanic presence in the South held in Mobile, Alabama, in June 1992, Rosendo Urrabazo, C.M.F., then president of the Mexican American Cultural Center in San Antonio, made an interesting comment on the use of racial and ethnic minority categories by the U.S. Census Bureau. His point was that by lumping together the Hispanic communities under one title as has been done with Black and Asian groups, the government, in giving aid to a particular segment of that large category, gives the appearance that help has been given to all members of that disparate group.

able. Another reason is that for some, "Latino," because it points to Latin America, a mixture of races, seems more inclusive of people of African, Portuguese, and Native American origin.[4] Allan Figueroa Deck, who has been writing about Hispanics for over two decades, has this to say about the distinction between the terms "Hispanic" and "Latino":

> There is no consensus among persons of Latin American origin in the United States regarding the most appropriate umbrella term. Church and government agencies have tended to use "Hispanic." In the western United States university, professional, and political leaders have preferred the term "Latino." The simple truth is that no single term is adequate.[5]

Deck uses the terms interchangeably. Fernando Segovia, in referring to a new group of U.S. Hispanic theologians, describes that group as "those persons of Hispanic descent, associated in one way or another with the Americas, who now live, for whatever reason, permanently in the United States."[6] The important thing to keep in mind at this point is the great religious, ethnic, and socioeconomic diversity that characterizes such peoples. Hispanics range from Catholic to non-Catholic and from the recently arrived to those well assimilated into the U.S. mainstream. Generalizations are helpful at times but also can be deceiving. My own resolution, feeling the need to move beyond what we choose to name ourselves, is to use the terms "Latino" and "Hispanic" interchangeably.[7]

Methodology

My way of proceeding is to engage a dialogue between theology and the social sciences, drawing on such fields as history, anthropology, economics, and sociology. In this way both contexts, that of Hispanics in the United States and some theological trends in the universal Church, assume a formative and integrative role. Despite its own perceptual biases, history affords *a* context for understanding the past. Sociology

---

4. María Pilar Aquino, in discussing Hispanic women, prefers the term "Latina," which she views as being more inclusive, especially in terms of the Black and indigenous women in the Latin American continent or the Caribbean. See "Challenge of Hispanic Women" (1992) 262.

5. Deck, *Frontiers* (1992) xxv, n. 1.

6. Segovia, "New Manifest Destiny" (1991) 102.

7. I have strived to use gender-inclusive language. I did not feel it fair, however, to insert *sic* where the writers did not. Language evolves, and those omissions represent an era that is hopefully coming to an end in correct English grammar usage.

and anthropology provide a contextual understanding of the present. The advantage of history is hindsight, which provides a type of social analysis.

The first step will be to situate the Hispanic in the ambiance of U.S. culture and Church. This is the aim of chapter 1. This is the most historical and sociological of the chapters. Its purpose is to provide a general background against which to view the writings of emerging Hispanic theologians in the United States. Chapter 2 provides a brief overview of U.S. Latino theology, rendering highlights of what has been written over the last twenty-five years by a group of fourteen authors. I chose these authors, all of whom are professional theologians, on the basis of the amount of material published relating to this area. An important assumption is that U.S. Hispanics can now generally be described as being both Protestant and Catholic. The increasing number of Latino Protestants warrants the incorporation of the works of several Protestant theologians in this chapter. The main themes that emerge from their work are mentioned, along with a bit of each one's background. Finally, some general trends in their work are noted.

To provide some type of overall perspective, the work shifts in chapter 3 from a brief overview of the writings of these Latino theologians to a description of the general trend toward contextualization in the Church today. Drawing from the thought of current missiologists along with that of systematic theologians, this chapter provides an analytical apparatus, presenting some current models of theological reflection that might prove suitable for an analysis of Hispanic theology.

Chapter 4 brings together chapters 2 and 3 by taking the various categories presented in the discussion of models and applying them to eight Hispanic theologians. In this manner, especially through the use of a common frame of reference, that is, the models formulated by Stephen Bevans, the contribution to contextual theology and the distinctiveness of each author can then be more readily assessed. Finally, chapter 5 summarizes the results of these comparisons and makes some overall observations in light of the future.

This study is not without its limitations. The study of fourteen Latino theologians over the course of thirty years seems like a mammoth task to undertake. Similarly, the specialization characteristic of the field of theology today seems to warrant a much more specific focus. The fact is, however, that the bulk of this writing has come in the last few years, and as the title of the present work suggests, this book introduces the reader to this plentiful harvest.

Another limitation that should be acknowledged is that only "professional" theologians are featured. If, in fact, theology is often born at the grass-roots level of the People of God, then much of it has not yet made it to the level of published works characteristic "of the academy." For example, there is a considerable amount of material on catechetics or, more recently, on how to adapt various aspects of parochial life to a growing body of Hispanic parishioners. Within this genre are the various incorporations of Latin customs, such as those of popular religiosity, within the parish's liturgical life. Various religious groups have also begun to direct their publications to, and have begun to feature, members of the Hispanic population. The American Missionary Society, Maryknoll, for example, publishes a Spanish version of *Maryknoll* magazine. Who knows how much "pamphlet theology" is waiting to be systematized!

On the other hand, the writings featured in this work often demonstrate that these theologians, far from being ivory-tower intellectuals, are actively engaged in pastoral ministry. Most are immigrant Hispanics in the United States who therefore are still quite close, by chance or design, to Latin American culture. Most in fact, see this living heritage and pastoral immersion as a constitutive element of their theologizing.

The value of the project at hand is that it provides a general framework or bird's-eye view of the type of contextual theology now being called "U.S. Hispanic or Latino theology."[8] Such a panoramic view makes possible the tracking of general trends and movements within this emergent theology. A discussion of the similarities and differences found in the writings of various authors provides a more accurate description of what this theology is saying and what shape it is taking. What follows is a detailed description of where this theological movement comes from and where it seems to be going. Its role within the larger picture of the theological scene, finally, reveals a contribution far beyond what some had termed an "advocacy theology."

8. As I will demonstrate in the latter part of this book, some of these Hispanic theologians did not agree with my calling their work "contextual theology," thus demonstrating a preference for their own terminology for their work.

1

Hispanics in American Culture and Church

Much of the theology written today is in dialogue with the social sciences. This is especially true of U.S. Hispanic theology. Following the Second Vatican Council's exhortation that we "read the signs of the times," the scope of this chapter is to provide a background, or type of social analysis, for understanding the emergence of U.S. Hispanic theology. An important component of this study is a brief overview of the history of Hispanics in the United States. Because this history spans several centuries, our overview begins with some salient points about the early Spanish period.

It is important to keep in mind, however, that many, if not the majority, of U.S. Hispanics are relatively recent immigrants or the children of immigrants. This fact points to the great diversity found among the Latino communities, as their countries of origin are multiple. At the same time, this recent connection to Latin America helps explain the common fabric of many aspects of U.S. Latino culture. Given this shared source of culture, especially from a religious standpoint, might it be possible to examine U.S. Hispanics as a theological entity? That is, do they share a common theological history that puts them in a position to contribute significantly to the present theological enterprise? The fourteen Latino theologians I have studied certainly think so. For the time being, this chapter uses history and economics to paint a contextual background for understanding their work. Later chapters are more explicitly theological.

As a type of preface, the initial sections offer a somewhat revisionist view of the colonial period. This more inclusive approach to history studies not only the chronology of individuals in authority but also the role that philosophical, religious, geographical, economic, and cultural factors played communally in the initial conquest and evangelization of the Americas.

In the latter part of the chapter the focus is a contemporary one. A current profile of Hispanics in the United States serves as a frame of reference for evaluating the writings of emerging Hispanic theologians. Despite the persistence of much poverty, numerous social scientists are pointing to various quality-of-life indicators, which testify that there is another factor operating here. In other words, given such dismal living conditions, one would not expect to find the resilience and stability that many of these communities are now exhibiting. What might this element be? Dr. David Hayes-Bautista, one of the leaders of this movement which is calling for a paradigm shift away from viewing Latinos solely in terms of the urban underclass model, answers emphatically, "It is their spirituality!" He maintains, in fact, that both the institutional and popular Church have provided a basis for the social construction of meaningful action.[1]

This time the context is no longer that of the first evangelization of the Americas but rather that of what some have called the second or, in the words of Pope John Paul II, the "new evangelization." Various perspectives, among them the sociological, economic, and political, are discussed as they relate to the formulation of a new theology that claims to be characterized by a praxis approach.

Some Historical Considerations

The "Discovery" Debate

One of the most controverted celebrations of the century was that held around the commemoration of the arrival of Europeans in the Americas. What before had been called the "discovery" of America by Christopher Columbus was reinterpreted by some to be more appropriately viewed as the "encounter" of two very different worlds: the Native American and the European. Among those critical of the celebration was a sector who demanded instead a very particular type of commemoration: a mourning for the historical massacre of so many indigenous peoples and cultures along with a call for the revindication of their rights today.

As the debate stirred across the Americas and across the Atlantic, politicians, theologians, and other academicians took the opportunity to wax eloquently on what was often seen as either the greatest bless-

1. Interview with Dr. David Hayes-Bautista, December 22, 1995, Rome.

ing of the last five hundred years, the "arrival of the Faith to the Americas," or the greatest curse since the fall of humankind in the Garden of Eden.

There were those who sought to integrate both aspects of this reality: the arrival of the gospel to the Americas and the sin that accompanied its proclamation. Leonardo Boff and Virgil Elizondo wrote an introduction to a collection of reflections by fourteen theologians, among them such well-known writers as Gustavo Gutiérrez, Hans Kung, and Johann Baptist Metz, with the following words:

> 12 October 1492 was the beginning of a long and bloody Good Friday for Latin America and the Caribbean. It is still Good Friday, and there is no sign of Easter Day. The dominant accounts were written from the ships which came to conquer and not by the victims waiting on the shore who suffered the effects of the domination. The victims cry out, and their suffering challenges us.[2]

The two theologians see the challenge posed not only by the atrocities of the past but also those of the present.

> The invasion represented the biggest genocide in human history. . . . The survivors are crucified peoples, enduring worse abuses than the Jews in Egypt and Babylon and the Christians under the Roman emperors, as was said many times by bishops who defended the Indians. Today this process continues in the two-thirds who suffer hunger, the submerging of our cities by shanty-towns, ecological aggression, in which the poor and the indigenous peoples are those most threatened with extermination; in the foreign debt, which represents the new tribute which countries kept in underdevelopment have to pay to their old and new masters.[3]

The arrival of the Spanish and the Portuguese on American soil brought about the birth of a new people, the Latin Americans. Spanish settlements were soon established in the Caribbean, and explorers were sent out to the neighboring islands and the mainland, which is now the United States, Mexico, Central America, and the South American continent. It was not long after that Portugal established itself primarily in what today is Brazil.

To give us an idea of the number and characteristics of aboriginal inhabitants in what was to become the United States, we turn to Jay

2. Elizondo and Boff, eds., *Voice of the Victims* (1990) vii.
3. Ibid. For a very different interpretation of the first evangelization, see Saranyana, *El Quinto Centenario.*

Dolan. What is particularly accented is the diversity of Native American peoples.

> Recent estimates place the number of Indians living in what is now the contiguous United States in 1492 at about 850,000, and they spoke at least two hundred languages. East of the Mississippi, native Americans lived in settled villages of substantial homes; they subsisted off the land, and their ceremonial life centered around the harvesting of corn. Farther west, the Plains Indians centered their life around the buffalo; they moved from place to place, setting up their tepees wherever they could find the buffalo. In the Southwest, the Indians lived in villages of multi-storied houses—pueblos, the Spanish called them—raised crops, wove cotton, and excelled in pottery.[4]

The significance of this monumental clash between the Native American and Spanish worlds is still being explored, as historians, theologians, and anthropologists strive to understand what happened and how this event is still relevant today. Areas of research, such as the types of indigenous cultures found and how they were subsequently modified by the Europeans, reveal much about why religion took the form it did in Latin America. Why, for example, did the missionary leadership not establish an indigenous clergy? How was the initial evangelization carried out in view of indigenous religious beliefs and cosmogonies? What were the biggest obstacles to a conversion to Christianity?

Since we no longer accept the *tabula rasa* belief that the minds of indigenous peoples could simply be reprogrammed in light of "Christian culture," it is important to explore the context.

An Appeal for a More Inclusive History

In the past historians have tended to focus on political and military factors that helped to shape the course of events. Until recently, for example, much of the writing focused on the armed conquest of these indigenous peoples. As previously stated, the story had most often been told from the perspective of the conquerors.[5] In a sense this is under-

4. Dolan, *American Catholic Experience* (1985) 22.

5. Essential sources for viewing the conquest and colonialization from another perspective have come out in recent years. Among them are J. L. Guerrero, *Flor y canto del nacimiento de México* (1990); Goodpasture, *Cross and Sword;* and the most famous, Leon-Portilla, *Broken Spears.* One of the most important aspects of their writing is that they make great use of firsthand reports, which were often written by "insignificant people." For an overview of the development of Latin American

standable because of the massive amount of documentation available due to the precise record-keeping methods employed by colonial Spain.[6]

With the dawning of social history and its increasing popularity in this century, however, other aspects of the historical reality of this encounter have begun to be explored; for example, more importance is given to the situation of the conquered, as well as to the emergent *mestizo*. Social science disciplines, such as sociology, anthropology, ethnohistory, and geography, have contributed a great deal to our more modern view of the confrontation between two very different worlds.[7] Among many other places in the Americas, the Spanish settled in what is now the United States. This is the overarching topic of David J. Weber's many scholarly works. He details the variety of topics examined by contemporary historians:

> The range and quality of current work on Spanish colonial North America is impressive. Between 1980 and 1986 American scholars have produced an astonishing number of studies of such traditional themes as exploration, administration and politics, economics and trade, ranching, Spanish-Indian relations, the church and the missions, military history and the presidio, international rivalry, historiography, and biography. Work published in the 1980s has also illuminated such relatively neglected areas as science, disease and medicine, material culture, architecture, cultural diffusion, the ownership of land and water, ecology, women, blacks, society, labor, demography, and urban areas. In listing these overlapping categories, I do not intend to provide an inventory of all writings on the Spanish borderlands in the 1980s, but I do wish to suggest the considerable variety of topics that has appeared in published works.[8]

---

culture, a captivating blend of Indian, Black, and European elements, see Fuentes' recent work, *Buried Mirror*. For a Peruvian perspective see Griffiths, *Cross and the Serpent*.

6. One of the foremost modern-day historians on colonial Mexico and Latin America, Richard E. Greenleaf, has made extensive use of such documentation. See *Mexican Inquisition* (1969) and the work he edited, *Church in Colonial Latin America* (1977).

7. Robert Ricard has written an exceptional treatment of the role religion played in early colonial Mexico. His classic, *Spiritual Conquest of Mexico* (1988), was first published in French in 1933. He covers the period before the arrival of the Jesuits. See Burgaleta, *José de Acosta, S.J.*, (1999) for an awe-inspiring account of de Acosta, a sixteenth-century "proto-evolutionist and sacred orator, a theologian and playwright, a missionary to Amerindians on the shores of Lake Titicaca in Peru, an economist, jurist, administrator, and a diplomat at the court of Philip II."

8. Weber, *Myth and the History*, 80.

Weber shows how these "Spanish Borderlands," as they have often been referred to by historians, provided a setting for the interaction of two very different worlds and how the more anthropological perspective of such trailblazers as Frederick W. Turner[9] are yielding much fruit for understanding this meeting of two worlds. Indeed, the frontier represented a new human encounter as well as a geographical one for the invader.

> Meanwhile, new and more satisfying explanations about frontier interactions have arisen on the foundation that Turner built, and historians have turned increasingly to them. The work of scholars such as geographer Marvin Mikesell, anthropologist Owen Lattimore, and ethnohistorian Jack Forbes have proved especially useful, for they remind us that a frontier represents a human as well as a geographical environment. We no longer think of the frontier as a line between "civilization and savagery" but as an interaction between two different cultures. The natures of these interactive cultures—both the culture of the invader and that of the invaded—combine with the physical environment to produce a dynamic that is unique to time and place.[10]

Besides expanding the scope of history, that is, by moving from a more military and political scheme to a more encompassing social one, current historical revisions are giving greater importance to the role of the masses in the making of history. Writing in the context of religious medieval history, the late Christopher Dawson, one of the century's great historians, had this to say about this more inclusive approach to historical analysis:

> [I]n the study of medieval culture it is necessary to remember that the higher levels of intellectual culture and political thought, on which the historian's attention always tends to be concentrated, form a very small part of the total picture, and that the creative activity of religion is more powerful where it is least recorded and most difficult to observe—in the minds of the masses and in the traditions of the common people. And thus in the fourteenth and fifteenth centuries, when the scholars were intent on the revival of learning and the statesmen were transforming the order of Christendom into a new state system, the mind of the common people is still immersed in the religious atmosphere of the past.[11]

---

9. Turner, *Beyond Geography.*
10. Weber, *Myth and the History*, 53.
11. Dawson, *Rise of Western Culture*, 219.

In some ways Dawson was most prophetic, for one of the major issues in pastoral theology today is popular culture and religiosity. A historical understanding of these phenomena cannot help but illuminate our approach to what is often simply dismissed as "the religion of the masses."

The Context of the First Evangelization

Archbishop Patricio Flores, having demonstrated why the initial evangelization of the Mexican Indian people was so traumatic, points out nevertheless what gave these people hope:

> The Indigenous people were deeply rooted in their tradition, their customs; they had a great love for their temple, for their dances, for their many practices; and the Spaniards came trying to bring about a conversion not only to European Spanish State, but to the Western culture. This was painful, very painful, for the Indian, since he was forced to learn a new language and to accept a new life style; yet, in the midst of all this, Our Lady of Guadalupe was there with these suffering people.[12]

Flores is well aware that the evangelization of the native Mexicans did not take place in a religious vacuum. Once again, it is a question of trying to understand the context of evangelization, whether it be religious, philosophical, or geographical. A focus on the history of the southwestern United States (called the "Spanish Borderlands" by some), the territory that has traditionally been the most Hispanic, reveals much about the religious and philosophical system that characterized the Spanish worldview of the colonial period.

In writing about the predominant philosophy and religion of the Spanish Borderlands we must be cautious against presuming that the mentality, or worldview, of the Spanish automatically became the only one at play. Such a simplistic approach ignores the complexity of human situations. Many historians, hastily describing Spanish rule, have used the term "Spanish absolutism" to speak about Spain's political, economic, and even religious ways of proceeding.[13] There is no doubt that Spain exerted a great deal of control over most aspects of colonial life. Under the *patronato real*, the Church became in large part another branch of the government. Church positions could not be filled without royal approval.

---

12. As quoted in Elizondo, *La Morenita* (1980) iii.
13. See Treutlein, "Non-Spanish Jesuits," 219–42.

Greed, which often blinds people's souls, was not the conquistadors' only motive, however. They were driven by the belief that they were crusaders on a divine mission: to win over new lands and peoples for the "one true God." After all, this crusade mentality had been responsible for the expulsion of the Moors and the Jews from Spain in 1492. There is no doubt, therefore, that they felt morally superior to the Native Americans they were subjecting. Christopher Columbus, writing to the Spanish king and queen in 1492, summarized this belief:

> Your Highnesses, as good Christian and Catholic princes, devout and propagators of the Christian faith, as well as enemies of the sect of Mahomet and of all idolatries and heresies, conceived the plan of sending me, Christopher Columbus, to this country of the Indies, there to see the princes, the peoples, the territory, their disposition and all things else, and the way in which one might proceed to convert these regions to our holy faith.
>
> And Your Highnesses have ordered that I should go, not by land, towards the East, which is the accustomed route, but by way of the West, whereby hitherto nobody to our knowledge has ever been. And so, after having expelled all the Jews from all your kingdoms and lordships, in this same month of January, Your highness ordered me to set out, with a sufficient fleet, for the said country of India, and to this end, Your Highnesses have shown me great favour.[14]

Dolan compares Columbus to John Winthrop, the founding father of the Massachusetts Bay Colony. Both felt called by God, as part of a new chosen people, to establish a type of new Israel, a Christian society in the New World, where, in the words of Winthrop, "we shall be as a city on a hill."[15]

> To acquire wealth was an obvious priority, but to establish a new Israel and extend the boundaries of the kingdom of God on earth was also a major impulse that propelled both the Spanish conquistador and the English Pilgrim across the ocean to America. Seen in this manner, the Spanish conquest of the sixteenth century, which inaugurates the history of Catholicism in the United States, evidences a striking resemblance to the Puritan colonization of the seventeenth century and the beginnings of American Protestantism. American Catholicism, like American Protestantism, was inaugurated with a millennial enthusiasm. It first surfaced on an island in the Bahamas, appropriately renamed San Salvador, and

---

14. Quoted in Goodpasture, *Cross and Sword*, 7.
15. Dolan, *American Catholic Experience* (1985) 16.

spread across Central and South America, eventually reaching Florida, Texas, Arizona, New Mexico, and California.[16]

It is interesting to note that this combination of greed and religious enthusiasm was also to play a role in the takeover of the Mexican Southwest two and a half centuries later by the United States' adherence to a similar ideology of "manifest destiny." The Roman Catholic ideology of the time was heavily influenced by scholasticism and the theology of St. Thomas Aquinas. Based on this fact, we might be tempted to look solely to scholasticism and Thomism for an explanation of why the Spaniards thought or acted as they did. But the explanation is necessarily more complicated, just as we would have to go beyond sixteenth-century Spanish religious pageantry to understand the basic teachings of Christianity. The popular religiosity of the day, quite medieval in inspiration, was in many ways just as traditionally Catholic as the Thomistic philosophical systems of academic theologians prevalent over the centuries.

Another engaging detail presented by some historians in regard to this plurality of religious beliefs is that despite the fact that the Spaniards were fiercely committed to Roman Catholic orthodoxy, some "simultaneously engaged in religious practices that resembled those of Indians, including pantheistic worship at pre-Christian shrines."[17]

Having said all this, however, it is important to keep in mind that the evangelization of the Americas was not carried out in a philosophical or religious vacuum. The Native Americans had their own languages and religious beliefs regarding the sacred and the cosmos. David J. Weber, summarizing the ideas of Turner, draws the following distinction between the Spaniards' religious tradition and that of the Native Americans. He concludes that, in a sense, the Spaniards' Judeo-Christian tradition had removed them from the world of myth:

> For Turner, the mythical world that Zunis and most, if not all, native Americans inhabited, teaches the interconnectedness of man and nature. In mythical religions, Turner suggests, spirits reside in the natural world, and the world itself has a cyclical, timeless quality. Spaniards, on the other hand, inherited a tradition in which human existence, divorced from nature and myth, moved relentlessly forward in history—that is, forward in linear time instead of

16. Ibid.
17. Weber, *Myth and the History,* 9. The author cites the following to support this assertion: William A. Christian, Jr., *Local Religion in Sixteenth-Century Spain* (Princeton: Princeton Univ. Press, 1981) 3–4, 42–7, 161; Christian, *Person and God in a Spanish Valley* (New York: Seminar Press, 1972) 181–2.

cyclical time. The Spaniards' otherworldly Christian god had created nature, but was not in nature. Christianity, Turner argues, "had effectively removed divinity from its [natural] world," leaving the world empty and devoid of spirit. Thus, Turner suggests, what the Europeans ethnocentrically and wrongly called the *New World,* could be despoiled as well as subdued—its forests leveled, its grasses grazed to the ground, and even its native inhabitants destroyed in the name of progress by a people bound for glory in another world.[18]

Whatever we may think of Turner's distinctions in regards to what he labels as "myth," there is no doubt that these religious and philosophical differences cannot be ignored in a contemporary study of such phenomena as religious syncretism.

Although the Native American cultures were by no means monolithic, certain common characteristics did prevail. Dolan lists three major ones: (1) a special love for the land and the natural environment, (2) a deep faith in the supernatural, and (3) the cultivation of various art forms, such as painting, dancing, and weaving, and a survival technology that included farming and hunting. In reference to the first characteristic, a love of the land, he gives some examples:

> "The earth is my mother," as one Spokane Indian put it. The Taos Indians, in New Mexico, so respected the land that they walked about in soft shoes during the spring, believing that the earth was pregnant at that time of the year and they should not harm their mother's body. Mountains were sacred shrines, and lakes were the dwelling place of the gods.[19]

Another aspect of the European conquest and early evangelization of the indigenous populations in the Americas relates to when they were conquered by the Europeans. For example, fierce exploitation and disease brought about almost the total eradication of the Indian in the Caribbean area, the first base of Spanish operations. The presence of so many persons of African descent there today reflects the fact that slaves were soon brought in to replace the indigenous population, which was quickly disappearing. Within a few decades the Spanish conquistadores, coming across monumental empires such as those of the Aztecs and the Incas, realized that Indian labor was a resource to be preserved, not carelessly exploited. In fact, intermarriage, or at least the fathering of what became known as *mestizo* children, became commonplace.

---

18. Weber, *Myth and the History,* 9–10.
19. Dolan, *American Catholic Experience* (1985) 23.

Focusing on the area that now is the United States, for example, disparity among indigenous peoples can similarly be noted. Some tribes, such as the Pueblos, had closer ties with the Spanish. Also, for centuries many of the Indian nations had occasionally warred with one another. J. Manuel Espinoza claims that "all in all, it is quite likely that Spain saved the Pueblo Indians from extermination" (at the hands of other Indian tribes).[20]

Perhaps Espinoza's contention is best left to be argued by historians. The point remains, however, that we must avoid lumping all the Native Americans together as if they were one united people at the time of the conquest. We must avoid a similar error, that of viewing the Spanish monolithically. The *leyenda negra,* that is, the constant unnuanced condemnation of the Spanish for their conquest and exploitation of the Americas, while at the same time making less of the exploitation in the same part of the world by other European nations, has reared its ugly head time and time again in U.S. and northern European history. Allan Figueroa Deck points to its presence even today.[21]

Almost three decades ago, similarly, in his first published article Deck was calling for such a nuanced interpretation of the history of the role of the Church in Latin America.[22] His point is that it is not fair to say that all the members of the clergy in the history of Latin America have always been on the side of the oppressor. As examples he lists such defenders of human rights in the Americas as Bartolomé de las Casas, Bernardino de Sahagún, and of more recent fame, Bishop Sergio Méndez of Cuernavaca, Mexico.[23] H. McKennie Goodpasture makes the same point in his collection of essays:

> The Europeans quickly dominated every area they entered. With the help of missionary friars, the conquerors pacified and evangelized the Indians, and also extracted their labor. The methods employed occasionally disturbed the European conscience. When protests arose, they usually came from the missionary orders. This was not surprising, for when the church was planted among the Indians, the process had involved not only coercion but also genuine pastoral care. Sensitive missionaries could see the destructive impact of forced labor. The few prophets among them, however, could not stop the slavery.[24]

20. Espinoza, *Crusaders of the Río Grande,* 370.
21. Deck, "Trashing of the Fifth Centenary" (1992) 499–501.
22. Deck, "New Vision" (1974) 87–93.
23. Ibid., 87.
24. Goodpasture, *Cross and Sword,* 2.

So far, an effort has been made to caution the reader against facile conclusions that come from a simplistic reading of history. Just as there was great diversity in terms of the composition and comportment of the Europeans, there were great differences among the indigenous populations. For one, some were nomadic while others were sedentary. Geography itself is a powerful force to be reckoned with, a factor not always taken into account. First, a look at the nationality of the missionaries is in order, then second, a mention of the role geography played in the conquest and evangelization of the Americas.

In many ways, the missionaries were the primary agents of evangelism and Spanish colonialism, yet, they were not always Spaniards. Theodore Edward Treutlein, using the Jesuits as an example, argues that "from a religious point of view, a Jesuit toiling in the mission fields of colonial Spanish America possessed no nationality. He was simply serving God and the king of Spain as an agent of Christendom among the American heathen."[25] Despite Spanish absolutism, which was greatly antagonistic to anything "foreign," many non-Spanish missionaries managed to make it to the Americas. In a system such as that characterized by the missions and the *presidios*, the presence of French, Flemish, Irish, German, Czech, Hungarian, Italian, and Polish missionaries should not be overlooked in understanding life in the colonial empire. These men brought with them many skills that shaped the new civilization in the Americas. Among the most skilled were the lay brothers, who made up a large proportion of the foreign Jesuits in Latin America.

> In the ranks of the lay brothers were to be found barbers, surgeons, apothecaries, turners, smiths, weavers, carpenters, tailors, metalworkers, architects, cabinetmakers, bakers, cooks, sculptors, painters, bell casters, masons, locksmiths, clothmakers, goldsmiths, organmakers, watchmakers, fullers, and tinsmiths. In the Chilean province, particularly, one notices a great number of lay brothers who were specialists in various arts and crafts. The presence of numerous Jesuit lay brothers in Chile may help to explain the accusations made against the Chilean Jesuits shortly before the expulsion, to the effect that the Society competed in trade, commerce, and manufacturing with Spanish merchants and artisans, to the detriment of the latter.[26]

The fact that many of these missionaries, for example, the Jesuits and the Franciscans, suffered one or more expulsions from these territories,

25. Treutlein, "Non-Spanish Jesuits," 219.
26. Ibid., 233.

moreover, raises the question of what happened when they were no longer in charge.

Geography played a crucial role in shaping the vast Spanish and Portuguese empires. In a situation where each headquarters was literally worlds apart, political and religious controls were not easily obtained. At times, for example, during the War of the Spanish Succession (1702–13), Spain, embroiled in domestic economic, political, and spiritual turmoil, had little energy or resources to devote to such outlying provincial posts as New Mexico.[27] The empires were immense and contained a great variety of terrain. From vast deserts to forests, from mountains to flat lands, these huge territories were not easy ones to administer. Areas such as New Mexico remained isolated. Spanish traditions became more fixed there. Even today some New Mexican inhabitants still speak a more archaic form of Spanish. A simplistic view of the Spanish and Portuguese empires over the various centuries ignores the role geography played in tempering European influence and developments in the Americas.

If anything, the previous paragraphs have shown the complexity involved in writing about the conquest and, to a certain extent, the evangelization of the Americas by Europeans. We are particularly indebted to social history and to historical anthropology for opening up a significant perspective that often had been ignored. Against this background, a clearer understanding of the emblematic role of religion during this period emerges. It is obvious, from our examination of religious, political, philosophical, and geographical factors, that this mass colonization did not take place in a social vacuum. It is more accurate to say that it was an encounter or, as some would say, a clash, between two very different worlds and worldviews. As theology looks increasingly to the social sciences for a dialogue partner, these findings will be of greater importance.

The Pre–U.S. Period in the Southwest

Up to this point, with some exceptions, the conquest and evangelization of the Americas has been taken together as a whole. What follows is a more specific focus on the history of Latinos in the United States. As is the case with any territory that has undergone innumerable political changes over the centuries, it is difficult to narrate here the entire history of U.S. Hispanics. Thus only a few points will be highlighted.

As previously mentioned, their presence in the Americas begins immediately with the arrival of Christopher Columbus in 1492. Spanish

---

27. Espinoza, *Crusaders of the Rio Grande*, 363.

settlements were soon established in the Caribbean, and explorers were sent out to the neighboring islands and the mainland, which is now the United States. After the conquest of the numerous Indian civilizations in Mexico in the first part of the sixteenth century and others soon after elsewhere in the Americas, the process of evangelizing the Native Americans began. The main vehicle for evangelization in the southwestern United States and northern Mexico was the mission, or the *reducciones*, as they were sometimes called.[28]

The National Pastoral Plan for Hispanic Ministry,[29] summarizing this work of the religious orders, describes the decades that followed:

> In the 17th century Franciscan missionaries raised elegant churches in the Pueblo towns of New Mexico; Jesuits along the western slopes of New Spain wove scattered Indian rancherias into efficient social systems that raised the standard of living in arid America. But the primacy of evangelization as a cornerstone of Spanish royal policy was swept away by political ambitions in the 18th century; the missions fell victim to secularism. First, the Jesuits were exiled and the order suppressed; Franciscans and Dominicans tried valiantly to stem the tide of absolutism, but their numbers dwindled rapidly and the Church's service to the poor crumbled.[30]

To further complicate matters this large area, which went from belonging to Spain to being part of the newly established independent country of Mexico in 1820, ended up as part of the territory the United States acquired with the Treaty of Guadalupe Hidalgo in 1848. This pact ended the Mexican American War, and as a result of it Mexico lost half its territory.

In many ways this takeover by the United States was disastrous for the native Hispanic population. Within a matter of years, many families who had lived in these territories for centuries lost their lands and native leadership as a new Anglo-American legal system engulfed them.[31] A traditional community that had known no separation of Church and state, for example, now found itself in a very different situ-

---

28. For an eyewitness description of mission life in seventeenth-century colonial New Mexico, see an excerpt of Fray Alonso de Benavides' writing found in Goodpastor, *Cross and Sword*, 57–8. For a more systematic treatment of the same during that and the following centuries, especially in terms of art, folklore, and the role of religion in daily life, see Hendren, "Daily Life on the Frontier," *Fronteras* (1983), ed. Sandoval, 103–39. Bolton's *On the Rim of Christendom* is a moving account of the work of the famed Jesuit missionary, Eusebio Francisco Kino, much beloved even to the present day.

29. National Conference of Catholic Bishops, *Pastoral Plan* (1987).

30. Ibid., 4.

31. See Acuña, *Occupied America*.

ation. Through years of long isolation, Spanish folk tradition had become fixed. Espinoza describes New Mexican life in the seventeenth century:

> The history of Spanish culture in New Mexico during the eighteenth century was not very different from that of the seventeenth. The social and religious activities continued as before. Always, it must be emphasized, New Mexico was an isolated frontier community, its people living simple village and rural life. Aside from labors in town and countryside, there were the Church festivals, Masses, marriages, baptisms, and military parades and exercises. The colonists often assembled publicly and privately in dances, prayers, penitential processions, *velorios* for the dead, and burials. During betrothal, marriage, and baptismal celebrations there was feasting, drinking, dancing, and singing of popular songs and ballads.[32]

In his book *Occupied America: A History of Chicanos* Rodolfo Acuña has entitled his chapter on the U.S. takeover of New Mexico "Freedom in a Cage: The Colonization of New Mexico."[33] This title describes vividly the situation of Hispanics in the Southwest during the second half of the nineteenth century. Virgil Elizondo, considered by many to be the father of U.S. Hispanic theology, notes emphatically that the Hispanic of the Southwest is an "exile who never left home."[34] Among the biggest disillusionments for the Hispanics during this era was the lack of support received from the Roman Catholic Church.

Incorporation into the United States

It was not long after the war that the U.S. Catholic hierarchy was given charge of the Church of these lands, which today encompass the southwestern part of the United States. Since the U.S. Church was still considered mission territory, prelates were brought in from Europe. Except in the case of San Antonio and Dallas, all the first bishops in the dioceses in New Mexico, Arizona, Colorado, and Texas were Frenchmen.[35] Fray Angelico Chavez, O.F.M., notes a certain irony in the fact that these prelates were Frenchmen, "given that the native priests, having been educated in Durango during the revolutions for independence, were very Mexican. There was a French invasion and they were

32. Espinoza, *Crusaders of the Rio Grande*, 365.
33. Acuña, *Occupied America*.
34. Stated at Mobile Jesuit conference, June 1992 (reference previously given; see introduction, n. 3).
35. Sandoval, *On the Move* (1990).

very anti-French. Then the one sent to them was a Frenchman!"[36] Moises Sandoval criticizes the behavior of some of these "foreign shepherds":

> These bishops, all but one born in Europe, attempted to create a church like the one they had left. The one who perhaps tried the hardest was Jean Baptiste Lamy, the first bishop of New Mexico. He boasted that he was creating a little Auvergne, the name of his province in France. Even the architectural style of the cathedral he started in Santa Fe was French, as were the artisans he brought in to build it.[37]

Sandoval, a layperson originally from New Mexico, is particularly critical of the lack of respect given to the indigenous church there:

> Lamy and his associate, Joseph P. Machebeuf, later the first bishop of Denver, have been credited for bringing Gallic discipline to the church in New Mexico. But he also caused division that took generations to reconcile. The Council of Baltimore had appointed Lamy to head the Vicariate of New Mexico *in partibus infidelium* (in the region of the infidels), a fixed phrase for any missionary territory. The designation was perhaps justified in Texas, considering how many indigenous peoples were not yet converted. But it was clearly an affront to the Catholicism that had existed in New Mexico for 250 years. The biased view of the American church and of the bishops sent to the Southwest was that there had been a glorious period of evangelization by the missionaries from Spain and an almost total collapse of the church during the Mexican period. Perhaps that explains why Lamy's relations with the native clergy were poor.[38]

Sandoval looks at the situations of the Hispanic Catholics in Texas and California and reaches the same conclusion: the Hispanic Church had lost its native leaders.[39] With the tremendous influx of non-Hispanics

36. In Stevens-Arroyo, *Prophets Denied Honor* (1980) 79.

37. Ibid.

38. Ibid., 31. See Bridgers, *Death's Deceiver.*

39. Among the most important of these leaders was the famed "Cura de Taos," Padre A. J. Martínez, a New Mexican priest active in education, publishing, and politics. His difficulties with Archbishop Lamy are the subject of many a writing. See *Reluctant Dawn: Historia del Padre A. J. Martínez, Cura de Taos* (San Antonio: Mexican American Cultural Center, 1976), by Juan Romero with Moises Sandoval. Also see De Aragon, *Padre Martínez and Bishop Lamy.* Archbishop Lamy's renown has spread with the publication of two books in recent history, *Death Comes for the Archbishop,* a novel by Willa Cather based on his life, and *Lamy of Santa Fe, His Life and Times* (New York: Farrar Straus & Giroux, 1975) by Paul Horgan.

into these territories, particularly after Texas was granted statehood and gold was discovered in California, Hispanics found themselves more and more on the fringe of not only the society in general but also of the Church.

> By the end of the nineteenth century, Hispanic Americans in the Southwest had no institutional voice in the church. The native Hispanic priests who had been their spokesmen in mid-century had all been purged or died out. The removal of the activists had been a powerful lesson for those aging priests who remained. They had realized that they could remain only on condition that they were submissive. They had faded away quietly.[40]

The New Mexican writer sees this loss of native leadership as one of the main reasons the Hispanic laypeople went their own way. "For almost 300 years in New Mexico, 200 years in Texas, and 100 years in California, they relied, of necessity, on their own homespun religious traditions. These served them well."[41]

During the second half of the nineteenth century, non-Hispanic immigration into the Southwest soon caused the native Hispanic population to become a minority. As a new system complete with its entirely different language and court system took effect, Hispanics found themselves pushed aside, often losing their land and consequently their political clout.

There was some migration north from Mexico in the years that followed, but these migrations became more numerous in the twentieth century. Many came to the United States during the time of the Revolution in the first decades of the twentieth century.[42]

Another Case of Internal Colonialism,
or the Growing U.S. Presence in the Caribbean

Antonio M. Stevens-Arroyo, an educator and cultural historian of Puerto Rican descent, describes a situation similar to that of the Southwest, in which the United States politically and militarily took over an entire region of Hispanic or Latino people:

---

40. Juan Romero, with Sandoval, *Reluctant Dawn*, 40.

41. Ibid. A good example of these native folk traditions is the *Penitente* movement, a lay confraternity whose origins and practices can be traced back to the penitential societies of medieval Spain. The movement has been quite controversial over the decades. See C. G. Romero, *Hispanic Devotional Piety* (1991); also see Podles, "Saint Makers in the Desert."

42. See M. García, *Desert Immigrants*; also see Acuña, *Occupied America*.

An understanding of Church history for Puerto Ricans in the United States does not begin when Puerto Ricans come to the continent but rather when the United States goes to Puerto Rico. The army troops which landed on the southern shore of Puerto Rico on July 25, 1898 ended four-hundred years of Spanish rule over the small Caribbean island and its multi-racial people. Valuable political studies demonstrate incontestably that the religion of the people of Puerto Rico was of prime concern to the new lords from Washington.[43]

Elsewhere the author points out the importance of Puerto Rico in the history of the U.S. Catholic Church:

Puerto Rico is the birthplace of the Catholic church in the Americas; it was the first diocese in the New World to receive its bishop, Alonso Manso, who arrived in 1513. When the easy wealth of Indian gold evaporated, the island lost population and the episcopal see suffered diminished importance. Nonetheless, throughout the years of the Spanish colonial empire, Puerto Rico served as first step for new bishops, including a high percentage of Latin American–born prelates. Only one of these was a Puerto Rican, however.[44]

One can only imagine the confusion that erupted with a changeover to a new political stem. After all, Puerto Rico had been under the Spanish flag for four hundred years. The parallels with New Mexico and the rest of the Southwest are numerous. As the political and economic system became more U.S. based, the thrust of government policies was to Americanize the population. English became the official language, and those politicians who opposed such a process of Americanization soon found themselves replaced by appointees of the military governor. The economic effects were almost immediate. "Puerto Rican merchants and land-owners lost much of their economic power when the peso was devalued and the newly established United States banks drastically limited credit on the island."[45]

The effects on the Catholic Church in the island were equally disastrous. Basing himself on the work of several historians, Stevens-Arroyo reports that "with the transfer of power and an insistence on the separation of Church and State, Spanish missionary priests and nuns left in great numbers and many hospitals, schools, and churches were confiscated. The argument used to justify these actions was that public tax

43. Stevens-Arroyo, "Puerto Rican Migration to the United States," *Frontiers*, ed. Deck (1992) 269–76.
44. Stevens-Arroyo, *Prophets Denied Honor* (1980) 76.
45. Stevens-Arroyo, "Puerto Rican Migration," *Frontiers*, ed. Deck (1992) 269.

money had built these Catholic institutions and that they were, therefore, public not religious buildings."[46]

The pastoral strategy of the hierarchy during the years that followed was to bring in, especially from the United States, missionary priests and religious, persons who set up missions and schools on the Caribbean island that was once known as Borinquen. Stevens-Arroyo characterizes their work as well intentioned but extremely deficient in adapting itself to a new reality:

> The efforts of these religious were directed, in large measure, at the establishment of a Catholic school system. These early missionaries belonged to their times and did not internalize the religious values of the Puerto Ricans as a conscious adaptation to the foreign missionary to the native Church. And although they recognized the Hispanic cultural roots of Catholicism by encouraging processions and devotions, this was more than offset by the conspicuous absence of success in recruiting Puerto Ricans to their ranks. The Protestants, on the other hand, were not only prepared to ordain Puerto Ricans to the ministry, but in many instances gave open entry to ex-Catholic priests.[47]

Thus the Catholic Church took more of an assimilationist stance than one of inculturation. This mistake has had repercussions today in the large percentage of Protestant Christians on the island.

Farther north, on the U.S. mainland, Latinos began to establish themselves. Toward the latter part of the nineteenth century refugees from Cuba's push for independence began to settle in Tampa, Florida. Even after Cuba received self-government as a result of the Spanish American War in 1898, Cubans kept migrating to the United States because of political unrest back on the island.

After the United States invaded Puerto Rico in 1898, as stated above, the Treaty of Paris, which brought an end to the Spanish American War, was signed, and the island became a possession of the United States. Some attention has already been given to the establishment of economic policies through which the peasants began to lose their land to U.S.–owned businesses that sought to develop the sugar cane industry. In the decades that followed these dispossessed peasants moved to the cities or migrated to the mainland.[48] Comparable economies and political instability brought people from the Dominican Republic to the United States' eastern seaboard. Joining the growing populations of

46. Ibid.
47. Ibid., 270ff.
48. Sandoval, *On the Move* (1990) 40.

Puerto Ricans and Cubans, they helped to create a significant part of the Hispanic presence in the United States.

Immigrant Church in a Protestant Country

Up to this point, what had been the situation of the Catholic Church in the United States? Church historian Thomas Bokenkotter distinguishes between the situation in the various territories that would eventually become part of the country and that of the thirteen English colonies. A brief history of the growth of the Church in the Spanish South and Southwest has already been given. Mention is now made, therefore, of that of the implantation of the Church in the French area to the north. Bokenkotter writes:

> Northward lay the huge French area, which also drew many Catholic missionaries, Jesuit, Capuchin, Recollect, and others. The Jesuit Pere Jacques Marquette, discoverer of the Mississippi, and the Jesuit martyrs Isaac Jogues, Jean de Brébeuf, and their companions were among the many who ministered to the spiritual and temporal needs of the Hurons and other Indian tribes. The missionaries also helped establish French Catholic outposts on the Great Lakes and down through the Ohio and Mississippi valleys, a chapter in Catholic history that is recalled by names like Detroit, St. Louis, Vincennes, Louisville, and Marietta.[49]

In reference to the thirteen English colonies, the historian writes about the gradual restriction of religious freedom for Catholics that took hold with the dawning of Protestant political hegemony. With the American Revolution many of these restrictions were lifted, and both Maryland and Pennsylvania passed religious freedom laws in 1776.[50]

Notwithstanding the difficulties met by the Hispanic Church in the Southwest in the nineteenth century, other missionary endeavors in the country met with great success.

> No missionary territory in the nineteenth century registered more sensational gains than the Catholic Church in the United States. Thanks to a massive influx of Catholic immigrants—Irish, German, Italians, Poles, and others—the growth of the Catholic Church far outstripped the nation's growth. The American bishops were able to successfully integrate these heterogeneous, polyglot newcomers into the Church structure and provide a huge network of schools, hospitals, and other institutions for them that were soon the envy of the entire Catholic world.[51]

49. Bokenkotter, *Concise History,* 378.
50. Ibid., 379.
51. Ibid., 378.

In a relatively short period of time the Catholic population, complete with all its diversity, grew beyond any foreseeable trend. Bokenkotter details this surge:

> This flood began in the 1820s, with the first wave of Irish immigrants. Largely because of Irish immigrants, the number of Catholics jumped from about 500,000 (out of U.S. population of 12 million) in 1830 to 3,103,000 in 1860 (out of a U.S. population of 31.5 million)—an increase of over 800 percent—with the number of priests and the number of churches increasing proportionately. So large was this increase that by 1850 Roman Catholicism, which at the birth of the nation was nearly invisible in terms of numbers, had now become the country's largest religious denomination.[52]

This tide of European immigration continued well into the latter part of the nineteenth century. German and Italian mass migrations soon joined those of the Irish:

> The next era, 1860 to 1890, was equally impressive, as the growth of the Church far outstripped the growth of the national population, the Church tripling in size while the nation was only doubling. By 1890 Catholics numbered 8,909,000 out of the nation's 62,947,000. German Catholics, who were previously far less in number, now began nearly to equal the number of Irish immigrants. The wave of immigration, lasting from 1890 to the immigration laws of the 1920s, brought a preponderance of Italians and eastern Europeans. Over a million Italians alone came during the two decades from 1890 to 1910.[53]

As stated above, the U.S. Church responded admirably to these waves of immigrants. True, controversies, such as those regarding the level to which the Church should function as an "Americanizer," abounded. The fact remains, however, that through its parishes, which provided some type of refuge within a new hostile environment, and its schools, which prepared a new generation for life in the United States, it became the defender of those who had come to America seeking a better life.

As these immigrants moved up the social ladder, so did the Church. Bokenkotter concludes his chapter on the American Church with an observation that by the middle of the twentieth century it too had found a home in the United States:

---

52. Ibid., 383.
53. Ibid.

By the 1950s it was quite obvious to most observers that the Catholic Church in the United States had became a thoroughly American institution. The era of Protestant domination was over. The political significance of this fact was underscored when John F. Kennedy was elected the first Catholic President of the United States, an event that, coupled with the reign of Pope John and the calling of his council, definitely marked the beginning of a new era in the history of American Catholicism.[54]

A New Wave of Hispanic Migration

As mentioned above, large numbers of people from Spanish-speaking countries migrated to the United States during the end of the nineteenth century and the early decades of the twentieth. Among this large group were those fleeing the political instability caused by the Mexican Revolution, which broke out in 1910. The passage of certain U.S. quota laws, which curtailed European immigration, in addition created a demand for labor during the first part of the century. Mexicans were recruited to fill this gap. In the years that followed many came as contract laborers, who were then forced to return to Mexico when their work was accomplished, or some entered the country illegally and stayed for a time or permanently.[55] Once their children were born in the United States (since birth in national territory entitles a person to U.S. citizenship), it was easier to obtain legal permission to stay.

The stories of other migrations of Hispanics, either within the country or from outside it, are similar. As some Mexican Americans went either westward or northward seeking employment after World War II, waves of Puerto Ricans and Cubans arrived on the mainland. One of the reasons people left Puerto Rico was the massive loss of jobs in the agricultural sector. From 1940 to 1970 the number of farm jobs dropped from 230,000 to 74,000.[56] From the time of the Cuban Revolution in 1959

54. Ibid., 396.

55. Various authors provide good historical sources for documenting this era. Among them are two works previously cited, that of M. García, *Desert Immigrants,* and Acuña, *Occupied America.* Timmons, in *El Paso,* describes one of these major guest worker programs, the *Bracero* Program, created by the United States in 1942. See page 242.

56. *Puerto Ricans in the Continental United States: An Uncertain Future,* a report of the U.S. Commission on Civil Rights (October 1976) 18. See Stevens-Arroyo's treatment of Puerto Rican migration to the mainland during this century in *Frontiers,* ed. Deck (1992). See also, for a perspective from the mainland, Ana María Díaz-Stevens, *Oxcart Catholicism* (1993). See also Díaz-Stevens and Stevens-Arroyo, *Latino Resurgence in U.S. Religion* (1998), for a very thorough treatment of Latinos in Church and society, told especially by two persons who have participated intensely in the recent decades' struggle for justice.

more than 875,000 Cubans have immigrated to the United States. As of 1980 the Hispanic population made up 39 percent of metropolitan Miami.[57] As recently as the last fifteen years Central Americans, particularly Nicaraguans, Salvadorans, and Guatemalans, have begun to migrate to the States in significant numbers. Like others before them, political unrest—in the cases of some, even death threats—as well as suffering economies have been the primary motivators.[58]

The Present "Signs of the Times"

The Current Socioeconomic Situation of U.S. Hispanics

The previous short summary of the history of Hispanics in the U.S. provides a useful backdrop for understanding the current situation of these peoples. The fact remains that great social progress for Hispanics, descendants of the first European group to set foot on the Americas, has been long in coming. Following a brief view of their socioeconomic situation is a discussion on the role of the Church vis-à-vis this Hispanic sociological reality.

First, a few statistics from the 1991 U.S. Census add some clarity to the Hispanic reality.[59] What ethnic clusters come under this name? Even though the largest group is the Mexicans (at 63 percent of the total), there are also people from nineteen Latin American republics, Puerto Rico, and Spain. The Puerto Ricans constitute the second largest group at 11 percent, while the Cubans are in third place with 5 percent. Persons from Central America and South America constitute 14 percent, while other Hispanics or Latinos number 8 percent.[60] The key point here is the tremendous amount of diversity that characterizes this population.[61]

This is an impressively young population. While the median age for the total population in the United States is thirty-four, the median age for Hispanic people is twenty-six. Within this category the youngest group are the Mexicans (twenty-four years), while the oldest group are

57. Sandoval, *On the Move* (1990) 106.
58. For a concise historical overview of the Latinos in the U.S. Church, see Jaime Vidal, "Hispanic Catholics in America," (1998) 635–42.
59. The U.S. Population Census is taken every ten years, marking 2000 as the next target date.
60. U.S. Census Bureau, *Hispanic Population*.
61. In a work edited by Cortina and Moncada, *Hispanos en los Estados Unidos,* the point of different histories and different socioeconomic status among the various Hispanic groups is highlighted. The authors decry a lack of social research that takes this large diversity into account. See, in this work, "El Sentido de la diversidad," 31–58.

the Cubans (thirty-nine years). In the same 1991 report the U.S. Census Bureau reports that about 30 percent of Hispanics were under fifteen years of age, compared with 22 percent of non-Hispanics.[62] It is essential that this fact not be overlooked by pastoral planners!

Hispanic families also tend to be larger than those of the general non-Hispanic population. The average size of Hispanic households (3.48 persons) in 1991 was larger than that of non-Hispanic households (2.58 persons). Among the various Hispanic subgroups the highest proportion of these large households was made up of Mexican families.[63]

Although Hispanics are less likely than the general population to be divorced or widowed, fewer Hispanic families live in husband-wife arrangements. About 69 percent of Hispanic families were married-couple families, compared with about 79 percent of non-Hispanic families. In the same vein, there are more Hispanic families than non-Hispanic families headed by women (24 percent vs. 16 percent).[64]

The greatest number of Hispanics live in the southwestern part of the United States. The state with the largest concentration is California, with almost 34 percent of the total U.S. Hispanic population. The next largest is Texas, with 21.3 percent. In third place is New York, with 11 percent.[65] Given the brief history of the Southwest, along with the migration trends furnished previously, this concentration comes as no surprise.

From about 1980 to 1988 the Hispanic population increased by 34 percent, or about five million persons (the population increase for non-Hispanics was only 7 percent). About half of the Hispanic population growth resulted from net migration and half from natural increase. The Hispanic population in general, therefore, is an extremely young one and will continue to increase significantly, since so many of the women are of childbearing age.[66]

Lack of education and professional training are serious problems that contribute to high unemployment. In 1988 only 51 percent of Hispanics twenty-five years or older had completed high school, compared with a 78 percent rate for the general population. The level of college education for that same year was also significantly lower: 10 percent for Hispanics vis-à-vis 21 percent for non-Hispanics.[67] Edmundo Rodríguez, a Mexican American who was pastor of the Jesuit

62. Ibid.
63. Ibid.
64. Ibid.
65. U.S. Census Bureau, *The Hispanic Population in the United States: March 1988 (Advance Report)* (Washington, D.C.: U.S. Department of Commerce, 1988).
66. Ibid.
67. Ibid.

parish in one of the poorest neighborhoods of San Antonio, Texas, has this to say about why so many young Hispanics drop out of school:

> In general, the reasons are economic, cultural, and structural. Economic in that many families cannot even afford to buy their children school clothes. Cultural in that Hispanic students are caught in a cultural crossfire, living with Hispanic culture at home while feeling pressured at school and work to assimilate and forsake their heritage. Structural in that the school systems are generally not equipped to deal with Hispanics.[68]

His reasons for Hispanics' overrepresentation in the prison population are also linked to social structures:

> Like Blacks, Hispanics constitute a disproportionately high percentage of the prison population in states with heavy Hispanic populations. The high rate of dropouts from schools, discouragement and frustration at not being able to get jobs, and lack of opportunities for those who have already been in prison, help enlarge the Hispanic population. The case of the devastating prison riot in New Mexico in 1979 shows how violently that frustration can explode.[69]

As one might expect, a large portion of Hispanics (almost 28 percent) lived below the poverty level in 1990. Their poverty rate was about two and a half times as high as that for non-Hispanics (12 percent). In addition, the Census Bureau reports that about half of all Hispanic persons in poverty were children under eighteen years (47.7 percent).[70] Such a high number of children living in poverty in a land of abundance seems to characterize modern national trends. A recent study by the United Nations Children's Fund, for example, found that children in the United States are more likely to live in poverty than children in any other industrialized nation. The same report ranked the murder rate for young people in the United States as being the highest in the industrialized world.[71]

Judging from the poverty figures quoted above, it is not surprising that Hispanics in general have a lower income than the rest of the population taken together. The median family income in 1990 was about $8,000 lower than that for non-Hispanics ($22,300 vs. $30,500). Among the Hispanic subgroups, Puerto Ricans had the lowest median household income.[72]

68. E. Rodríguez, "Realities for Hispanics" (1988) 9.
69. Ibid.
70. U.S. Census Bureau, *Hispanic Population* (1991).
71. *San Francisco Chronicle*, September 23, 1993.
72. U.S. Census Bureau, *Hispanic Population* (1991).

What, then, is the socioeconomic state of the Latino population in the United States? In general, it is a young, working-class population that is still much poorer and less educated than the rest of the nation. It is also characterized by larger families, a good number of which are not only made up of the traditional nuclear family but are much more likely to include members of the extended family, such as a grandparent. Another important quality is its diversity in terms of the various subgroups, which all come under the "Hispanic" or "Latino" umbrella, along with the variety of assimilation into U.S. culture that shows itself across generational lines.

Does the fact that Latinos are generally poorer and less educated than the general population therefore mean that their culture can best be understood in light of what some have described as "the culture of poverty" or the "urban underclass model"? This theory, whose proponents include such writers as Oscar Lewis, Nicholas Lehmann, and Lawrence Mead, basically holds that a poor person, as a member of the underclass, is either a social deviant or has low morals, for example, suffers from laziness, apathy, and the like and tends to experience much social alienation.[73] Until recently, this notion went virtually unchallenged.

This high level of poverty, however, does not necessarily mean that Latinos' quality of life is inevitably lower. In a fascinating study of Latinos in California directed by medical sociologist David E. Hayes-Bautista, the team of researchers presents substantial evidence to challenge many of the myths perpetuated about the Latino in California. Their conclusions show that, contrary to popular perception and even previous sociological studies, the Latino does not fit into the "underclass and cultural deficit paradigms" that supposedly characterize other poor populations in this country.

For example, despite their poverty, Latinos have high levels of labor force participation. In terms of education, there are significant signs of progress if generational differences are observed. The researchers did

73. J. G. Fernández, basing herself on the work of Moore and Pinderhughes (*In the Barrios*), summarizes the history of the term: "Among social scientists and other scholars there is as yet no consensus about the term 'underclass.' During the 60s, urban analysts began to speak of a new dimension to the urban crisis in the form of a large subpopulation of low-income families and individuals whose behavior was different from the general population. In the late 70s and early 80s the underclass were considered an urban group with tendencies of criminal acts, welfare dependency, mental illness, alcoholic, and drug dependency and it included the poorest of the poor." See J. G. Fernández, "Latina Garment Workers," 1. See Moore and Pinderhuges, *In the Barrios;* Lewis, *Children of Sanchez;* Lehmann, "Origins of the Underclass," (June 1986) 31–55, and (July 1986) 54–68; Mead, "New Politics," 3–21. I am indebted to Juanita García Fernández for this discussion of the underclass model as applicable to Latinos in the United States.

not find a sense of alienation or loss of identity in terms of mainstream culture, as some social scientists have posited in the past. Among the most positive traits they uncovered besides the previously mentioned high labor-force participation were strong family formation, good health indicators, and low welfare utilization. The researchers state the crux of their argument:

> There is an apparent contradiction in this situation: a group with the highest poverty and lowest education rates demonstrates some of the most markedly positive behavior regarding family, work, health and the community. Under most current assumptions about the way minority groups are assumed to behave, this should not be the case.[74]

Another study done on Latina garment workers in El Paso, Texas, from 1992 to 1994 reached the same conclusion. The researcher, Juanita García Fernández, describes the results of her study, whose purpose it was to examine the Latinas' workplace (small, medium, and large clothing factories), community, personal and home issues, "in order to quantify the necessities and progress needed for the garment worker population."[75]

> The survey shows that these women demonstrate middle class attitudes and behavior toward the basic institutions in our society, especially family, work, and education. The women demonstrate[d] . . . high labor participation, low welfare and government assistance dependency, strong health indicators, awareness of the need of education, strong family unity. These characteristics . . . demonstrate that Latino garment workers do not comply with the expected profile of the UUM [urban underclass model]. Although the population in the study did have low levels of education and a high poverty level, it is wrong to assume from these facts alone that they conform to the UUM.[76]

Elsewhere she concludes that one of the major reasons for their poverty is simply that they "work in the garment industry which offers low-paying, dead-end jobs that give little opportunity for occupational mobility and advancement."[77]

---

74. See Hayes-Bautista and others, *No Longer a Minority* (1992) xi. The companion book, by the same authors, is *Redefining California* (1992). While their findings must be limited to Latinos in California, the questions they raise are very significant for studying Latinos in other areas of the country.

75. J. G. Fernández, "Latina Garment Workers," vi.

76. Ibid.

77. Ibid., 89.

While the work of these researchers is still at the pioneering stage, they definitely represent a challenge to the urban underclass model. From a sociological standpoint then, what is the factor that accounts for the resiliency of U.S. Latinos? Again, their theologians are now beginning to explore an inherent world of meaning—a spirituality, one might say—that provides an unmistakable source of strength. More of that in the next chapter. For now, a look at Latinos and the institutional Church helps to round out this overview.

The Role of the Church

According to a sociological study done in 1985 by Roberto González and Michael LaVelle, 83 percent of the Hispanic Catholics sampled considered religion important, yet 88 percent are not active in their parishes.[78] Their study, nonetheless, also found that Hispanics have high levels of adherence to orthodox Catholic beliefs and that they engage in many folk religious practices, some of Marian inspiration. The study also found that a higher percentage of Hispanic Catholics appear to attend Mass on Sundays and holy days of obligation than is generally acknowledged by conventual pastoral wisdom.[79]

To what extent has the Church been present and actively involved in the service of the Hispanic community in the United States over the decades? Several writers on this subject would seem to say that the Church's record for being in solidarity with this marginal population is mixed. Among the critics is Moises Sandoval, the previously mentioned editor of *Maryknoll*, the monthly magazine of the Catholic Foreign Mission Society of America, as well as its bilingual counterpart, *Revista Maryknoll*. Extensive use of his history of the Hispanic Church in the United States, entitled *On the Move*, has already been made.[80]

In an article published prior to this account Sandoval traces the history of the *campesino* and the Catholic Church in the southwestern United States.[81] His overall conclusion is that the Church, aside from its influential intervention in the farm-labor negotiations of the late 1960s and early 1970s, has consistently taken a more conservative position in respect to social change. A brief history of the Church in the Southwest since the arrival of the first evangelizers in the sixteenth century reveals a Church with too few resources to tend to its Hispanic flock. Even as

---

78. See R. González and M. LaVelle, *Hispanic Catholic.* For a summary of their findings, see especially pages xi–xiii.
79. Ibid.
80. Sandoval, *On the Move* (1990).
81. Sandoval, "El Campesino" (1988).

late as the nineteenth century the Church hierarchy viewed the Hispanic as the object of evangelization, never the subject.

Sandoval concludes that the Church, instead of making a radical option for the poor today *(acompañamiento)*, has chosen to offer some relief aid *(caridad)* and to devote the majority of its resources to the middle class, its biggest financial backer. Sandoval reminds us of the need to look back to history for social analysis. True, the Church lacked resources, but part of that dearth was caused by its failure at a fuller inculturation (as evidenced by its imported clergy over the last four centuries).[82]

Leveling similar charges that the Church has failed to fully inculturate within the culture of U.S. Hispanics, Yolanda Tarango, a Mexican American woman religious, brings home the point that while the Church has reached "the ends of the earth" geographically, it is still struggling to be universal.[83] Tracing the emergence of the Mexican American historically and culturally in the Southwest, she criticizes the American Catholic Church, especially in Texas, for promoting "Americanization" along with evangelization.

She believes that the lingering feeling of Mexican Americans toward the official Church is that it is an Anglo institution. Such alienation has, consequently, caused people to transfer religious practices to the home. The system of evangelization in which most Hispanics have been subjected, therefore, is a circular one in which religion is taught through feeling and example. On the other hand, the official Church's method is linear and individualistic. Hispanics are still viewed as objects of mission, and the emphasis remains on assimilation.

A New Exodus

The discontent with the Church has led some Hispanics to gravitate toward Protestant groups and sects.[84] True, Protestantism, as Justo

---

82. In an address delivered at the Western Vocation Directors Association Convention in 1973, Roger B. Luna, S.D.B., basing himself on a survey of Mexican American priests, gave the following four reasons, which had surfaced from the inquiry: "1) The Spanish tradition of not creating a native clergy, 2) Open discrimination against Mexicans by priests, 3) Taking Mexicans for granted on the part of the church; no special effort to keep them Catholic, and 4) the lack of education, especially higher education, among Mexican young people" (text was printed in Stevens-Arroyo, *Prophets Denied Honor* [1980], as "Why So Few Mexican-American Priests?" 160–3).

83. Tarango, "Church Struggling" (1989) 167–73.

84. U.S. sociologist and priest Andrew Greeley reports a defection rate of 8 percent among Hispanics during the last fifteen years, which is nearly one million Hispanic men and women. See Greeley, "Defection Among Hispanics" (1988) 61–2.

González notes, had existed for some time in Latin America, but the fact remains that the Catholic Church has lost and is continuing to lose much of its flock. González describes some of the historical appeal of Protestantism to U.S. Hispanics:

> But not all Protestant Hispanics in the United States entered the country as Protestants. Many were converted in the United States, through processes similar to those that took place in Latin America. In the nineteenth century, Protestantism appeared to be as the vanguard of progress, while Roman Catholicism, especially under Pius IX, was going through its most authoritarian and reactionary period. After the Mexican-American War, the Roman Catholic hierarchy in the conquered territories was in the hands of the invaders, and generally in their service. Actually, the first Mexican-American bishop was not named until well into the second half of the twentieth century. These circumstances gave rise to anticlerical feelings similar to those which appeared in Latin America at the time of independence. And this in turn opened the way for Protestantism.[85]

Thus during the nineteenth century many perceived the Catholic Church as being backward and anti-Hispanic, while Protestants were seen as being progressive.

Today the trend to abandon the Roman Church has only escalated. As the saying goes, "people vote with their feet." There are some who feel that these non-Catholic groups have done a much better job than has the Catholic Church of catering to Hispanics and immigrants in general. Allan Deck, one of the foremost experts in the field, stresses that since there is not one single cause for this mass exodus, not one remedy exists. In an article that appeared in 1985 he offers numerous reasons and suggests various possible solutions.[86]

He discusses the results of several meetings that attempted to deal with this flight of Hispanic Catholics. The single most prominent aspect that emerged from the dialogue of bishops in Alta and Baja California was the need for more personalism in all dealings with Hispanic people. The Church has often failed to inculturate, often being too territorial and coming across as lacking in focus.[87]

The fundamentalists, on the other hand, "offer the Hispanic an attractive, coherent package." Fixed doctrines, simple morality, com-

---

85. J. L. González, *Mañana* (1990) 71–2.

86. Deck, "Fundamentalism and the Hispanic Catholic" (1985) 64–6.

87. On a more positive note, the U.S. Catholic Church at various times in history took a strong advocacy role. Among these champions is Robert E. Lucy, archbishop of San Antonio from 1941 to 1969. See Privett, *U.S. Catholic Church and Its Hispanic Members*.

bined with emotionally charged worship, make fundamentalism very attractive to a Hispanic largely ignored by his or her native church. Deck challenges the Catholic Church to open its eyes to why it is that the fundamentalists are making such inroads with Hispanics, that is, they have made more of an effort to inculturate into a less cerebral milieu.

Edmundo Rodríguez, the Jesuit pastor previously mentioned who later became provincial of the New Orleans Jesuit Province, raises the question from another perspective:

> The Protestant and Pentecostal churches are making great inroads into the Hispanic community. They are perceived as churches of the poor and for the poor (whether this be the reality or not); many of them take in chemically dependent people and turn their lives around. Generally their buildings are much simpler, and often these are "storefront" churches; they are basically lay churches in which anyone willing to spend time in training can become an apostle. There is also a perception that the people who belong to these little churches are not afraid to come into people's houses and deal with the worst problems they find there: addictions, violence, and strained relationships between family members. The Catholic Church, on the other hand, is seen as being uncomfortable with poverty and as not dealing with the real problems that poor people generally experience. That, in my opinion, is why the fundamentalist churches are so attractive to poorer Hispanics.[88]

In short, then, the Church's ministry to Hispanics has been plagued with many difficulties. Among the two most difficult ones has been how to make, in the words of Puebla, a "preferential option of the poor" and how to inculturate better the message of the gospel in a Hispanic context.

A Prophetic Presence

The U.S. bishops wrote a pastoral letter in 1983, following it with a "pastoral plan" in 1987. Although issued by the hierarchy, this work, the *National Pastoral Plan for Hispanic Ministry*, is the culmination of three *encuentros*, or national meetings, held in 1972, 1977, and 1985 to collect input and feedback from the grass-roots Hispanic Church.[89] The one held in 1985, the *Tercer Encuentro*, was particularly characterized by

88. E. Rodríguez, "Realities for Hispanics" (1988) 9. See also his article "Hispanic Community and Church Movements" (1994) 206–39.

89. See Galerón et al., *Prophetic Vision.* The work is a collection of essays written by leading pastoral theologians.

consultation, study, and reflection at all levels. It was attended by 1,150 delegates.[90] As the *Pastoral Plan* notes, Hispanics, despite their economic poverty, have much to offer the U.S. Church:

> This same people, due to its great sense of religion, family, and community, is a prophetic presence in the face of materialism and individualism of society. Since the majority of Hispanics are Catholic, their presence can be a source of renewal within the Catholic Church in North America. Because of its youth and growth, this community will continue to be a significant presence in the future.[91]

Other writers add their assessment of the spiritual riches of the Hispanic culture to the bishops' statement. Kenneth G. Davis, a Conventual Franciscan, sees the presence of Hispanics in the Church as a blessing. In them he finds less of a modern, secularistic taint. "It is precisely because Hispanics are Catholic and not part of our dominant society that they are in a unique position to help us distinguish between what is authentically Catholic in our society and what is the trappings of purely civil religion or cultural convention."[92]

In a similar vein, Allan Deck describes some of the differences between the Hispanic and the dominant North American culture. His analysis fleshes out the bishops' hope that Hispanics are a prophetic presence in the Church:

> The North American culture is one closely wrapped in personal development, in individualism, in secularism, while the Hispanic culture stresses the collective aspects of personal life: the extended family, the interrelatedness of people's spiritual and temporal lives. The Anglo-American world stresses the independence of the individual, while the Hispanics' world is hierarchical and stresses the dependence and interdependence of the individual on the family, the church, and the community. Hispanic culture, with its strong emphasis on the religious aspect of life, feels a definite attraction to a family- and community-based approach to religion. The Hispanic looks for more expressive ways of living his or her faith.[93]

Some theologians have taken a serious look at Hispanic spirituality, of which popular religiosity is an important part, and have begun its systematization. Rosa María Icaza, for example, a Sister of Charity of the Incarnate Word, describes the spirituality of Mexican and Mexican

90. For a description of the *encuentros* and a characterization of their spirit, see J. L. González, *Mañana* (1990) 65.
91. National Conference of Catholic Bishops, *Pastoral Plan* (1987) 5.
92. Davis, "Father, We're Not in Kansas Anymore" (1990) 16.
93. Deck, "As I See It," *Company* 6 (Fall 1988) 28.

American Catholics. Her observations probably hold true for Latin American spirituality in general. She concludes that for Hispanics "spirituality is translated into the love of God which moves, strengthens and is manifested in love of neighbor and of self."[94]

Numerous examples prove her point. Drawing greatly from popular religiosity, she describes an incarnational spirituality where symbols and relationships are of utmost importance, whether between the individual and God or the individual and others. She succeeds in showing that both women and priests play an important role within the culture and concludes that a Hispanic pastoral theology is still in the process of development.[95]

As the above article by a Hispanic theologian suggests, there is today an emerging U.S. Hispanic theology that is attempting to identify and promote Christian values within Hispanic culture. Although, in the words of the bishops' pastoral, "no other European culture has been in this country longer than the Hispanic,"[96] it is only until recently, with the advent of such Hispanic theologians as Virgil Elizondo, Allan Deck, and María Pilar Aquino, that these voices are being heard in the area of theological scholarship.[97]

The Academy of Catholic Hispanic Theologians of the United States (ACHTUS) was formed in 1989 and is already serving an important role in the development of this emerging local theology. What is interesting to note about this group of Hispanic theologians is that at least a quarter are female, a significant number are laypersons, and just about all are actively engaged in a pastoral area.

This last fact helps to guarantee that their reflection is coming out of pastoral experience. The need for insertion and dialogue, acknowledged in Puebla (nos. 650, 122, 1307), is summarized in the phrase *pastoral de conjunto*. The bishops' letter describes this strategy as "a pastoral focus and approach to action arising from shared reflection among the agents of evangelization."[98]

The Challenge Remaining

An examination of Hispanic Catholics in the U.S. Church has led us through a brief history that revealed both an old and new presence; a social analysis that rendered the image of a young, generally poor and

---

94. Icaza, "Spirituality" (1989) 232.

95. Ibid.

96. National Conference of Catholic Bishops, *Hispanic Presence* (1984) no. 6.

97. See Elizondo, *Future Is Mestizo* (1988); Deck, *Second Wave* (1989); Aquino, *Our Cry for Life* (1993).

98. National Conference of Catholic Bishops, *Hispanic Presence* (1984) no. 11.

uneducated population very much in need of the Church's assistance; yet, as the theological reflection highlighted, a people not without innumerable social and religious gifts. In fact, the evidence for debunking the urban underclass model as it has been applied to Latinos in the United States calls for the development of new paradigms, ones that take into account their spirituality, or their world of meaning in relation to the sacred. Religion may very well provide a unifying factor for the tremendously diverse Latino communities.

For these and other reasons they will continue to play an important role in the U.S. Church. Despite the present exodus of Hispanic Catholics from the Church, it is said that by the year 2010 the majority of Catholics in the United States will be Hispanic or of Hispanic origin. It is not the first time that the U.S. Church has been made up of a large immigrant population. The great successes with the waves of poor Europeans who came to America in the second half of the nineteenth and the early part of the twentieth centuries were not obtained without faith, creativity, and adaptation. Through these struggles the Church matured and grew to encompass a great diversity, surely the most diverse in the world. Parochial schools, seminaries for a native clergy, hospitals, orphanages, and national parishes were a welcome sight for immigrants who had left everything to come to America and form part, not only of a new country, but also of a new Church.[99]

Once again, it has an opportunity to be a Church of the poor, the poor who are already within its dioceses. Will it welcome them and see them as a blessing and not a problem to be solved—or as just another ethnic group to be assimilated? The question remains. We now turn to a more detailed survey of the history of U.S. Hispanic theology, a theology that takes into account not only suffering but also God's infinite grace. In the words of Paul's letter to the Hebrews, "For land which has drunk the rain that often falls upon it, and brings forth vegetation useful to those for whose sake it is cultivated, receives a blessing from God" (Heb 6:7, *RSV*).

---

99. See Fitzpatrick, "Hispanic Poor" (1988) 189–200.

2

The History of U.S. Hispanic Theology: 1972–1998

At a presbyteral ordination that took place in a small, old mission town in West Texas, a group of Mexican folk dancers adorned the liturgy with their presence. The joyfully sung *Gloria,* led by *Mariachis,* came alive as the dancers whirled in praise of a God who is often found in the grace and color of popular celebrations. In response to the first reading the congregation prayerfully sang Psalm 34 as adapted by John Foley's "Cry of the Poor." Mexican shawls in hand, the women dancers, standing before the faithful, moved gracefully in dance and gesture. In unison these young women portrayed, gently yet powerfully, a God tender and compassionate, a God incarnate in the suffering of human-kind.

Two very different cultures, the Latin American and the North American, came together in that majestic dance. Together they helped convey the power and compassion of a God who creates, loves, and sustains all, especially the poor. There is another dance being created today in the Church. Its choreographers are a new generation of U.S. Hispanic theologians who are demonstrating that an important facet of this dance is the resonant faith experience of Hispanics in the United States. In attempting to convey this Latina and Latino experience of the divine, their new voices, seeking to articulate the ineffable, join with other non-Hispanic theologians. As articulators of a long faith tradition, these Hispanic theologians are confident that their contribution to what might be called mainstream theology will be for the enhancement of all. Although the Latino presence in what is now the United States goes back centuries, it has only been recently that these Latino voices have started to be heard in theological circles, a point made in chapter 1.

During the last thirty years or so, various theologians have begun to produce a Hispanic theology, one often rooted in poverty and marginalization yet not without its salvific element.[1]

This chapter describes in considerable detail the writings of U.S. Hispanic theologians during this formative period, from 1972 to 1998. The writers featured are presented in four groups: (1) Virgil P. Elizondo, the earliest and certainly the most prolific of the Catholic writers; (2) several theologians writing after Elizondo who are members of ACHTUS, the Academy of Catholic Hispanic Theologians (María Pilar Aquino, Allan Figueroa Deck, Orlando O. Espín, Roberto S. Goizueta, Ada María Isasi-Díaz, Jaime R. Vidal, and Alejandro García-Rivera); (3) one of the most published of the Protestant Hispanic theologians, Justo L. González; and (4) other Protestant Latino theologians (Orlando E. Costas, Harold J. Recinos, Eldin Villafañe, Samuel Solivan, and Ismael García).[2]

1. An overview of this emerging theology is the topic of my licentiate thesis. See E. C. Fernández, "Towards a U.S. Hispanic Theology" (1992). The bulk of the thesis consists of a cursory analysis of a bibliography of most of the material written so far by U.S. Hispanic Catholic theologians. I am indebted to Arturo Bañuelas, in whose seminar I participated the previous year at the Jesuit School of Theology in Berkeley, California, for the formulation of this approach. Among the most comprehensive articles written on the subject are Segovia's "New Manifest Destiny" (1991) 102; Bañuelas' "U.S. Hispanic Theology," (1992) 275–300; Deck's introduction to *Frontiers* (1992) ix–xxvi. The *National Catholic Reporter* (September 11, 1992) dedicated its fall book section to the works of Hispanic theologians. The article, by Dawn Gibeau, is quite succinct and interestingly sprinkled with quotations from the various authors. See also E. C. Fernández, "Reading the Bible in Spanish" (1994) 86–90; Lara Medina, "Broadening the Discourse at the Theological Table: An Overview of Latino Theology (1968–1993)," *Latino Studies Journal* 5, no. 3 (September 1994) 10–36. One of the first articles to synthesize U.S. Hispanic theology within a certain area, namely, sacred Scripture, is Ruiz, "Beginning to Read the Bible in Spanish," 28–50. The work includes the writings of J. L. González, Deck, and Romero. See also Segovia, "Reading the Bible as Hispanic Americans" (1994) 167–73. Two recently edited works of the writings of Latino Protestants are *Teología en Conjunto,* ed. J. D. Rodríguez and L. I. Martell-Otero, and *Protestantes/Protestants,* ed. David Maldonado, Jr.

2. To my knowledge the only U.S. Protestant Latina theologian to have published a theological book is Loida I. Martell-Otero. I refer above to her co-edited work, *Teología en Conjunto.* This dearth is not surprising, given that it was not until 1996 that Daisy Machado became the first U.S. Latina Protestant to earn a doctorate. A graduate of the University of Chicago Divinity School, she was the first Latina in the U.S. ordained in the Christian Church (Disciples of Christ), in 1981. She is the recipient of the 1999 Orlando E. Costas Award, given by Andover-Newton Theological School. Among her works is "Being Ecumenical in the Barrio," *Journal of Hispanic/ Latino Theology* 3, no. 2 (November 1995) 6–13. Machado is presently working on a history of Latina/o Disciples in the United States and Canada to be published by Chalice Press. As of this writing there are three others: Elizabeth

Besides influencing each other, they are now beginning to make their presence felt in the academic theological world.[3] The purpose of this overview is to give a general idea of emerging U.S. Hispanic or Latino theology, in the process exposing some of the basic issues surrounding its evolution. While this scope may seem somewhat broad at first, later chapters will draw from this general exposition, demonstrating in particular how this theology can be understood as a contextual theology.

"Reading the Bible in Spanish"

Latin America's theology of liberation has contributed much to our understanding of perspective in theological methodology. The world looks very different from a palace than it does from a dilapidated shack. Protestant Hispanic theologian Justo González, trying to propose a more contextualized biblical theology, calls this approach "reading the Bible in Spanish."[4] By this expression González does not mean literally reading the Bible in a Spanish translation but bringing to the interpretation of Scripture a particular perspective. He hopes that such a perspective will help not only Hispanics but also the Church at large by tapping into the theological richness present in Hispanic Christianity.[5]

Early Hispanic theologians were not as much concerned about making a contribution to the wider Church as they were about developing a pastoral theology to help guide ministry to Hispanics. Many consider Virgil Elizondo, a Mexican American diocesan priest from San Antonio,

---

Conde-Frazier (Boston College, 1998), Zaida Maldonado Perez (St. Louis University, 1999), and Esther Díaz-Bolet (Southwestern Baptist Seminary, 1999). I am indebted to Dr. Machado, program director of the Hispanic Theological Initiative until August 1999, for this information.

3. Several historical and theological journals have devoted entire issues to discussing the U.S. Hispanic reality. See *U.S. Catholic Historian* (winter/spring 1990); *Listening: Journal of Religion and Culture* (winter 1992); *New Theology Review* (December 1991); and *Missiology* (April 1992). One of the key figures behind several theological journal issues published later is Kenneth Davis. The Conventual Franciscan friar guest-edited (with Virgilio Elizondo) the fall 1997 issue of *Listening;* the December 1997 issue of *Chicago Studies* (with Allan Figueroa Deck); and the January 1998 issue of *Theology Today* (with Justo González). Among the recent anthologies published are Deck's *Frontiers* (1992); Goizueta's *We Are a People* (1992); Hemrick's edited work *Strangers and Aliens No Longer;* J. L. González, *Alabadle!* (1996); Peter Casarella and Raúl Gomez, eds., *El Cuerpo de Cristo: The Hispanic Presence in the U.S. Catholic Church* (New York: Crossroad Herder, 1998).

4. For an interesting approach to biblical theology from other cultural perspectives, such as that of Southeast Asia, see Abesamis, *Core of Biblical Faith,* and Fung, *Shoes-Off Barefoot We Walk.*

5. J. L. González, *Mañana* (1990) 75.

Texas, to be the major pioneer of Roman Catholic Hispanic theology. He first gained wide acclaim for his reflections on religion and culture.[6] Following his example, yet bringing to bear their own perspective, a handful of others have begun to create a theology rooted in the Hispanic experience of Church and of U.S. society. The year 1974 saw the publication of two articles, one by Jesuit priest Allan Figueroa Deck and the other by Marina Herrera, an expert on multicultural catechesis.[7]

Since the early writings of Herrera, other women theologians have responded to the challenge of how to speak of God from a Latina woman's stance. The publication of many articles and some books, especially during the last few years, provides a much needed contribution to a theological perspective that too often has been solely male. Deck and Bañuelas helped bring together these theologians to form the Academy of Catholic Hispanic Theologians of the U.S. (ACHTUS) in 1988.[8] Protestant Latino theologians, probably the most noted of which is J. L. González, mentioned above, also have been writing. Their perspective is significant not only because a large number of Hispanics are now Protestant but also because they, in a sense, are outside the Latino religious and cultural majority, which until recently tended to be Roman Catholic.[9]

1. Elizondo: Herald of U.S. Hispanic Theology

Elizondo, the founder of the Mexican American Cultural Center in San Antonio, Texas, having served as its first president (1972–87), was rector of the Cathedral of San Fernando in San Antonio for twelve years. Holding a doctorate from the Institut Catholique in Paris, he has served as an editor of *Concilium*. A 1992 bibliographic study of U.S. Hispanic theology revealed that, with his various books, innumerable articles, and edited collections, he is responsible for 30 percent of its 227 entries. He has authored or co-authored more than ten books and more

6. Elizondo, "Educación Religiosa" (1972). See also his *Christianity and Culture* (1975).
7. Deck, "New Vision" (1974) 87–93; Herrera, "La Teología en el Mundo de Hoy," (1974).
8. For a description of how ACHTUS was born, see Deck's introduction to *Frontiers* (1992) ix–xxvi.
9. The years between 1972 and 1989 witnessed a 7 percent increase in the number of Hispanic Protestants in the United States. In 1972, this group made up 16 percent of the Hispanic population. In 1989, they numbered 23 percent (Source: National Opinion Research Center; Gallup Poll as quoted in *Statistical Handbook*, compiled and ed. F. L. Schick and R. Schick).

than forty articles.[10] His writings are now so prolific that a later generation has begun to write about them.[11]

Several of Elizondo's works have already been mentioned. Among these, the two most well known are *Galilean Journey* (1983) and *The Future Is Mestizo* (1988). The first is structured more analytically, while the second is basically autobiographical. That is, the first explains the story told in the second.

In *Galilean Journey* Elizondo combines two identities that at first seem to have nothing in common. Taking the notion of what it meant to be Galilean in Jesus' time and what it means to be *mestizo* today, he bases his entire book on the similarities of these two identities. One might assume that the bicultural background of St. Paul, a product of Judaism and Hellenism, seems to lend itself much more to a comparison with modern day *mestizos*. Elizondo's work, however, goes beyond the bicultural aspect of the *mestizo*, although he does discuss it at some length. Instead, he uses the term *mestizo*, one some might equate with "half-breed," to designate marginal status. In this sense, both the Galileans in their day and *mestizos* today are marginalized people. It is the role of these individuals in God's salvific plan that Elizondo highlights.

The book is divided into three parts: the Mexican American experience, the gospel matrix, and the interaction of both. The operational theological method views human experience as foundational. Affirmed is the value of recognizing that all theologizing comes out of a particular context. If we are to interpret the meaning of the gospel for our times, therefore, what is needed is a thorough understanding of the multiple aspects of this context.

The author begins this process of contextualization by presenting a brief historical overview of what the Mexican experience has been. The Chicano, or Mexican American, is seen as a product of two *mestizajes:* the first having occurred during the Spanish-Catholic Conquest of Mexico, during which both Spanish and Indian blood along with culture was intermingled, and the second having taken place at the time of the United States' takeover of the Southwest. The Nordic-Protestant Conquest had more political ramifications, since blood, culture, and religion largely remained distinct even to this day.

Of great importance anthropologically is the emergence of the *mestizo*. While it took centuries for such an identity and culture to develop in Mexico, with many wanting to ignore either the Indian or the Spanish contribution to the forging of the Mexican nation, it is only in the last few decades that such an awareness has begun to develop in terms of the

10. See E. C. Fernández, "Towards a U.S. Hispanic Theology" (1992).
11. Matovina, "Liturgy and Popular Expressions of Faith," 436–44.

Mexican American.[12] Indeed, Elizondo comments that such a *mestizaje* is "feared by established groups because it is perceived as a threat to the barriers of separation that consolidate self-identity and security."[13]

The result is that the *mestizo* is left having to make a conscious or unconscious choice between either assimilating into one of the parent cultures or creating an identity that is a product of both. The difficulty comes from not being accepted totally by either of the parent cultures—hence a type of cultural marginalization. In the case of the Mexican American, the *pocho* often feels that he or she is neither totally a part of the dominant Anglo-American culture nor the Mexican culture because of having been socialized into life as lived in the United States.

Before going on to show specifically how this marginalization is related to that of Galileans in the time of Jesus, Elizondo outlines some of the symbols of Mexican American Catholicism that speak of belonging, identity, struggle, suffering, death, and a new creation. Among them are ashes on Ash Wednesday, Good Friday, the *Posadas*, the *Pastorela*, the saints—especially St. Martin de Porres—baptism, and Christ the King and Our Lady of Guadalupe. Each is explained from the perspective of popular religiosity.

In the third section of the work, the Mexican American theologian develops what he calls the "Galilee principle," namely, "what human beings reject, God chooses as his very own."[14] The son of God comes from an area that was insignificant in the view of the sociopolitical powers of the time. Considered by the people of Jerusalem to be "country bumpkins," the Jewish people of Galilee can be compared to the *campesinos* of today. Elizondo notes that they were considered psychologically and sociologically inferior even by their own people and were considered culturally inferior by the great powers of the world.

In the final section of the book Elizondo introduces two other important principles that he wishes to pursue. The first is the "Jerusalem principle": "God chooses an oppressed people, not to bring them comfort in their oppression but to enable them to confront, transcend, and transform whatever in the oppressor society diminishes and destroys the fundamental dignity of human nature."[15] The marginated person, therefore, who in this case happens to be the *mestizo*, is crucial for the transformation of society, just as confronting Jerusalem is crucial to Jesus' redemptive act. In this manner, Elizondo understands *mestizaje* as prophetic mission. The *mestizo*, although in many ways alienated

---

12. See Lafaye, *Quetzacóatl and Guadalupe;* Fuentes, *Buried Mirror.*
13. Elizondo, *Galilean Journey* (1983) 18.
14. Ibid., 91.
15. Ibid., 103.

from the parent cultures, is called upon by God to be the bridge between the oppressor and the oppressed and to convert oppressors and their system of values. A bicultural background is a tremendous gift for her or him. Far from simply being passive, the *mestizo,* in this case the Mexican American, is being challenged to help transform unjust social, political, and economic institutions.

Paradoxically, however, because of the Christian belief of "death unto life," the *mestizo* is guaranteed final victory. The "resurrection principle," the last of Elizondo's tenets, states that "only love can triumph over evil, and no human power can prevail against the power of unlimited love. Out of suffering and death, God will bring health and life."[16]

Elizondo mentions various signs of hope, concrete ways in which the unselfish service of some Mexican Americans is giving birth to a society that is striving to be more just, for example, through the formation of community organizations or through the United Farm Workers. Another great sign of hope throughout Latin America is the formation of *comunidades eclesiales de base.* The challenge for the *mestizo* remains clear: not to seek power for the sake of personal gain but power for the sake of all the oppressed and thus for the sake of a better future for all.

The second most important work of the Mexican American theologian is *The Future Is Mestizo,* published in 1988.[17] This autobiographical book further develops insights from *Galilean Journey.* Fernando F. Segovia shows the relationship between Elizondo's two principal works:

> Five years separate the publication of *Galilean Journey* (1983) from that of *The Future Is Mestizo* (1988), two works that complement one another quite well. The former follows a familiar pattern from the hermeneutics of liberation: a critical reading of a particular sociocultural situation (the Mexican American experience) and of the Scriptures in light of one another; the latter follows another familiar pattern from the theology of liberation: the use of the personal story or autobiography in the description and critical analysis of the particular sociohistorical situation in question. In effect, the later work provides a detailed background for the earlier and more systematic work.[18]

---

16. Ibid., 115.

17. Elizondo. The work was first published in French under the title *L'avenir est au métissage* (Paris: Nouvelle Editions Mame, 1987). The Meyer-Stone edition cited here is an edited version of the original English manuscript. Rosa María Icaza translated the English text into Spanish. See *El Futuro es Mestizo: Vivir donde se juntan las culturas* (San Antonio: Mexican American Cultural Center, 1998).

18. F. Segovia, "New Manifest Destiny" (1991) 103.

In both works Elizondo spells out what happens, or can happen, when faith confronts culture. In *The Future Is Mestizo,* Elizondo's story, as the son of Mexican immigrants to the Southwest, unfolds.[19] The Latino priest from San Antonio, Texas, describes what it was like to grow up living between two very different worlds: the Mexican and the American. While early memories of basking in the warmth of a Mexican American community evoke a paradise, later years brought feelings of rejection and discrimination from Anglo culture.

> The paradise existence of the neighborhood came to a halt the first day I went to a Catholic grade school operated by German nuns in what had been a German parish. There the pastor still told Mexicans to go away because it wasn't their church. My parents had sent me there because it was the nearest Catholic school. Mexicans were tolerated but not very welcome.[20]

In another passage from the book Elizondo reflects on how he came to see himself not in terms of someone who didn't belong, whether as a "pure Mexican" or a "pure American," but rather in terms of something entirely new.

> Between the school years at the seminary and the summers at the store [the family business located in a Mexican neighborhood], I gradually became more and more aware of the many things that I was not; I was not and would never be, even if I wanted to, a regular U.S.–American. Yet neither would I be a *puro mexicano.* There were identities that I knew that I was and was not at the same time: U.S.–American, Mexican, Spanish, Indian. Yet I was! My very being was a combination. I was a rich mixture but was not mixed-up! In fact, I was more and more clear that my own inner identity was new and exciting. I started to enjoy the feeling of who I was: I was *not just* U.S.–American and *not just* Mexican but fully both and exclusively neither. I knew both perfectly even though I remained a mystery to them. And I was threatening to them since they knew I knew them, but they did not know me fully. I lived in two worlds, and the two worlds lived in me. That was wealth.[21]

From this personal insight Elizondo moves to grappling with the larger picture. In the final chapter, "Towards Universal Mestizaje," he

19. Kenneth G. Davis describes this work in the following words: "This book is sacramental; it effects what it signifies. Of all of Elizondo's writings this is the book which is itself most mestizo, a synthesis of what appear to be opposites; at one and the same time it weds a very popular autobiographical style with Elizondo's most potentially far-reaching reflections." See *Apuntes* 9, no. 3 (fall 1989) 68.

20. Elizondo, *Future Is Mestizo* (1988) 15.

21. Ibid., 26.

describes a mixture, or *mestizaje*, not only at the cultural level but also at the religious. Jesus is described as the great universalizer.

> The radical universalizing newness of the way of Jesus of Nazareth is that it offers people the possibility of a hyphenated existence: Jewish-Christians, Gentile-Christians, Afro-Christians, Asian-Christians, *Mestizo*-Christians. Thus the way of Jesus affirms local identity while opening it up to fellowship and free exchange with all others. Jesus' way is the opposite of the abstract universals of philosophy or ideology; it is concrete, specific socio-cultural identity no longer threatened by others or afraid of being contaminated by others.[22]

This *mestizaje* is not one of dominance but rather one of cultural and religious pluralism, a combination of the particular and the universal. Through the integration of various cultural riches, people become more human and therefore more Christian.

Specific aspects of Elizondo's thought will be examined further on in this work. For now, however, it is helpful to summarize his basic contribution to the emergence of U.S. Hispanic theology. The Mexican American theologian has tried to bring about, in the case of Latinos in the United States, a dialogue between theology and anthropology. His two main themes are *mestizaje* and popular religion. Beyond the shadow of a doubt, he is a pastoral theologian and an activist. While his model is chiefly anthropological, he is also quite praxis-oriented in that he is concerned with the identity of a people for their eventual empowerment. Thus he is concerned with societal change.

2. Various Other Roman Catholic Hispanic Theologians in ACHTUS

While the formation of ACHTUS has already been mentioned, it is helpful here to describe some of the factors behind its creation.[23] Besides Jesuit Allan Figueroa Deck, the other person most responsible for its formation is Arturo Bañuelas, a diocesan priest from El Paso, Texas. He presently is the director of Tepeyac Institute, a lay ministry formation center, as well as pastor of a large parish in his home diocese. His doctorate is from the Pontifical Gregorian University in Rome.[24] In addition to his hands-on work in pastoral ministry and training he has

22. Ibid., 108ff.

23. As previously mentioned, see Deck's introduction in *Frontiers* (1992).

24. Arturo José Bañuelas, "The Exodus in the Theologies of Liberation of Gustavo Gutiérrez and J. Severino Croatto" (S.T.D. diss., Pontifical Gregorian University, 1987).

been attempting to synthesize U.S. Hispanic theology, particularly one appropriate for the U.S.–Mexico border region.[25]

In the mid 1980s both Deck and Bañuelas were concerned about the need for serious theological reflection on the part of Hispanics in the United States. Deck writes:

> It seemed to us that the lack of articulate Hispanic theological voices was a basic and alarming symptom of the marginality that characterized the Hispanic presence in the U.S. Catholic Church. While the Hispanic communities' lack of "hands on" pastoral care and outreach was of deep concern to us, the failure to raise up a more critical and theologically grounded voice seemed to us to be especially serious in the North American Catholic Church context. The fuller participation of Hispanics in the church especially at the levels of policy and planning, a fairer distribution of the church's resources, and a more valid vision of the U.S. church's identity and destiny would never come about without the contribution of thinkers and theologians. But not just any thinkers and theologians. We were concerned about professionals interested in and capable of doing what Clodovis Boff calls "feet-on-the-ground" theology.[26]

The late 1980s witnessed the realization of their dream to form such a group. In 1994 the association counted sixty regular and associate members. Besides representing Hispanics from different national origins, the group comprised almost two-thirds of all U.S. Hispanic Catholics with or completing doctorates in some theological discipline.[27]

It is significant that of the thirty-seven authors listed in a bibliographic study of Catholic U.S. Hispanic theology done in 1992,[28] twenty, or 54 percent, are members of the Academy. The newly founded organization, therefore, has succeeded in bringing together a significant number of published U.S. Hispanic theologians. The core of the association's mission statement is given below:

> The Academy of Catholic Hispanic Theologians of the United States is an association of scholars dedicated to promoting research and critical reflection within the context of the United States Hispanic experience.

25. Bañuelas, "U.S.Hispanic Theology (1992) 275–300. His *Mestizo Christianity* (1995) is a collection of essays by principal figures in U.S. Hispanic theology, both Catholic and Protestant. The work introduces each contributor with a brief biography and also provides what was then the most comprehensive bibliography of U.S. Latino theology.

26. Deck, *Frontiers* (1992) xxii.

27. Ibid., xxiii.

28. E. C. Fernández, "Towards a U.S. Hispanic Theology" (1992) 67.

While influenced by other theologies, the articulation of the faith experience of United States Hispanics is a distinct theological enterprise whose depth and richness remain largely untapped by the Church. The urgency of providing a theological voice for the lived faith of the United States Hispanics is further underscored by the rapidly increasing demographic significance of the Hispanic population.[29]

Noteworthy in this statement is the importance given to articulating the faith experience of the Hispanic people. Its commitment to grass-roots theology is thus explicitly stated.

What kind of people make up ACHTUS? The requirements for admission allow for other than those with doctorates to join. Similarly, non-Latinos are also members.[30] As revealed below by viewing several individually, they are people with vision who are publishing fresh insights in theology from a U.S. Latino perspective. Two ACHTUS women theologians will be discussed after, because, while agreeing with much of the men's thought, they also make a serious critique of it.

Allan Figueroa Deck

Another well-published Mexican American priest, Deck has published two books, edited one, and has in addition over twenty-five articles to his credit. A native of Los Angeles, he served as pastor in Santa Ana and for six years was Director of Hispanic Ministry for the Diocese of Orange. He holds a Ph.D. in Latin American Studies from St. Louis

---

29. As stated in the ACHTUS Membership Directory, 1991, 1.

30. Article 2, Section 1 of the *Bylaws and Constitution,* which were amended in July 1998, describes the different types of memberships: "*Active* membership is open to Roman Catholic Hispanics who possess a doctorate in theology, scripture, ministry or general religious studies and are knowledgeable and actively engaged in the North American Hispanic religious experience. In exceptional cases the committee on Admissions may recommend for active membership those whose education and scholarly achievements could be considered as meeting the standards customarily demanded for the doctorate. *Associate* membership is open to Roman Catholic Hispanics who are enrolled in a doctoral program in theology, scripture, ministry, or general religious studies; or to others with doctorates who are engaged in the U.S. Hispanic religious experience. *Affiliate* membership is open to Roman Catholics who have completed or who are enrolled in an accredited non-doctoral graduate program in theology, scripture, ministry, or general religious studies, and who are engaged in the U.S. Hispanic religious experience. *Honorary* membership is conferred, upon recommendation of the Board of Directors, by majority vote of the active membership present at the annual business meeting in recognition of special services to the Academy or the elaboration of a U.S. Hispanic theology" (emphasis mine). As of Spring 1999 the total membership was close to one hundred.

University and an S.T.D. from the Pontifical Gregorian University in Rome. Besides serving as adjunct faculty at Loyola Marymount University in Los Angeles, he directs a multicultural center for spirituality, Loyola Institute of Spirituality, in Orange, California.

The Jesuit's most commented upon work to date is *The Second Wave: Hispanic Ministry and the Evangelization of Cultures.*[31] Through this work, Deck has constructed a framework for understanding Hispanic ministry in the Catholic Church today. It is an effort to surface pastoral issues. Extremely well received, the book was awarded first place in the 1989 Catholic Press Association professional books category. By "second wave," Deck is referring to the demographic trend of Latin Americans and Asian-Pacific peoples coming to the United States that started after World War II and continues today. This trend has been changing the face of the U.S. Catholic Church. Once heavily populated by immigrants chiefly from Europe or their descendants, tomorrow's U.S. Catholic Church will be Hispanic in the majority.

Deck notes that the "first wave" of immigrants to the United States consisted of the traditionally Catholic ethnic groups—Irish, German, Italian, and Slavic. In many ways these groups assimilated well into U.S. cultural mainstream.

> U.S. Catholics have become comfortable with their hard-earned identity. Sons and daughters of the teeming masses—the "first wave"—that disembarked in the last century or early in this one, they achieved acceptance in a predominantly Protestant and rather anti-Catholic country. The struggle was long and often bitter. World War II gave these immigrants and their offspring an opportunity to demonstrate their Americanism. They performed their civic and patriotic duties with distinction. By and large, they ceased speaking their native languages. And by 1960 the United States was able to elect a Catholic president. Roman Catholics were becoming "as American as apple pie."[32]

But with the more recent arrival of the large new groups of immigrants, many of whom are Catholic, the Church has found itself in a different position.

> At this moment in time, consequently, the U.S. Catholic Church is schizophrenic, caught between two identities. One is the achievement of the mainstreaming process, the other is the result of a new migration that shows no sign of abating. This migration will trans-

31. Deck, *Second Wave* (1989).
32. Ibid., 1.

form that Church by the next century into a predominantly Hispanic American institution just as today it is predominantly Irish
American.[33]

From the beginning, Deck sets the stage for what today is the most important challenge for the Church in the United States: "This book is
written with the conviction that what is done to promote the effective
pastoral care of Hispanics today will determine to a degree still not
fully appreciated the vitality and effectiveness of the U.S. Catholic
Church of the twenty-first century."[34] Sheer numbers, to say nothing of
the challenge of the gospel, dictate a careful revision of pastoral strategy that takes into account not only the good of the Hispanic community but also that of the entire U.S. Church. For Deck, a true
evangelization of the North American Church calls for a consistent attentiveness to such gospel values as mutual respect, dialogue, and pluralism.[35]

Deck's method and motivation for doing theology, evident in *The
Second Wave* and elsewhere, is basically one of praxis. Theory is at the
service of practice, and practice must influence theory.[36] Fernando
Segovia describes the book's method in the following words:

> The book represents a critical exercise in pastoral theology, written
> from what Figueroa Deck describes as a transformative perspec-
> tive, as distinct from both a functionalist or assimilationist and a
> Marxist or conflict approach—an analysis of the Hispanic Ameri-
> can reality from a utopian vision of God and humanity and with
> specific goals and actions in mind.[37]

Deck is quite eclectic in his approach, a mastery he has demonstrated
well in his previous writings, the bulk of which are in the form of articles. In the first part of *The Second Wave,* the first two chapters, he uses
sociology, economics, and history in order to introduce the Hispanic

33. Ibid., 2.
34. Ibid.
35. See Deck, "La Raza Cósmica" (1993) 46–53.
36. J. Holland and P. Henriot in *Social Analysis* describe this method as the "pastoral circle." This method incorporates the well-known "see/judge/act" trilogy of
Joseph Cardijn, a Belgian priest responsible for founding Catholic social action
groups prior to World War II. Its strength is its emphasis on the ongoing relationship between reflection and action. Like the "hermeneutic circle," that is, a method
of interpretation in which older theories are questioned in light of new situations,
the pastoral circle allows for ongoing renewal of both theory and practice. These authors credit both Freire, *Pedagogy of the Oppressed,* and Segundo, *Liberation of Theology,* for their contributions to this model of analysis.
37. Segovia, "New Manifest Destiny" (1991) 105.

American phenomenon. In the second part of the book, the last three chapters, he identifies the major issues in Hispanic ministry and assesses the Church's present pastoral work with Latinos, particularly focusing on the State of California although not limited to it. Concerned about evangelization and other missiological issues, he discusses the role of tradition, the magisterium, and the appropriateness of certain pastoral strategies.

In an edited work published in 1992, Deck provides a platform for a new generation of U.S. Latino theologians. Readers of this collection of essays sample the writings of such ACHTUS theologians as Roberto S. Goizueta, María Pilar Aquino, C. Gilbert Romero, Orlando O. Espín, Sixto J. García, Virgil P. Elizondo, and Gloria Inés Loya. Deck's introduction to the series of essays is a good "state of affairs" presentation for the situation of U.S. Hispanic theology today. In part he intends here to show how this new perspective in theology done from U.S. shores is both similar and dissimilar to Latin America's theology of liberation. The challenge of U.S. Hispanic theology is not to mimic the southern continent's liberation theology but to take seriously its method. Deck reports on both the progress and the task that still lies ahead:

> U.S. Hispanic theologians have thus deepened their respect for the accomplishments of Latin American and other third-world theologies. They have acknowledged an important debt. Yet there has been a gradual recognition of the need to do something different: to affirm the originality of theology grounded on the unique experiences of Hispanics specifically in the U.S. Gustavo Gutiérrez reminded us over and over again of the need to do this. He suggested that it was not a question of replicating the work of Latin Americans in the considerably different North American context, but of truly taking their method seriously—that is, doing theology out of this particular U.S. Hispanic reality. The resulting theology would surely be something fresh and original.[38]

A good example of how these two theologies, the Latin American theology of liberation and U.S. Hispanic theology, are different is how they have stressed different aspects of what is most important. According to Deck, Latin America's theology of liberation has stressed a praxis approach, one more committed to social change, over a more anthropological one. U.S. Hispanic theology, on the other hand, has tended to lean more, especially as seen in the writings of Elizondo and Deck, on

---

38. Deck, *Frontiers*, (1992) xv.

an anthropological perspective. This preference has seemed more appropriate because of the struggle of U.S. Hispanics to maintain their identity. A question that remains on the table, however, is whether social change is any less necessary in a U.S. context.

According to Deck, Latin America's liberationist thinkers have had to rethink their strong praxis orientation, wondering if too much attention was given to praxis and not enough to anthropological concerns, for example, to popular religiosity. In referring to Elizondo's treatment of Our Lady of Guadalupe in his writings, for example, Deck writes that

> Elizondo reinterpreted the story of Our Lady of Guadalupe as a myth in the deepest anthropological sense of the word, a myth which allows us to get at the heart of the Mexican and the Mexican-American culture and identity. In this Elizondo actually anticipated the criticism that was going to be made of liberation theologians for their disregard for the anthropological core of popular culture. A theology which purports to be "of the people" cannot take seriously only or mainly the socio-economic and political factors; it must attend to the people's religion, to their devotions, rituals, and customs. Among the Latin American peoples that means paying attention to their profound interest in the Virgin Mary. The contribution that Elizondo has made to the understanding of the Guadalupe event as it is celebrated and lived by Hispanics of Mexican origin shows that he possessed the insight long before many of his contemporaries.[39]

Although Deck would never dismiss the importance of attending to social and economic oppression, he laments the fact that often not enough attention on the part of Hispanic thinkers has been paid to the anthropological. Such concern for the *whole* person, that which includes the spiritual, artistic, and all that is human, is much more encompassing than mere ideology. Thus Deck is warning against a narrow focus on action dictated by ideology.

In general, his writings reveal a dialectic between theory and practice. That is, he brings theological sources, such as the Bible, present reality, and the magisterium, to bear on practical issues and practical concerns to bear on theological sources. For example, in writing about illegal migration into the United States, he engages theological and biblical concepts regarding aliens, Catholic social teaching, and present sociological reality.[40]

---

39. Ibid., xiii.
40. See Deck, "Christian Perspective" (1978) 39–53.

Orlando O. Espín

President of ACHTUS during the period of 1992–93 and one of its founding members, Espín teaches at the University of San Diego and directs the university's Center for the Study of Latino Catholicism. Born in Cuba and reared in the United States, he has worked in the Dominican Republic and in Brazil as well as in the United States. He is also founding editor of the *Journal of Hispanic/Latino Theology.*

Espín, whose main medium of expression has been articles and conferences, has distinguished himself through his reflections on the role of culture in theology and the importance of incorporating popular religiosity in our theologizing.[41] In his work he has dealt with such topics in systematic theology as grace, sin, the Trinity, and Christian anthropology. He argues that popular religiosity, which he considers to be a privileged means of understanding the *sensus fidelium,* is a key source for constructing an adequate theology of grace and providence. By *sensus fidelium,* Espín refers to the living witness of the faith of the people, that is, a certain intuition that springs from a Christian way of life.[42]

---

41. For a thorough history of Latino popular Catholicism in the United States, see his chapter "Popular Catholicism among Latinos," Dolan and Deck, *Hispanic Catholic Culture* (1994) 308–59. In "A 'Multicultural' Church? Theological Reflections from 'Below,'" *The Multicultural Church: A New Landscape in U.S. Theologies,* ed. W. Cenkner (Mahwah, N.J.: Paulist Press, 1996) 54–71, Espín expounds on the role of culture in theology. See his "Popular Religion as an Epistemology (of Suffering)" (1994) 55–78. In this article he dialogues with other theologians and social scientists to present a hypothetical position in search of an authentic Latino epistemology. "The problem . . . is how [Latinos] explain their suffering, know it as suffering, and make sense (at least some sense) of it" (p. 74). Here he argues that popular religion plays a very important role epistemologically. Finally, in "Popular Catholicism: Alienation or Hope?" *Hispanic/Latino Theology: Challenge and Promise,* ed. F. F. Segovia and A. M. Isasi-Díaz (Minneapolis: Fortress Press, 1996) 307–24, Espín presents a critical view of popular religion, one that takes into account both its alienating and liberating potential. He is not so naive as to think that hegemonic influences have not made their way into popular religion. In 1997 Espín published a collection of six of his key articles, which he entitled *The Faith of the People: Theological Reflections on Popular Catholicism.* Both the foreword by Roberto Goizueta and the introduction by Espín provide a framework for understanding his contribution as well as where his research is leading him.

42. Espín explains what he means by *sensus fidelium:* "Just as important as the written texts of tradition (or, in fact, more important), however, is the *living witness and faith* of the Christian people. This living witness and faith do not seem to be taken seriously by those who study tradition. It is difficult to limit the object of one's study when it is supposed to be found mainly at the experiential level in every faith community. Cultural differences, diversity of languages, and all sorts of other variations make the actual theological study and interpretation of the life and faith of real Christian people a very difficult task indeed. And to complicate things even

Espín explains the uniqueness of popular religiosity for getting at the soul of Hispanic culture:

> It has always been my contention that popular religiosity is a privileged vehicle for Hispanic cultures. Popular religiosity has been, and still is, the least "invaded" cultural creation of our peoples, and a locus for our most authentic self-disclosure. It is through popular religiosity that we have been able to develop, preserve, and communicate deeply held religious beliefs. Through it we experience profound encounters with God. While popular religiosity is not the only means for the development and preservation of our cultures, it would be extremely difficult (if not impossible) to think about or understand Hispanic cultures without finding the crucial role that popular religiosity has played (and still plays) in our midst as a matrix and vehicle for our most authentic values and selves.[43]

Like Deck, Espín bemoans the lack of serious attention given to the study of popular religiosity by systematic theologians. Often perceived as pertaining to the work of anthropologists or social scientists, the role of popular religiosity in the Church has been downplayed even by some liberation theologies. Espín notes, "It is not an exaggeration to say that, in Catholic theological circles, popular religion is either treated as an example of what should not be, or it is simply ignored as of no value for the serious theological enterprise."[44]

In an interview with *National Catholic Reporter*, Espín explicates the difference in an approach where popular Catholicism is studied "not as an anthropologist would study it, but as a theologian."[45] He continues, describing some of the characteristics of this popular religiosity, "an

---

further, the object of the study (though expressed through cultural categories, languages, and so forth, that run the gamut of human diversity) is found at the level of *intuition*. It is this 'faith-full' intuition that makes real Christian people sense that something is true or not vis-á-vis the gospel, or that someone is acting in accordance with the Christian gospel or not, or that something important for Christianity is not being heard. This intuition in turn allows for and encourages a belief and a style of life and prayer that express and witness to the fundamental Christian message: God as revealed in Jesus Christ. This 'faith-full' intuition is called the *sensus fidelium* (or *sensus fidei*)." See Espín, "Tradition and Popular Religion" (1992) 64.

43. Espín, "Grace and Humanness" (1992) 148. See also some of his works written in collaboration with Sixto J. García: "Hispanic-American Theology," (1987) 114–9; "Sources of Hispanic Theology" (1988) 122–5; "Lilies of the Field" (1989) 70–90. Also noteworthy is "Trinitarian Monotheism" (1992) 177–204.

44. Espín "Tradition and Popular Religion" (1992) 62.

45. Dawn Gibeau, "Hispanic Theology Aims Church at Poor," *National Catholic Reporter* (September 11, 1992).

emphasis on compassion and solidarity, an emphasis on the affective and, literally on the popularity of it—it's people's Catholicism," with clergy less important than laity as leaders.[46]

In his writings Espín singles out two key symbols found in popular religiosity, symbols he calls "bearers of the Christian gospel": the crucified Christ and Mary. "These two symbols are present in every Catholic Hispanic community in the United States with very similar functions and meaning, giving us a religious connecting link amid Hispanic diversity."[47] Over the centuries, the suffering Christ, as evidenced by Hispanic iconography and popular devotions such as those focused on the passion, has appealed to Latinos. Espín explains why, linking the history of oppression with an intuitive sense of the transformative power of the cross today:

> The Christ of Hispanic passion symbolism is a tortured, suffering human being. The image leaves no room for doubt. This dying Jesus, however, is so special because he is not just another human who suffers unfairly at the hands of evil humans. He is the divine Christ, and that makes his innocent suffering all the more dramatic. He is prayed to as one speaks with a living person, and not merely mourned or remembered as some dead hero of the past. His passion and death express his solidarity with all men and women throughout history who have also innocently suffered at the hands of evildoers.[48]

Taking the image of Our Lady of Guadalupe, Espín demonstrates in the same article why this great example of the inculturation of Mary through the religious symbols of ancient Mexico is consistent with the message of the gospel.[49]

---

46. Ibid.

47. Espín, "Tradition and Popular Religion" (1992) 69–70.

48. Ibid., 71.

49. For an intriguing discussion of the connection between the Holy Spirit and Our Lady of Guadalupe, see Espín's introduction to *Faith of the People* (1997). Espín poses some thought-provoking questions: "Why can't we understand the 'Mary' categories of Latino Catholicism as *orthodox popular pneumatology?* Is there something inherent in the divine nature of the Spirit that prevents it from being imaged, spoken of, and related within feminine categories? If colonial Mexico (and Tridentine Spain) were not really free to choose a pneumatological language truly adequate to proper evangelization about the Spirit (and not just to superficial pneumatological ortholalia) among the natives and *mestizos* of Mesoamerica, then I could wonder if the Mexican population might not have borrowed culturally meaningful Marian language (symbols, imagery, etc.), readily available in and through Catholic speech and practice, thereby allowing orthodox pneumatology to *understandably* speak with and to them. The ecclesiastical establishment convinced itself that Guadalupe

Elsewhere, the Cuban-born theologian, after having examined historically some of the means used in the early evangelization of indigenous Mexico, illustrates why the crucified Christ became so popular: vanquished people could relate to a suffering Christ. Incorporating history, anthropology, and theology, Espín masterfully relates this suffering Christ to trinitarian monotheism in sixteenth-century Mexico.[50]

Roberto S. Goizueta

This theology professor at Boston College, like Orlando Espín, was born in Cuba. A layperson, husband, and parent, he is also a charter member of ACHTUS and one of its past presidents. He has been publishing since 1984.[51] His first book, *Liberation, Method, and Dialogue: Enrique Dussel and North American Theological Discourse*,[52] which was translated into Portuguese, in many ways sets the tone for his future work. It marks a willingness to engage Latin American theology, especially the theology of liberation. In this work, the product of his dissertation, Goizueta explains Dussel's method, suggesting an analogue in the thought of Bernard Lonergan.[53]

Like Virgil Elizondo, Roberto Goizueta's story is one of finding himself very much between two worlds, that of the U.S. mainstream and that of Latin America, in neither of which he felt perfectly at home. Dawn Gibeau reports on her interview with him:

> Goizueta "got interested in trying to struggle with this whole issue of U.S. Hispanic identity as somehow being a combination of both

---

is Mary of Nazareth; but is this the more correct, orthodox, or only interpretation? Instead of an inculturated mariology, don't we have a superbly inculturated pneumatology?" (p. 9).

50. See Espín, "Trinitarian Monotheism" (1992). For a similar trinitarian discussion, see Sixto J. García's "A Hispanic Approach to Trinitarian Theology: The Dynamics of Celebration, Reflection, and Praxis," *We Are a People!* ed. Goizueta (1992) 107–32. A recent collection Espín co-edited with Miguel H. Díaz is *From the Heart of Our People: Latino/a Explorations in Catholic Systematic Theology* (Maryknoll, N.Y.: Orbis Books (1999).

51. Goizueta, "Liberation Theology: An Analysis of Two Critiques," *Verbum* (fall 1984).

52. Goizueta, *Liberation, Method, and Dialogue* (1988).

53. Among his numerous articles are "History of Suffering as Locus Theologicus in German Political Theology" (1985); "Liberation Theology: Retrospect and Prospect" (1988) 25–43; "Liberating Creation Spirituality," (1989) 85–115; "Theology as Intellectually Vital Inquiry" (1991) 58–69; "Challenge of Pluralism" (1992) 1–22; "*Nosotros*" (1992) 55–69; "U.S. Hispanic Mestizaje and Theological Method," *Migrants and Refugees* (1993/4 Concilium edition, ed. Dietmar Mieth and Lisa Sowle Cahill and published by Orbis Books).

a Latin American and a North American experience" out of his
own history. . . . [B]orn in Cuba, he grew up in various places
throughout the Southeast [USA]. "First, he tried to assimilate and
intellectually become like Anglos". . . . But recognizing "a certain
alienation between who I was and this culture I was trying to become assimilated to," he said, he turned to Latin America to find
identity. "Gradually, I became aware that I wasn't Latin American
either," he said. People like himself "live in a 'both/and' world
rather than an 'either/or' world," he said. "We have what some
have called a binocular vision. . . . We're always aware, constitu-
tionally almost, that there's more than one way of looking at
things."[54]

Like so many of the other U.S. Hispanic theologians, most of his energy
so far had been spent in teaching and in writing short works, such as
articles and chapters for collections. He edited a compilation entitled
We Are a People! Initiatives in Hispanic American Theology.[55] More recently
he published *Caminemos con Jesús: Toward a Hispanic/Latino Theology of
Accompaniment.*[56]

Among other U.S. Hispanic theologians, Goizueta seems most concerned about theological method. Well versed in philosophy, he engages such thinkers as Aristotle, Marx, Lonergan, and Habermas. In
many ways, because he dialogues with what other theologians are
proposing, his work bears the mark of what has come to be known as
teología de conjunto.[57] In discussing the concept of praxis as it relates to

54. Gibeau, *National Catholic Reporter,* September 11, 1992.
55. Goizueta, *We Are a People!* (1992). See also the collection he co-edited with
Aquino, *Theology: Expanding the Borders* (1998).
56. Goizueta, *Caminemos con Jesús* (1995).
57. Arturo Bañuelas explains the term, linking it with *pastoral de conjunto* in the
following manner: "U.S. Hispanic theologies are the result of a process called *pastoral de conjunto.* This process implies a method that stresses direct involvement and
analysis of reality as necessary first steps to the author's option to theologize from
within the Hispanic social and pastoral context. *Pastoral de conjunto* assures that Hispanic theologizing is grounded in human experience, especially the experience of
oppression. U.S. Hispanic Theology attempts to give a voice to the voiceless. As
members of the community, in the *pastoral de conjunto* process theologians also see
themselves as *mestizos,* articulating their own theology. This process calls for a new
kind of theologian with a new type of consciousness and commitment, so that theology will not emanate from ivory-tower abstract positions, but from engagement
with other Hispanos articulating their struggles and hopes for liberation. Immersed
in the Hispanic reality of oppression, these theologians understand how their cultural bias influences their theological presuppositions. They admit the non-neutrality
of their theology since their common project, their *teología de conjunto,* is the liberation of Hispanics as part of God's salvific plan for a new humanity." See Bañuelas,
"U.S. Hispanic Theology" (1992) 292.

theological method, for example, he draws on the work of Virgil Elizondo, Orlando Espín, Sixto García, Ada María Isasi-Díaz, and Yolanda Tarango. He finds in these theologians an emphasis on aesthetics, especially as manifested in popular religion and in Latino culture in general.[58]

Goizueta is grappling with some of what is behind such a radical difference in perception and comportment for the Hispanic, that is, in comparison with other North Americans. While the history of oppression cannot be overlooked, something Elizondo has repeatedly pointed out, Goizueta focuses on some philosophical propositions. He notes, for example, that the aesthetic paradigm has played an important role in the history of Latin American philosophy, in many ways as an alternative to the Cartesian epistemological paradigm.[59] Popular religiosity, therefore, which engages the senses and does not simply appeal to reason, will be more attractive than other ways of encountering the sacred.

This preference for the aesthetic paradigm does not deny the ability to be rational. Goizueta is critical of a certain tendency of U.S. dominant culture to stereotype Latinos:

> Portrayed as amiable, fun-loving people of warmth, feeling, and fiestas, i.e., people of "the body" over against the Anglo-Saxons, people of "the mind," we have been denied our minds and deemed incapable of serious, rational thought. Despite the fact that some of the greatest literature, philosophy, theology, poetry, etc. has been written in Spanish, the language itself continues to be perceived as less "scholarly" than French or German.[60]

While looking back at this great cultural heritage found in Spain and Latin America, Goizueta acknowledges the birth of a new people, the *mestizo* Elizondo has described so eloquently. It is within this new world, this new context, that the Latino theologian must work. Anthropology plays a crucial role in this process of contextualization. Goizueta writes:

> By examining the nature of subjectivity and community from within a U.S. Hispanic worldview, and the consequent role of such an anthropology in U.S. Hispanic theological method, we will explore the significance of a Hispanic anthropology, or understanding of the person, for the theological method.[61]

58. See Goizueta, "Rediscovering Praxis" (1992).
59. Ibid., 67, n. 33 for a reference to such Latin American thinkers as José Vasconcelos.
60. Goizueta, *"Nosotros"* (1992) 67.
61. Ibid., 56.

Goizueta maintains that a Hispanic contextual theology will not only reap benefits for Hispanics but also for the Church at large:

> Our claims on the theological establishment are not pastoral but theological: the admission of U.S. Hispanics into the broader theological dialogue is important, not because such inclusion would be the Christian thing to do (though this is also true), but because it would be the theologically and intellectually responsible thing to do. If the inherently communal character of historical praxis implies the obligation to engage in dialogue, it likewise implies the possibility of common understanding and interpretation. To marginalize some voices, such as those of U.S. Hispanics, by excluding them from the possibility of rational discourse is to undermine our common enterprise of understanding and interpretation.[62]

For these reasons Goizueta engages the dominant theological paradigms in order to critique them. According to him, the advantage of U.S. Hispanic theology is that, like Latin America's liberation theology, it specifically acknowledges the perspective of the person theologizing. It acknowledges that, in a sense, all theology is done perspectivally.

> The terms *U.S. Hispanic theology* and *U.S. Hispanic theologian* are appropriate only if we are clear that these are but shorthand ways of saying that a U.S. Hispanic theologian is a theologian who does theology from a self-consciously U.S. Hispanic perspective rather than from an unconsciously Anglo American perspective.[63]

Goizueta, conscious of his own bicultural background, argues that theory, praxis, and the aesthetic are interrelated. Arturo Bañuelas, in describing Goizueta's most recent project,[64] asserts that it will be a valuable resource:

> A principal thesis of this work is the importance of the aesthetic dimension of praxis as the ground for theology, most evident in popular religiosity. His contention is that Hispanic popular religiosity embodies the dialectical unity of reason, justice, and beauty as mutually implicit dimensions of Christian faith. In so doing, it offers a radical critique of mainline North American Christianity, at

---

62. Goizueta, "Rediscovering Praxis" (1992) 76.
63. Ibid., 77.
64. *Caminemos con Jesús* (1995).

the same time suggesting possible avenues for the latter's renewal and transformation. This promising work will undoubtedly have a major impact as an indispensable source of reference on any discussion of U.S. Hispanic Theologies.[65]

This combination of theory-praxis-aesthetic, which Bañuelas highlights above, can be summarized as the cycle of knowing the truth (theory), doing justice (praxis), and feeling the beautiful (aesthetic).

Jaime R. Vidal

Despite the fact that Puerto Ricans, at 11 percent of the Hispanic population in the United States, constitute the second largest group (Mexicans make up 63 percent of the total),[66] few Roman Catholic theologians have emerged among this Latino group.[67] The writings of Jaime R. Vidal, a layperson born in Puerto Rico who received his doctorate from Fordham University in 1984, are therefore extremely important for filling this gap. Vidal, having taught at the Catholic universities of Fordham and Seton Hall, has also worked in New York's *Instituto Pastoral Hispano* and in the Hispanic deacons' training program at St. Joseph's Seminary in Dunwoodie, New York. In addition, he was director of the Hispanic Community of Our Lady of Guadalupe in St. Patrick's Church in Jersey City. Among other positions held are Associate Professor/Director of Hispanic Ministry at the Pontifical College Josephinum's School of Theology, located in Columbus, Ohio, assistant director of the Cushwa Center for the Study of American Catholicism at the University of Notre Dame, and the Msgr. James A. Supple Chair of Catholic Studies at Iowa State University.

As the above posts indicate, Vidal demonstrates a wide range of expertise, ranging from the academic to the pastoral. He has applied his training in medieval studies (his doctoral dissertation is entitled "The Infancy Narrative in Pseudo-Bonaventure's *Meditationes Vitae Christi:* A Study in Medieval Franciscan Christ-Piety, c. 1300") to the task of understanding modern popular piety among Hispanics, particularly those living in the northeastern part of the United States.

---

65. Bañuelas, "U.S. Hispanic Theology" (1992) 290.

66. U.S. Census Bureau, *Hispanic Population* (1991).

67. My 1992 bibliographic study, "Towards a U.S. Hispanic Theology," found five Puerto Rican authors among the thirty-seven listed: José Dimas Soberal, Roberto O. González, Antonio Stevens-Arroyo, Jaime R. Vidal, and Dominga Zapata. The group most represented, next to the Mexicans, are the Cuban writers.

In addition to a substantial amount of writing for religious pastoral periodicals in Spanish over the years, Vidal has produced two very valuable studies of popular religion as manifested among Latinos whose origins are Caribbean. In the first of these studies, "Popular Religion in the Lands of Origin of New York's Hispanic Population," Vidal contributed to a study on Hispanics in New York conducted by the archdiocese.[68] His approach, which is directed basically to pastoral ministers in New York, is to describe and explain the role popular religion has served in various countries of origin. His overall treatment of popular religion in the Spanish Caribbean, followed by individual treatises on it as manifested in Puerto Rico, the Dominican Republic, Cuba, and Colombia, the four areas most represented in the northeastern United States, makes the diversity existent in the Hispanic communities apparent.[69]

There are those who say that this type of descriptive approach to religion is more anthropological, specifically ethnographical, than it is theological. Certainly, it is more characteristic of anthropology than of traditional theology to describe such social phenomena as the family as focus and matrix, religious ignorance, the role of the elite, the effect of urbanization, and the different cultural influences from Spain, Africa, and the United States. Yet as demonstrated above by the work of Elizondo, Deck, and Goizueta, anthropology, in fact, all of the social sciences, have become U.S. Hispanic theology's main dialogue partner.

This work, despite its brevity and tentativeness (points Vidal himself acknowledges in his introduction and conclusion[70]) is reminiscent of Espín's words previously cited in an interview with the *National Catholic Reporter*. Both hold that U.S. Hispanic theology studies popular reli-

---

68. Vidal, "Popular Religion in the Lands of Origin of New York's Hispanic Population" (1982).

69. For a similar study of popular piety in the Southwest, see *Faith Expressions of Hispanics in the Southwest: Workshops on Hispanic Liturgy and Popular Piety,* a small booklet published by the Mexican American Cultural Center in San Antonio (1977). For a treatise of some of the same but from a more biblical perspective, see Romero, *Hispanic Devotional Piety* (1991).

70. In his introduction to "Popular Religion in the Lands of Origin of New York's Hispanic Population," Vidal writes, "The reader should be warned that, since interest in the field of popular religion is relatively recent, the subject is seriously underresearched, and in some ways not yet ripe for the kind of overview that this paper is attempting. This is therefore by necessity a most emphatically tentative presentation, and it is our hope that it will motivate others to do research in the field, and to publish any data they may discover that will corroborate, modify or even contradict what is here presented. Meanwhile, it is hoped that this paper may be of use to those engaged in pastoral work, and that its very weaknesses may be an eloquent plea for the research that will eventually correct them" (p. 9).

gion, not, in the final analysis, anthropologically but theologically. The references to Puebla and to Church tradition which Vidal makes indicate an ecclesial consciousness:

> It must be stressed that popular religion is not necessarily—although it *can* be—a debased or heterodox form of the official religion of a people. In the case of Latin America, as the Puebla conference has recognized, popular religion is on the whole, an expression of orthodox Catholicism, colored by the environment and history of the people in perfectly legitimate and even desirable ways. Latin American popular religion, however, includes also in certain areas syncretistic mixtures of Christianity and native American or African religions, and popular Protestantism is also a genuine and important factor. Even in its Orthodox form Latin American popular religion shares in the problems of devotionalism, etc. which have plagued the Church in general since the later middle ages.[71]

Vidal defends popular religiosity, yet does not see it as an absolute, encouraging the reader to "approach popular piety in a spirit that will be neither condescending nor uncritical; with an awareness of its gaps but also of all it has that can fill the gaps in our own élite religiosity; ready to teach and to learn, and to grow together in the ways of the Incarnate Wisdom of God."[72]

In the same way that some theologians have called for a wider recognition of popular religiosity's ability to involve the whole person, Vidal writes about such a holistic spirituality. What is interesting to note is that he is writing in the early 1980s, a time when U.S. Hispanic theology still had not blossomed. Vidal believes that ever since the twelfth century "the spiritual quest in Western Christianity has been increasingly dichotomized into a focus on intellect and will (as has usually been the case of the élites), or else a focus on the emotions in the form of shallow sentimentality."[73] He proposes a solution to this false dichotomy:

> This divorce between mind/will (élite) and emotions (people) leaves both sides impoverished. What the Church needs, and may be ready to do in our age, is to re-marry these divorced elements, and work at creating a rich, all-around, holistic spirituality, which will cater to body and soul, mind, will, emotions and senses, in an integrated whole; which would be accessible to the intellectual and

71. Ibid., 3ff.
72. Ibid.
73. Ibid.

the common man at different levels of meaning, but would be the same spiritually, equally satisfying to all and at all levels. We need a spirituality which will start from and culminate in the liturgy, as a sensual expression and celebration of our Gospel—faith in the Paschal Mystery of Christ's death and resurrection, and our sharing in his death and risen life—not expressed in the jargon of the liturgical theologian, but in color, music, poetry, movement; in eating, drinking, embracing, singing. To this synthesis the common people must contribute their sense of the concrete, their beautiful and earthly traditions of celebration, while the élite must contribute the theological solidarity that has been so sadly missing from people's devotional life. The result, we hope, will be infinitely better than either or than the sum of both.[74]

Like Goizueta and Espín, Vidal defends the virtues found in popular religion not solely for the sake of those who practice it but also for the good of the entire worshiping community.

In his second, lengthier study of popular religion published in the book *Presencia Nueva: A Study of Hispanics in the Archdiocese of Newark*[75] Vidal continues along the same lines of describing popular religion as manifested by Hispanics of that area but this time in a more North American context.[76] Also, as he sought in his first study, Vidal's aims are explicitly pastoral. Most recently he has co-edited a work on Puerto Rican and Cuban Catholics in the United States.[77] The work is part of a project in which Hispanic theologians, working with professor of history Jay P. Dolan, have studied Hispanic history from a Hispanic perspective, a perspective that, according to Vidal, gives much importance to spirituality.[78]

Alex García-Rivera

Elected president of ACHTUS in 1998, this Cuban-born theologian teaches at the Jesuit School of Theology at Berkeley. In his first book, *St.*

---

74. Ibid., 33.

75. Vidal, "Popular Religion Among the Hispanics in the General Area of the Archdiocese of Newark," (1988) 241–352.

76. See also his article, "American Church and the Puerto Rican People" (1990) 119–35. It contains an excellent discussion on the value of national parishes.

77. Vidal and Dolan, *Puerto Rican and Cuban Catholics* (1994). Another of Vidal's recent works explores popular religiosity from the angle of a continuity and new synthesis of Iberian practices with those in the Americas. See "Toward an Understanding of Synthesis" (1994) 69–95.

78. *National Catholic Reporter* (September 11, 1992). The two other books in the Notre Dame History of Hispanics in the U.S. Series, published in 1994 by the University of Notre Dame Press, are Dolan and Hinojosa, *Mexican Americans and the Catholic Church* (1994); and Dolan and Deck, *Hispanic Catholic Culture* (1994).

Martín de Porres: the "Little Stories" and the Semiotics of Culture (1995), García-Rivera argues, in agreement with U.S. Hispanic theology, that in the violent and unequal encounter of cultures that took place in the evangelization of the Americas, the anthropological dimensions of culture became accentuated. As examples he gives the notions of the "other," ethnicity, and *mestizaje*. He stresses emphatically that it was not only the literate and the powerful who reflected on this encounter, although their perspective, because of its literary quality, has often been the one most articulated. His goal is to accentuate the thought of the popular folk, a thought made manifest in popular religiosity, through the use of new methods provided by the linguistic and cultural anthropological sciences.

García-Rivera draws on both the work done by Elizondo (in the area of *mestizaje*) and that done by Robert Shreiter (in semiotics). The method employed by the systematic theologian, in the case of semiotics, for example, is to study the beatification process of the Peruvian mulatto, San Martín de Porres, who lived from 1567 to 1634. By examining the world of meaning behind certain signs that appear repeatedly in the ecclesiastical process, García-Rivera examines the symbolic-cultural and sociohistorical contexts that gave rise to the form of popular piety so prevalent throughout Latin America. This world of meaning is embodied in what García refers to as the "little stories," that is, those testimonial accounts that are part of San Martín de Porres' beatification process.

These "little stories" unlock the imagination and provide access to the "big story," or the universals that help create our world of meaning. García-Rivera explains the need for both, although he detects a tendency to diminish the importance of the "little stories."

> Scholars and theologians make up a select group of individuals who have been trained in the art of disclosing the universals of human being and its place in the cosmos. There is nothing wrong with such a specialized group. Their contributions are essential to any society. Nonetheless, in recent centuries, the "Big Story" they tell is increasingly understood only by other members of the same specialized group. More often than not, the "Big Story" account of reality turns out to be not so much a universal tale of human being, but merely a skewed or specialized story, an insider's story that makes sense only to those who tell it. Such a complaint is more than a call for clarity or a recall of technical language. More is at stake.[79]

79. Alex García-Rivera, *St. Martín de Porres* (1995) 1–2.

And certainly more was at stake in the sixteenth-century discovery of the new world. One of the critical issues being debated, in fact, was the very meaning of what a human being is. As García-Rivera says in the eloquent opening to his book,

> All human beings are essentially the same. Or are they? The Old World believed human beings were distinguished from the animals by their reason. Reason was the universal principle that bound human beings in fellowship. This assumption was challenged at Lima. New questions were asked and new answers given. Are there true differences between human beings? If so, on what basis can there be true human fellowship? The mystery lies in that this important debate did not take place in the halls of a university but, rather, in the beatification process of the mulatto saint, Martín de Porres. At issue was the very meaning of human being.[80]

As an alternative to this stress on reason for the definition of what it means to be human, more specifically as it relates to the testimonies given about God's humble saint, San Martín, García-Rivera seizes on a Spanish phrase that comes up repeatedly in the investigation, *criatura de Dios* (a reference to God's creation):

> The ultimate mystery of human being is not so much reason but that the human is a creature of God. What is human cannot be known without reference to God, and that reference lies not with the distinctiveness of the human but with the connectedness of creation.[81]

Nancy Angela Pineda not only describes García-Rivera's assimilation of Latino theology's themes but also his unique contribution to its evolution:

> As a text within U.S. Hispanic/Latino theology, García-Rivera's work incorporates many of the field's pivotal themes (*mestizaje,* identity and change, human difference, popular religion, hegemony), taking them a step further through his use of semiotics. Semiotics is the study of "signs and the relationship between signs. . . . The task of a semiotic analysis of culture consists in reading the cultural text, which means 'locates its signs, the codes that place the signs in dynamic interaction, and the messages that are conveyed.'" While others, such as Virgilio Elizondo, have implicitly used a quasi-semiotic analysis in their theological work,

80. Ibid., 1.
81. Ibid., 94.

García-Rivera makes the use of semiotic theory explicit, further re-fashioning and sharpening both semiotic theory and Latino theology.[82]

In his current writings, Alex García-Rivera continues to employ semiotics, together with other philosophical and theological strands, to call for a revival of some ignored or forgotten elements in the Christian tradition.[83]

Two Latina Theologians in ACHTUS

A small group of women are making an indispensable contribution to U.S. Hispanic theology by expanding the horizons of perspectival theology. It is clear that Hispanics are increasingly constituting a larger percentage of the U.S. Catholic Church. What is often not perceived is that Latina women are very much at the heart of this Church. In fact, as Ana María Díaz-Stevens notes, even now little has been written about Latinas and religion:

> Thanks in great measure to the sacrifices of earlier generations of Latinas, their daughters and granddaughters have been able to secure important positions at different levels of the political, economic, educational, and general social structure of U.S. society, in parallel with the rise of women's status over the past two decades. These positions present the opportunity to exert a certain influence not only upon Latino communities but upon general society as well. Yet, the sphere of religion has been generally neglected by scholars of the Latino community. This is unfortunate, because beyond affording women the opportunity for influence, religion has oftentimes given Latinas affirmation as leaders, especially at the grassroots level. Even the contradictions inherent in a religious system which purports to accept everyone on an equal basis while reserving its positions of authority and decision making to males only have proved incapable of destroying or negating the legitimacy of women's roles in the religious sphere.[84]

82. Nancy Angela Pineda, "Book Review of *St. Martín de Porres: 'The Little Stories' and the Semiotics of Culture* by Alex García-Rivera," *Journal of Hispanic/ Latino Theology* 5, no. 3 (February 1998) 68–71.

83. In *Community of the Beautiful* (1999), García-Rivera draws on other U.S. Hispanic theologians, North American pragmatism, the theological aesthetics of Hans Urs von Balthasar, and the semiotics of Jan Mukarovsy.

84. A. M. Díaz-Stevens, "Latinas and the Church." In *Hispanic Catholic Culture*, Dolan and Deck (1994) 241. In a footnote on page 277, Díaz-Stevens writes, "*Sociology of Religion* dedicated its Spring 1992 edition entirely to the question of women in religion. As I scan through it I find not one article, not one quote, not even one cited source on the question of Latinas and their religious experience. In the eyes of

The fact that Latinas have begun to write theology from their perspective is good news, for it makes for a more inclusive understanding of church. More importantly, it challenges the church's very theology, even that of Latino men.

A recent bibliographic study revealed that 27 percent of those U.S. Hispanic authors featured were women.[85] Such Latina theologians as María Pilar Aquino, Ada María Isasi-Díaz, and Yolanda Tarango are writing theology from a woman's perspective.[86] Their work combines cultural, feminist, and liberation aspects and joins that of other women theologians in the U.S. and outside whose views have gone unnoticed in theological circles for centuries.

What is also noteworthy, aside from quantity and themes explored, is that Hispanic women theologians started to make their contributions early in the history of U.S. Hispanic theology.[87] The two most published

---

certain sectors of the institutional church and of academia, we either simply do not exist or are not interesting enough to be studied."

85. E. C. Fernández, "Towards a U.S. Hispanic Theology" (1992) 89. In terms of the topics written about, feminist theology, with twenty-eight entries, ranked second (the greatest number of works written fell into the category of pastoral theology/ Hispanic ministry/catechesis). At first, of the authors in general, this high ranking among the topics covered might seem only to reflect the ten female writers. A further consideration, however, reveals a strong concern for identity issues, which crop up especially when North American and Latin American cultures come face-to-face.

86. In "Mujeristas: A Name of Our Own," by Ada María Isasi-Díaz, published in *Yearning to Breathe Free: Liberation Theologies in the U.S.*, ed. Mar Peter-Raoul and others (Maryknoll, N.Y.: Orbis Books, 1990), Isasi-Díaz acknowledges how she was influenced by Black feminists who took the term "womanist" to distinguish themselves from the feminism of Anglo women. In *En La Lucha* (1993) Isasi-Díaz explains the dilemma Hispanic feminists face and the reason for the name *mujeristas*. She writes, "*Feministas hispanas* have been consistently marginalized within the Anglo feminist community because of our critique of its ethnic/racial prejudice and its lack of class analysis. Though Anglo feminists have indeed worked to correct these serious shortcomings in their discourse, in my experience their praxis continues to be flawed in this regard. The phrase *feministas hispanas* has also been rejected by many in the Hispanic community because they consider feminism a concern of Anglo women. Yet Latinas widely agree with an analysis of sexism as an evil within our communities, an evil made into a touchable reality through the different ways in which Hispanic women are repressed and exploited. In spite of our understanding of sexism and its role in our oppression, however, Latinas have not had a way to name ourselves until recently when some of us came up with the word *mujerista*" (p. 3ff.).

87. The same year in which Deck published his first article, "New Vision" (1974), Dominican-born Marina Herrera came out with "La Teología en el Mundo de Hoy." Herrera, an expert in multicultural education, teaches part-time at the Washington Theological Union in Washington, D.C. She also serves as a consultant, writer, translator, and workshop designer and director. My bibliographic study lists forty-eight of her published works, most of which are articles or chapters in the area of

Latina theologians in the United States are Ada María Isasi-Díaz and María Pilar Aquino.[88]

Ada María Isasi-Díaz

The Latina who has come the furthest in developing coherently a Hispanic theology from the perspective of women is this Cuban-born theologian. Currently she is professor of ethics and theology at Drew University in Madison, New Jersey. She was the first Latina to earn a doctorate at Union Theological Seminary in New York in 1990. Having begun publishing in the late 1970s, she has written on women's ordination and worked in numerous ecumenical circles. In the fall of 1986 she published "'Apuntes' for an Hispanic Women's Theology of Liberation," an article that set the tone for the evolution of *mujerista* theology.[89]

Soon after, together with Yolanda Tarango, a Sister of Charity of the Incarnate Word from El Paso, Texas, she produced a work that is destined to be a classic for its methodological innovation. In *Hispanic Women: Prophetic Voice in the Church*,[90] the two Latina theologians expound their theory of what constitutes a theology from the perspective of Hispanic women and proceed to illustrate this process with examples.

Their approach was to reflect with groups of Hispanic women in order to know and understand their beliefs about the divine.[91] From what emerged during these discussions, they sought to identify recurring themes. Since they maintain that *mujerista* theology is a liberative praxis, behavior remains an important constituent. The researchers, therefore, examined the ethical understandings of these Hispanic women and looked for recurrent themes. The final part of the process included a type of feedback to the contributors for the purpose of verify-

---

pastoral theology and education. Her essay "Context and Development of Hispanic Ecclesial Leadership" appears in volume 3 of the University of Notre Dame Cushwa Center's history of Hispanics in the United States, *Hispanic Catholic Culture*, ed. Dolan and Deck (1994) 166–205.

88. Some of the other Catholic Hispanic women currently writing in theology are Rosa María Icaza, C.C.V.I. (catechesis and spirituality); María de la Cruz Aymes, S.H. (catechesis); Ana María Pineda, R.S.M.; Gloria Inés Loya, P.B.V.M.; Ana María Díaz-Stevens; and Jeanette Rodríguez. For information on Protestant Hispanic women, see note 2, above.

89. Isasi-Díaz, "Apuntes" (1986) 61–70. It was reprinted in the collection edited by Justo L. González entitled *Voces: Voices from the Hispanic Church* (1992) 24–31.

90. Isasi-Díaz and Tarango, *Hispanic Women* (1988).

91. Their book, *Hispanic Women*, is the fruit of a decade of listening and reflecting with eleven different groups.

ing that, in fact, what the researchers recorded and analyzed was representative of their beliefs.

They adopted this method for collecting data, known as "ethnomethodology," from Harvard social psychologist Harold Garfinkel. Isasi-Díaz explains his approach, demonstrating why it differs from conventional sociological studies:

> His primary criticism is that in professional sociology there is no "actor," but rather an ideal type, a dummy. Ethnomethodologists argue that it is difficult to find in sociological studies a real person with a biography and a history. The person to whom the studies keep referring is the creation of the social scientist. The self-understanding and everyday life of that person are absent from consideration. Ethnomethodology, on the other hand, is a theory of everyday life.[92]

Yolanda Tarango and Ada María Isasi-Díaz have adopted this method, which in many ways is quite anthropological, for doing theology. This "let the women speak for themselves" approach guards against an idealized community perspective when speaking about Hispanics. Goizueta explains:

> The dangers of an idealized community are nowhere more evident than in the experience of many U.S. Hispanic women. Too often, the emphasis on community (e.g., family) among Hispanics can devolve into an ideological rationalization for the suppression of genuine intersubjectivity. Women are especially susceptible to such victimization since, having been traditionally viewed as the guardians of community, they have often been expected to submerge their own identity within the collective, that is, to sacrifice their own historical subjectivity to the collective subject. The idealization of community has often been accompanied by an idealization of women. In turn, what is idealized is thereby distorted since its concrete historicity is rejected in favor of the idea, or the romantic illusion.[93]

At the heart of dealing with one's own historical subjectivity are self-awareness and consciousness. This self-reflective process is key to doing *mujerista* theology. It is a way of taking seriously the faith experience, or as Isasi-Díaz labels it, the "lived experience," of Hispanic women:

92. Isasi-Díaz, "*Mujerista* Theology's Method" (1992) 42.
93. Goizueta, "*Nosotros*" (1992) 61.

> Though the expression "lived-experience" might seem tautological to some, in the context of *mujerista* theology it refers not only to what has happened—what a person has endured or made happen—but also to that experience upon which she reflects in order to understand its significance and to value it accordingly. Because of the centrality of religion in the day-to-day life of Hispanic women, our understanding about the divine, and about ultimate meaning, play a very important role in the process of giving significance to and valuing our experience. It is imperative for us, therefore, to comprehend better how religious understandings and practices impact our lives. In order to do this, we need to start from what we know, ourselves, our everyday surroundings and experiences.[94]

From the beginning, the women theologians make it clear that their goal is liberation. Thus they make no pretensions of proceeding from an objective, passionless stance:

> First and foremost we are activists—Hispanic Women committed to the struggle for justice and peace. Our lived experience has pointed us in the direction of being theologians. We see no conflict in being both theologians and activists; this follows our understanding of the intrinsic unity between what has been classically referred to as systematic theology and moral theology or ethics. This will become obvious as we clarify what it means for us to do theology.[95]

Isasi-Díaz's book, *En la Lucha/In the Struggle: A Hispanic Women's Theology,*[96] uses the same methodology to further elaborate a *mujerista* theology. Like *Hispanic Women: Prophetic Voice in the Church* it makes clear the need to take seriously the emotive when theologizing.[97] Isasi-Díaz and Tarango take to heart anthropologist Clifford Geertz's definition of religion as "a system of symbols which acts to establish powerful, pervasive, and long-lasting moods and motivations in men by formulating conceptions of a general order of existence and clothing these conceptions with such an aura of actuality that the moods and motivations seem uniquely realistic."[98] The stories told by the women they interviewed, whose recurring themes often involve community and family,

---

94. Isasi-Díaz, "*Mujerista* Theology's Method" (1992) 49.

95. Isasi-Díaz and Tarango, *Hispanic Women* (1988) ix.

96. Isasi-Díaz, *En la Lucha* (1993).

97. See J. Rodríguez' treatment of religious emotion as developed in the thought of William James in *Our Lady of Guadalupe* (1994) 51. For a sublime incorporation of Latinas' faith stories, see Rodríguez, *Stories We Live* (1996).

98. Geertz, *Interpretation of Cultures*, 90.

reveal much of the "moods and motivations" behind their faith as well as their ethical behavior.[99]

María Pilar Aquino

This theologian, born in Ixtlán del Río, Nayarit, Mexico, grew up in Sonora, Mexico, and was educated in Mexico, Costa Rica, Peru, and Spain. She bears the distinction of being the first Catholic woman to obtain a doctorate in theology from the Pontifical University of Salamanca, Spain. Her publications are extensive.[100] Her first book, *Aportes para una Teología desde la Mujer* (1988), was an edited work. In 1992 she published *Nuestro Clamor por la Vida: Teología Latinoamericana desde la Perspectiva de la Mujer.*[101] A fuller version of this work, *Our Cry for Life: Feminist Theology from Latin America,* was published in 1993 in English.[102] She is currently a member of the faculty of the Department of Theological and Religious Studies at the University of San Diego.

Like Isasi-Díaz, Aquino is attempting to develop a theology of liberation from the viewpoint of Latinas.[103] Her article "Doing Theology from the Perspective of Latin American Women,"[104] summarizes ideas that are expanded in her book. At the core of her work is a critique of some of the dominant theological methods employed today, including that of some Latin American liberation and U.S. Hispanic theologians. Like Isasi-Díaz, whose *mujerista* theology prompts her to make a distinction between North American and Latina feminism, Aquino is critical of the North American variety. In presenting her essay the editor, Roberto S. Goizueta, makes the following remarks:

> Sympathetic to Latin American liberation theology and Anglo American feminism, Aquino nevertheless proffers a critique of both: the first for its male-centered perspective, and the latter for

99. See the introduction to *Mujerista Theology: A Theology for the Twenty-First Century* (Maryknoll, N.Y.: Orbis Books, 1996), a compilation of previously published articles, in which she presents in the introduction a type of road map for understanding her work. Her treatment of such areas as liturgy, Scripture, and ethics is an example of how a Latina perspective sheds light on each of these theological specialties.

100. Among Aquino's most recent work is "Challenge of Hispanic Women" (1992); "Perspectives" (1992); "Doing Theology" (1992); and "Santo Domingo Through the Eyes of Women" (1993).

101. M. P. Aquino, *Nuestro Clamor por la Vida: Teología Latinoamericana desde la Perspectiva de la Mujer* (San José, Costa Rica: Editorial DEI, 1992).

102. Aquino, *Our Cry for Life* (1993). See also "Santo Domingo Through the Eyes of Women" (1993) 212–25.

103. One quickly gets the impression, given her interlocutors, that she is a great believer in *teología de conjunto.* Note her strong reliance on Latin American authors.

104. Aquino, "Doing Theology" (1992).

its failure to make explicit the causal link between sexism and classism, between the privileges of First World women and the exploitation of Third World women. Such a critique is essential as Latinas develop a theological reflection which affirms them as historical subjects in their own right. In turn, this reflection contributes to the development of an integral theological perspective which will be liberating for both women and men.[105]

She also shares with Isasi-Díaz a criticism of any theology that does not take the affect seriously along with any that is not based on lived experience.

Two realities become increasingly obvious as one reads her writings: (1) within one of the poorest minority groups in the United States (although her frame of reference includes all of Latin America), Latinas are among the most needy and oppressed;[106] (2) Latinas are, in reality, the driving force behind most of the work being done in evangelization and social advocacy today. To substantiate the first reality, that of the oppression of Latina women, she quotes I. Gebara, who asserts that in Latin America

> the poor have many faces: laborers, farmworkers, beggars, abandoned children, the marginalized and dispossessed youth, and others. They are men and women, but among them we should give precedence to one group: *the women*. . . . The poor woman today is poor even among the poor. She is truly other: the overburdened woman, the menstruating woman, the laboring woman, mother, daughter, and wife. She is at the same time, both subject and object of our option for the poor.[107]

When one considers the number of Latin American women who, in order to provide for their families, are forced to migrate to developed countries, especially to the United States, her description quickly becomes applicable to a North American context.

To this reality Aquino brings the light of the gospel, a gospel that proclaims life in all its fullness. It is this promotion of the gospel and of life that should be the locus of theology:

> [T]he aim of theology from the point of view of women must share the aim of God's re-creative activity in history and must be inspired by it. Moreover, it must illuminate and activate the response of faith by the one who embraces it. In accordance with the core of

105. Goizueta, *We Are a People!* (1992) xv.
106. Isasi-Díaz documents well this socioeconomic poverty among U.S. Latinas in the first chapter of *En la Lucha* (1993).
107. As quoted in Aquino, "Doing Theology" (1992) 96.

the liberating biblical vision, this aim is on the path toward the attainment of the fullness of life, human integrity, shared solidarity, complete liberation, and common enjoyment of the goods of the earth. The biblical formulation of this aim is found succinctly in John 10:10: "I have come that they may have life, and that they may have it abundantly."[108]

Despite their poverty and oppression, Aquino demonstrates how these faith-filled Latinas are not without hope. Far from it, they are heavily involved in the transformation both of the society and of the Church:

For Latina women, Christian faith is not a fragmentary aspect of their life or of their own cultural identity. The struggle of these women for a new earth and for new ways of being and living in the church, where they can participate as members in their own right, is inspired by their conviction of faith, and affects their whole life. To state just a few of their activities, many Latina women are committed to human rights groups, to the defense of the undocumented, to solidarity movements, to peace, to ecological, artistic, and cultural movements, to liberating evangelization groups, to the affirmation of indigenous communities, to the defense of civil rights, to the affirmation of women, young people, children, and the aged, and so on. Consequently, theological reflection must take into account their multiple interests as believers, as poor, and as women, together with their religious and cultural values.[109]

Given their oppressive situation, yet also their committed work for faith and justice, Aquino argues that Latinas have much to contribute to the theological enterprise. Yet, writing in 1992, she bemoans the lack of Hispanic women theologians, commenting, "It is absurd that after five hundred years of Christianity on this continent, there are fewer than eight Latin American women holding the doctoral degree in theology."[110] She is likewise critical of the lack of leadership opportunities available for women in church settings.[111]

She faults male Latin American liberation theologians for often not taking into account the role of women. She is also critical of the direction U.S. Hispanic theology seems to be taking in terms of being too quick to dialogue with modern/liberal theological currents instead of offering other horizons. In the words of Deck,

she cautions us against the unanalyzed acceptance of or complicity with the culture of modernity. She claims that U.S. Hispanic theo-

---

108. Aquino, "Perspectives" (1992) 24.
109. Aquino, in *Frontiers*, ed. Deck, 36.
110. Aquino, "Doing Theology" (1992) 84, n. 6.
111. Aquino, "Perspectives" (1992) 39, n. 12.

Using the existence of various Gospels in sacred Scripture as an example, he illustrates the authenticity of unity amidst plurality:

> The truth is that the early church included these four gospels in the canon precisely because they were different. In the struggle against various Gnostic interpretations of Christianity, which denied some of the crucial historical events of the life of Jesus, there was strength in the argument that these four witnesses, while differing in detail, agreed on the crucial matters under attack. In a court of law, it is difficult to impugn the testimony of a multiplicity of witnesses who, while differing in matters of detail, agree on the basic issue at hand. Indeed, if they agree in every detail their authority is questioned, for there is the likelihood that their testimony has been prearranged. Likewise, in the debates of the second century, the church found support for its insistence on the historical events of the life of Jesus, and for its rejection of Gnostic speculations, precisely in this multiform witness of the four gospels.[125]

In short, González is saying that the tradition is much greater than any particular perspective (i.e., the givenness yet the unsuitability of any one, exclusive perspective), especially those that are the product of a type of Constantinian, imperialist sociopolitical project that is not conscious of its own shortcomings or sinfulness. This type of Christendom often tries to justify its political goals religiously, for example, in the case of "manifest destiny" in U.S. history. González reminds us that we can be very selective in terms of what we extract from the tradition, often consciously or unconsciously rationalizing our behavior. He cites examples of this distortion in the past, and warns against it in the present, especially in the case of North America.

In *The Liberating Pulpit*, which he co-authored with his wife, Catherine G. González, González gives another example of how selectivity, in terms of what we draw from the tradition, can be misleading:

> We have already referred to Eusebius' attempt to show that the persecutions were little more than a grave misunderstanding on the part of the Roman Empire. More recent historians have also read history in a similar manner. For instance, treatises on the ethics of the early church deal almost exclusively with sexual mores, lying, homicide, and so forth, but fail to take into account the astonishing teachings of early Christian writers regarding property, the use and distribution of wealth, and the like. The reason for this is that the definition of what are "ethical" questions has

125. J. L. González, *Out of Every Tribe* (1992) 19.

been narrowed in our capitalist society, precisely so as not to include issues such as whether private property is morally correct, or what are the rights of the poor. On the basis of such a definition, historians of Christian ethics tend to ignore the very radical things that have been said in earlier centuries of Christian history, and thus give us the impression that today's radical questioning of the rights of property, for instance, is a new phenomenon, about which Christian tradition has little to say.[126]

Their examples from the writings of such early Christians as Ignatius of Antioch, Hermas, Ambrose of Milan, Basil the Great, and John Chrysostom illustrate that the early Church was very concerned about the morality of the use and distribution of wealth.[127]

It is particularly within this environment that Hispanic theology can point the way back to the heart of Christian tradition: an acknowledgment of a need for redemption from our sinfulness:

Therefore, part of our responsibility as Hispanics, not only for our own sake but also for the sake of other minorities as well as for the sake of the dominant group, is constantly to remind the group of their immigrant beginnings, of the Indian massacres, of the rape of the land, of the war with Mexico, of riches drawn from slave labor, of neocolonial exploitation, and of any other guilty items that one may be inclined to forget in an innocent reading of history.[128]

The same can be said for failing to recognize modern-day versions of such ancient heresies as Gnosticism, Adoptionism, Docetism, and Nestorianism. In the case of Nestorianism, for example, González elucidates the gift Hispanics represent for the Church:

Nestorianism has never been a temptation for Hispanic Christians. The reason for this is that we feel the need to assert that the broken, oppressed, and crucified Jesus is God. A disjunction between divinity and humanity in Christ that denies this would destroy the greatest appeal of Jesus for Hispanics and other groups who must live in suffering. North Atlantic Christians have often criticized Hispanics for representing Jesus and his sufferings in gory detail. This, they claim, is a sign of a defeatist religion, or of a sadomasochistic attitude that delights in pain. But this is not the case. The suffering Christ is important to Hispanics because he is the sign that God suffers with us. An emaciated Christ is the sign that God is with those who hunger. A flagellated Christ is the sign that

126. J. L. González and C. G. González, *Liberating Pulpit* (1994) 52–3.
127. See also J. L. González, *Faith and Wealth* (1990).
128. Ibid., 79ff.

God is with those who must bear the stripes of an unjust society. Blood and suffering have long been the lot of the impoverished masses in Latin America. Blood and suffering are the history of Mexican-Americans in the Southwest. Nestorianism denies that God took these up. For this reason, the Nestorian Christ can never be the Lord of our devotion.[129]

González brings home the point that theological doctrines were not formulated in a sociopolitical vacuum and that we cannot assume a real impartiality vis-á-vis what is exalted from the tradition. Hispanic theology, therefore, can function as a corrective to an incomplete or distorted reading of the Christian tradition.[130]

4. Additional Protestant Latino Theologians

Orlando E. Costas

Described by Justo González as the "dean of Latino Evangelical theologians,"[131] the late Orlando E. Costas' figure appears prominently in the writings of most of the Latino Protestants. Having authored several books, including *The Integrity of Mission* (1979) and *Christ Outside the Gate* (1982), he served as dean of Andover Newton Theological School until his untimely death in November 1987.[132] In the preface to the Puerto Rican's last book, which was published posthumously, his wife, Rose L. Feliciano Costas, speaks of his life's contribution:

> Orlando's zeal to write at different stages of his missiological development was part of his desire to share—especially with the Latin American world—the research and insights of his own journey of

---

129. J. L. González, *Mañana* (1990) 148–9.

130. Among the non-Hispanic writers who hold a similar position of the importance of Hispanics for doing Catholic theology is Kenneth G. Davis. In "Father, We're Not in Kansas Anymore" (1990) Davis writes: "It is precisely because Hispanics are Catholic and not part of our dominant society that they are in a unique position to help us distinguish between what is authentically Catholic in our society and what is the trappings of purely civil religion or cultural convention" (p. 16).

131. J. L. González, in *Teología en Conjunto*, ed. J. D. Rodríguez and L. I. Martell-Otero (1997) 88.

132. See David Traverzo Galarza, "Emergence of a Latino Social Ethic in the Work and Thought of Orlando E. Costas: An Ethico-Theological Discourse from the Underside of History" (Ph.D. diss., Drew University, 1992). See also Traverzo Galarza's chapter, "Sin: A Hispanic Perspective," in *Teología en Conjunto*, 112–24, in which he draws heavily from Costas' work to describe what Traverzo Galarza terms a "Latino radical evangelical tradition" approach to sin.

faith as a pastor, evangelist, and missiologist. "One must put things in writing because time is running out," he would often say to me. His mind was never at rest. Daily experiences with and challenges from laity, pastors, and theological peers spawned ideas for new writing projects. Old ideas took new forms; new ones were revised. Indeed, the driving force of the last decade of my husband's life was to piece these ideas together in a book on a contextual theology of evangelization.[133]

In this same work, Costas argues that "all religious communities have their theologies, be they explicit or implicit."[134] In the book's conclusion, therefore, he advocates for a greater awareness of the contexts in which these theologies are formulated:

Unfortunately, the evangelistic practice of many churches, both in the Americas and elsewhere, has suffered from the absence of a clear vision of their sociohistorical contexts. Consequently, their evangelistic practice has been contextually shallow. Recognizing this, we have been arguing not so much for a new type of evangelization as for a new way of understanding and practicing contextual evangelization. This implies a sociohistorical approach to the biblical roots of evangelization, a communal theological ground, and an ecclesial vision informed by the theological and social base of the church.[135]

Much of what other Latino Protestants write after Costas uses this contextual method. In his view a contextual reading of the Bible is not simply concerned with how to apply Scripture to a given situation but how that situation, particularly in the case of the poor and the oppressed, presents an opportunity for returning to the context for the formulation of that Scripture in the first place, or, as he states, "[contextual evangelization is] the communication of the good news from the 'base' or 'margin' where we find the absentees of history, the most vulnerable and needy people of society."[136] The social sciences contribute significantly to this sociohistorical method, as the importance of the community and sociopolitical factors quickly become evident.

Although in some ways Costas is not necessarily focusing on the reality of U.S. Latinos, his contextual method provides much of the legitimization for what will follow.[137] In proposing that the marginalized can

133. Rose L. Feliciano Costas, quoted in Costas, *Liberating News* (1989) ix.
134. Ibid., 2.
135. Ibid., 148.
136. Ibid., 149.
137. It is interesting to note that next to Justo González, Orlando Costas is the most cited in *Teología en Conjunto*'s index. González has twenty-two references,

not only be the object of mission but also its proponents, he has shifted the focus of what we understand by mission.[138] Such Latino Protestant theologians as Eldin Villafañe, Harold Recinos, and Samuel Solivan also stress the important role the poor and marginal play in the evolution of theology, particularly the poor in our U.S. inner cities.

In many ways Costas models a theological method that is not only praxiological,[139] as well as one that opts for the poor, but also one that gives great importance to prayer so as to be in tune with the Spirit:

> The preacher-teacher needs to be a person of prayer, because prayer is the means by which we express our dependence on the Holy Spirit, seek his guidance and submit to his will. Thus, through submission and intense supplication we may claim the empowering presence of the Spirit in our preaching and teaching and thus we may anticipate believers being motivated for witness.[140]

Harold J. Recinos

This United Methodist minister, who teaches at Wesley Theological Seminary in Washington, D.C., demonstrates a remarkable ability to theologize from experience. Whether in terms of his own past, which includes living alone as a heroin addict at age thirteen in New York City, or through the tragic stories of people in his congregation, one cannot help but be moved by the authenticity of his writing. In the foreword to Recinos' first book, *Hear the Cry! A Latino Pastor Challenges the Church* (Louisville: Westminster/John Knox Press, 1989), Richard Shaull describes the author's method, a method he employs in his two later books:

> The book captures and holds our interest because of the way the author is able to present his case by weaving together his story and the stories of other men and women in the ghetto, by careful analysis of economic and social realities and creative theological reflection, and by his own poetry portraying life in the South Bronx.[141]

---

while Costas has fifteen. Incidently, in the same index, Virgilio Elizondo has fourteen references.

138. Costas, *Christ Outside the Gate* (1982).

139. Costas employs Juan Luis Segundo's hermeneutical circulation. In the words of Segundo, "Each new reality obliges us to interpret the Word of God afresh, to change reality accordingly, and then go back and re-interpret the Word of God again" (as quoted in Costas, *Liberating News*, 8).

140. As quoted in *Teología en Conjunto*, 158.

141. Shaull, in Recinos, *Hear the Cry!* (1989) 9–10.

The son of Puerto Rican *campesinos* who migrated to New York City, he was fortunate to survive in a neighborhood where "out of a group of fifteen decent kids, four have survived into their thirties."[142] As an adolescent Recinos was befriended by a Presbyterian minister and his family. Eventually he studied theology at Union Theological School in New York. His experience of growing up in the inner city in many ways collided with that of the seminary. It was precisely at this crucial time that membership in a local faith community proved to be very beneficial.

> I became a member of Broadway Temple-Spanish, a [United Methodist] congregation that was then under the leadership of the Rev. Noé Torres. The tension between Latin American liberation theology and Latino evangelical piety developed as a major theme of my faith perceptions. Generally, it is assumed that evangelical faith is conservative and reactionary, especially around issues of left-oriented social action. Many traditional Latino church groups in the United States would fit the conservative description because they have tended not to be influenced by the sweeping theological changes initiated by the Latin American bishops' conferences of the last two decades. Until very recently, the North American Latino church has led an isolated life cut off from the new theology coming out of the Third World. As a student pastor at Broadway Temple-Spanish, I was convinced that the Latino evangelical in the United States, or any evangelical, could recover the social-witness dimensions latent in the pietistic tradition.[143]

In terms of a contextual approach to theological method, Recinos follows in the vein of Costas. In his second work, *Jesus Weeps: Global Encounters on Our Doorstep* (1992), Recinos demonstrates a desire for dialogue with Jewish, *Mujerista*, Womanist, Native American, and Asian theologians. Like Costas, he views the whole enterprise of evangelization in terms of expanding globalization:

> Globalization implies that the church is ready to discern God's presence in the contrast of cultural experience. Hence, critical reflection on the gospel in light of human diversity requires greater attention to cultural realities. The gospel is never heard outside of cultural systems of belief and behavior. The history of Christian thought from the advent of the patristic writings to the present, confirms that theology has always been contextual or culture-bound. Surely, the great insight of the process of globalization is its admission that human beings devise systems of meaning through their cultures.[144]

142. Ibid., 30.
143. Ibid., 39.
144. Recinos, *Jesus Weeps* (1992) 99.

The topic of globalization appears again in Recinos' most recent work, *Who Comes in the Name of the Lord? Jesus at the Margins* (1997). His concern, particularly in this work, is the disregard of the Latino poor living in the inner cities on the part of the mainline churches. He contrasts this indifference with passionate concern in recent years about the war in Central America:

> [F]or over a decade, mainline churches' progressive wings were particularly solidarized with the political struggles of the poor of El Salvador and their Salvadoran counterparts in the United States. The solidarity movement was a genuine reflection of a new way of thinking about God and the Scriptures. Mainline Christians did theology from below by reading the Scriptures from the perspective of the oppressed, giving sanctuary to Salvadoran and Guatemalan refugees, and demanding an end to the U.S. government's involvement in Central American civil wars. Mainline churches' contact with Latinos issued forth in an alternative understanding of the political conflict in Central America that featured issues of wealth and poverty.[145]

Recinos decries the lack of commitment to these same persons today, however, many of whom are now living in the United States:

> Although Central Americans and Salvadorans are now living in cities all across the United States, mainline churches are presently ignoring them. Salvadorans have simply become another group of "hispanics" in the States that are simply no longer seen as a moral focus in mainline church life. Because many progressive mainline Christians believe that peace and democracy are being established in El Salvador, their ethical interests have turned to other long-neglected matters. Indeed, mainline denominations are replacing social gospel interests with a new privatized Christianity that emphasizes personal spirituality. The faithful are increasingly evacuating the world of political conflicts to build a more subjectively grounded church.[146]

Recinos proposes a solution for the mainline churches, one that calls them back to the whole reason for being Church: the imitation of Jesus, who reached out to the "uninvited guest."

> As congregations gather for Bible study, worship, and to celebrate the sacraments, they acknowledge the revelation of God-in-Christ. Yet, this visible community needs to be in ministry precisely where

145. Recinos, *Who Comes?* (1997) 83–4.
146. Ibid.

the risen Christ is already hidden and waiting to be found: with uninvited guests. Mainline churches will restore meaning to their identity when they recall the gospel's requirement to identify with the barrio. Discovering Jesus in the barrio, hidden in the sick, poor, imprisoned, homeless, hungry, downtrodden, undocumented alien, and underemployed, negates the idea that solidarity with disdained people is optional for Christian ministry. The true church knows it works for justice on behalf of the least of humanity (Matt 25:31-46; James 1:27).[147]

As will be evident in the treatment of Eldin Villafañe, which follows, Recinos' contribution is to keep Latino theology focused on its implications for ministry. At a time when the role of institutional religion is diminishing and therefore religion is becoming marginal to society, he proposes a focus on the suffering Christ in the barrio as a solution to this crisis.[148]

Eldin Villafañe

Among the most well known of the Latino Pentecostal theologians, Eldin Villafañe teaches at Gordon-Conwell Theological Seminary near Boston. An ordained minister with the Hispanic Eastern District of the Assemblies of God, his primary published work to date is *The Liberating Spirit: Toward an Hispanic Pentecostal Social Ethic*. In the opening paragraph of the book he succinctly states his purpose in writing:

> For many years now an overriding passion has motivated my research—the construction of a social ethic for the Hispanic Pentecostal Church in the United States. This social ethic, though, must cohere with the Hispanic American socio-cultural experience as well as be consistent with Hispanic Pentecostalism's self understanding of ethics emerging from its experience of the Spirit. This has been the not too modest goal of this book. You, the reader, will be the judge whether I have made some contribution towards that end.[149]

As an experienced pastor, he appreciates the reality of grass-roots Hispanic Pentecostals who are marginated[150] yet combines in his analysis insights gained from sociology and scholarly theological research. In a sense, he is speaking to two audiences: to his Pentecostal sisters and

147. Ibid., 144–5.
148. For a critique of Recinos' and Elizondo's use of Scripture, see Valentin, "Nuevos Odres para el Vino," 30–47.
149. Villafañe, *Liberating Spirit* (1993) xi.
150. Villafañe describes a certain social stigma that often accompanies these communities: "The tendency of Hispanic Pentecostals to easily attribute all opposition

brothers, urging them to take the social dimension of Christianity seriously, as well as to other Christians, demonstrating the gifts that Pentecostals bring to the wider Church.

He reminds the second group, other Christians, that Pentecostals now constitute the "third force" of Christianity. His statistics say that in 1991 one out of every five Christians in the world belonged to a Pentecostal/charismatic Church. The growth of this movement has been phenomenal.

> The beginning of the 20th century heralded the arrival of the Pentecostal Movement into the religious scene. Its rapid growth and worldwide scope—a true missionary phenomenon—has challenged both friend and foe to take note of this "ragged" (and not so "ragged" in many places today) group of "disinherited." The significance of the Pentecostal Movement as a new reformation, emerging alongside Roman Catholicism and mainline Protestantism as the third major type and branch of Christendom, has been called "The Third Force."[151]

Much of the book is a general description of Pentecostalism, particularly as it is found among Hispanics. This focus demands a broad social analysis and historical overview, which he promptly provides. In trying to explain the appeal of Pentecostalism to Hispanics he applies the conclusions of Paul A. Pomerville[152] by mentioning the lack of engagement on the part of mainline churches, and then relating this phenomenon to Latinos:

> Among the many reasons for the emergence of Pentecostalism as a worldwide renewal movement at the turn of the century was "its emphasis on the experiential dimension of the Christian faith, the dynamic experience of the Spirit" [the phrase is Pomerville's]. Pentecostalism in the U.S.A., as well as worldwide, emerged in the context of the "oppressed of the 'spirit,'" reflecting the cold and formal state of Christianity; and in the context of the "spirit of the oppressed," reflecting the poor and disinherited. Hispanic Pentecostalism in the "barrios" also participated in this dual oppressive situation: an experience of a "distant" Christianity, and an experience of a "distant" social-cultural enfranchisement.[153]

---

to their faith experience of 'glossolalia,' oftentimes hides a deep opposition and rejection; one rooted on their being a "class church"—a church of the poor—with all the cultural and social baggage which it carries. To be Hispanic, poor, and Pentecostal is to be an easy 'scapegoat' target for many in the 'barrios'" (ibid., 150).

151. Ibid., 84–5.
152. Pomerville, *Third Force in Missions* (1985).
153. Villafañe, *Liberating Spirit*, 164.

In light of the context affecting the emergence of Pentecostalism, one characterized by a need to offer an alternative to a "distant" Christianity as well as one coming from those society has relegated to the margins, Villafañe refers frequently to the many contributions that this relatively new movement in the Church is making worldwide. Often this contribution is presented as that which often is already a reality, such as the presence of small, tightly knit communal structures that provide a type of safety net for church members who need social services, together with the identification of the Pentecostal community's growing edge, in this case, a need for the development of a social ethic that confronts social problems structurally.

Villafañe illustrates another contribution the Latino Pentecostal community is making in terms of the healing of the individual human person. Pentecostals are known for their belief in healings: "The power of the Spirit of God to heal physical impairment is crucial."[154] Yet the Pentecostal theologian chides the acceptance of a spirituality that is dualistic:

> The Pentecostal's intolerance for sickness—a physical, not "spiritual" condition—should extend to other non-spiritual areas of life, (i.e., intolerance for bad housing, unemployment, injustice). The potential for radical social change is within the bosom of Hispanic Pentecostals in the "barrio" given the radical experience of baptism in the Spirit.[155]

This potential is none other than that of a person who comes to the realization that she or he is endowed by God with an irrevocable dignity.

> The baptism in the Holy Spirit profoundly influences the self-worth of the person. In the "barrio" Pentecostal church, the impact is noticeable as believers, "new creatures in Christ," in touch with the power of the universe, find new status and personal worth. Their evangelistic or recruitment zeal owes no small measure to this new self-image and its motivating power.[156]

154. Ibid., 149.
155. Ibid.
156. Ibid., 148. Previously, in a footnote, Villafañe quotes Boff to accent Pentecostalism's emphasis on human dignity: "In a meeting with Latin American liberation theologians in Petrópolis, Brazil on January 24, 1991, I raised the question of the role, if any, of the Pentecostal Church to Liberation. Leonardo Boff responded quickly with four positive points, noting the significant role played by the Pentecostal Church in the 'favelas' of Brazil: 1) 'Rescata dignidad mínima'; 2) 'Religión de resistencia'; 3) 'Liberación espiritual'; y 4) 'Lanza un reto al pueblo.'" *Liberating Spirit*, 127, n. 208.

All in all, Villafañe is calling for a more integral spirituality, one that is not dualistic. Basing himself on sacred Scripture, he concludes that the main reason Hispanic Pentecostalism must develop a social ethic is so that it will be "a 'community of the Spirit' *in* the world and a 'community of the Spirit' *for* the world, but not *of* the world" (emphasis his).[157] He devotes much of the book to an elaboration of this ecclesial vision.

Samuel Solivan

Like Villafañe, this "New Yorican" (northeastern Puerto Rican) Pentecostal theologian, who teaches at Newton Theological School and at the Harvard School of Medicine Mind Body Institute, has written a book challenging both Pentecostals and other Christians. In *The Spirit, Pathos, and Liberation*[158] he describes his position, one that is dually critical of conservatives and liberals and therefore places him on the margins of both:

> The perspective that informs me is one tempered by a modern critical spirit and some liberation insights, by love for God and neighbor and Pentecostal tradition and passion. I raise questions that critique the traditional conservative theology of Pentecostalism as well as the theological perspectives of liberal and liberationist theologies are raised as a loyal critic of both sides of the issues, as one who lives on the boundaries.[159]

Not simply a case of "what happens when Pentecostalism meets theology of liberation," his work strives to uphold the unique contribution Pentecostals are making to Christianity today. In describing the "Hispanic Protestant Ethos," Solivan highlights a return to a more radical reliance on God's Spirit and less on rational discourse:

> History has taught the poor that the objective tools of rational discourse have often become the instrumentation of oppressive forces that keep them hungry and ignorant. Thus, the Hispanic religious ethos is not solely dependent on the rational, theological discourse of well-trained theologians. It has had to learn to see and hear the inner voice of the Spirit of God. It has had to take leaps of faith in its long journey of darkness.[160]

Solivan calls this transforming presence of the Spirit "orthopathos." Described as "the power of the Holy Spirit in one's life that transforms

157. Ibid., 161.
158. Solivan, *Spirit, Pathos, and Liberation* (1998).
159. Ibid., 35.
160. Ibid., 26.

pathos, suffering and despair into hope and wholeness,"[161] orthopathos is the missing component of a three-legged stool, one in which orthodoxy and orthopraxis are already present. These terms, often presented as opposites and therefore part of a continuum, are not an adequate way to describe the Christian vision.

> Orthodoxy and orthopraxis are terms with varied usage. Doubtless, they frame the faith and mission of the church. Yet by emphasizing their difference, a cleavage is drawn that has polarized, rather than empowered, further reflection. Orthodoxy has become a sterile term which reduces the power of the Word to a set of faith statements posited by a given religious community in a given time. Thus, orthodoxy is manipulated to defend and maintain certain vested interests of class and gender.[162]

Orthopraxis, which often has been presented as the solution for an excessively "idea oriented" approach to Christianity, unfortunately, according to Solivan, is also falling short. He sees it as often lacking an existential link to the poor. Termed "cognitive praxis," it too errs by being overly rationalistic.

> Whatever interest or concern the mainline church has had for suffering peoples is a "cognitive praxis"; it is a kind of retreat. Several of those who employ praxis as a methodological principle are "absentee advocates" in the church and communities they claim to represent. Most North American liberation praxis has been reduced to scholarly theological forums, removed and distant from actual suffering. Conceived rationally and divorced from the experience of oppression, this kind of praxis defends the vested interests of a middle class that substitutes cognition for pathos. It reduces orthopraxis to a slogan that maintains control in the arena of theological exchange.[163]

Solivan proposes the need for a bridge between orthodoxy and orthopraxis, a connector that will work against the polarization of these two essential elements. As mentioned above, orthopathos provides the element often lacking in mainline churches.[164]

161. Ibid., 27.

162. Ibid., 60–1.

163. Ibid., 66.

164. While acknowledging the positive impact of the streams of "American orthodoxy found in Wesleyan and non-Wesleyan traditions, as well as the orthodox traditions of the Protestant Reformation and post Vatican II Roman Catholicism," Solivan criticizes both: "These have stretched and enriched my understanding of God, Jesus and the Holy Spirit. Yet at times the waters have been bitter, even pol-

The polarization of orthodoxy and orthopraxis has been detrimental to the poor and the suffering who often find that they must choose between their piety and their sociopolitical survival. This is inconsistent with the Christian world-view that both orthodoxy and orthopraxis seek to represent. A bridge between these two is needed, not the leap of despair which seems now to be required. I propose that orthopathos can be that bridge between piety and social engagement, between proper thinking and proper doing. I hope to show that orthopathos is a theological epistemology, which humanizes cognition as well as critical reflection about engagement. Scholars who allow themselves to be in touch with and touched by the pain and suffering of others humanize and deobjectivize them. This contact provides an entrée to the voices and vision of the disinherited and a location for legitimate discourse by those whom orthodoxy seeks to save and orthopraxis seeks to represent. Like the cross that stood between the incarnation and the resurrection, the possibilities of orthopathos stand between orthodoxy and orthopraxis, seeking to be a resource to incarnate orthodoxy and to resurrect and relocate orthopraxis.[165]

Throughout the book Solivan argues that Pentecostalism, which today may be "perhaps the largest church of the poor, in the world,"[166] engages suffering in a way that mainline churches have not. Their living out of this "orthopathos," moreover, provides a witness to the power of the Spirit, who "works in and through our brokenness to bring to us the benefits of Christ."[167] Although not necessarily limited to Hispanic Pentecostals but, more generally, to those imbued with orthopathos, Solivan eloquently describes the hope of these faith communities:

This transformation expressed in orthopathos occurs in spite of the present systemic presence of evil and does not require that these structures be overcome in order for our pathos to be transformed into orthopathos. The hope of overcoming the structures of evil in our society resides in those who, in spite of these structures, have begun to overcome them by the power of the Holy Spirit; a power manifested in them in a manner that has taken their pathos, suffering and pain and has converted their weakness and suffering into power for liberation.[168]

---

luted, because of orthodoxy's failure to live up to its promise of representing the whole counsel of God. . . . Both Catholic and Protestant orthodoxy's partnership with the dominant culture, and their propensity to uphold at all costs the status quo, have marred their integrity and undermined their claims" (ibid., 35).

165. Ibid., 37–8.
166. Ibid., 30.
167. Ibid., 147.
168. Ibid.

Ismael García

Another Latino theologian, who like Villafañe, focuses on ethics and the Latino community, teaches at Austin Presbyterian Theological Seminary in Texas. His perspectival lens in his recent work, *Dignidad: Ethics Through Hispanic Eyes*,[169] is clearly a Hispanic one:

> Feelings, traditions, cultural habits, and religious convictions are part of the act of thinking about moral behavior. Therefore, our perceptions of God, our differing social experiences and cultural manners influence and shape the ways we feel, practice, and think about the moral life. The purpose of this book is to clarify how these various elements become part of the Hispanic moral point of view.[170]

Proceeding from a position that the interpersonal is more important for Hispanic ethical decisions than the rational, García describes how this type of behavior differs from other ways of ethical comportment:

> The Hispanic focus on intimate relationships and our sensitivity to the needs of others cement our conviction that we have moral obligations beyond those defined in terms of rights and impartial universal laws. Within the family and the comunidad it is not the language of benefience and utility, nor the language of law, rights, and contracts between free agents that makes moral sense, but the language of commitment, mutual dependence, care, love, and compassion that communicates what is morally required. In these contexts obligation and responsibility take precedence over rights.[171]

Much of the book is descriptive. García is attempting to explain how it is that Hispanics make moral decisions, not an easy task. Aware of this complexity, he is striving not to identify the moral theory out of which Hispanics respond but rather to bring to light the "dominant motifs found in the moral language by which Hispanic Americans express their moral views and commitments."[172] Some type of critique is in order as he points to the strengths and weaknesses of each.

A case study that features prominently in the work is the film *Mi Familia* (My Family), produced by Francis Ford Copola and directed by Gregory Nava. The film chronicles the story of a Mexican family's three generations in California. Using this rich story allows García to demon-

---

169. I. García, *Dignidad*.
170. Ibid., 15.
171. Ibid., 44.
172. Ibid., 21.

strate the impact of environment on decision making. "The dominant motifs that inform the different ethical views of Hispanics are, to a great extent, a response to the social condition lived by our people."[173] The theme of oppression, which other Latino theologians stress, is certainly not absent here.

> We appeal to the terms "oppression" and "domination" to both describe and evaluate the social conditions in which our people are forced to live. In using the terms oppression and domination, our purpose is to point to a multilayered social condition that covers the diverse social harms inflicted on us as a social group. It is important to specify and describe each of these social harms in order to understand better how different manifestations of oppression relate to one another and how each one is unique. Different subgroups within the larger Hispanic community are affected more by one or another form of oppression and domination; to be freed from them, each form of oppression must be dealt with on its own terms. To be oppressed is to be subjected to a social structure in which the power and freedom needed by one social group to forward its self-realization is controlled or possessed by another social group.[174]

The various types of oppression discussed are economic, social, political, and cultural. Although socioeconomic views of the Latino community in and of themselves often reveal a discouraging picture, García, like some of the other Latino theologians mentioned thus far, demonstrates that the real scene is much larger. The sin of oppression may abound, but so does the reality of grace. In describing this grace García points to the contribution Hispanics can make to the larger Church and society:

> One of the contributions Hispanics can make to the community of faith is to keep alive the collective, public dimension of sin, since the personal, private dimension is already overemphasized. Sin has a political, public dimension since at its core sin violates the power of love that calls us to be for and with others. We can also make a contribution by helping members of the community of faith see how the private dimension of life is related to and significantly affected by the public dimension.[175]

This social understanding of sin emerges partly out of the Hispanic sensitivity to the interpersonal, which was described above. Aside

173. Ibid., 21.
174. Ibid., 21–2.
175. Ibid., 142.

from this emphasis on the social, García holds that most Hispanics have a "strong sense of personhood which shapes [their] moral point of view."[176]

> This [sense of personhood] is particularly true among Hispanics who ground their moral point of view on religious convictions. We do not conceive of God primarily in philosophical categories; rather we use the language and imagery of personal relationships. We view God as companion, a friend, a source of care, support, and hope. Our everyday language is full of God talk: "hay Dios," "Dios te bendiga," "que sea la voluntad de Dios," "Ave María." We express ourselves in ways that reveal our sense of the ever-presence of God in our lives.[177]

García joins other Latina and Latino theologians in stressing the need for the affect in our theologizing. His book is an exposition of how such elements as the social and the affect play key roles in shaping and executing Hispanic moral values.

A point that appears time and time again in the writings of both Protestant and Catholic Hispanic theologians is that the often marginal perspective of the Latino community provides an immeasurable resource for theological reflection. Roberto Goizueta, summarizing the contributions of Hispanics to theological parlance, makes the same point: at stake in the emergence of this theology is the good of everyone, not just Hispanics:

> U.S. Hispanic theologians have already made important contributions to this critical dialogue. While engaging the Tradition, the ongoing theological scholarship has as its wellspring the popular traditions of our communities. These traditions are, in turn, examined from within the context of a mestizo community. Traditional scriptural themes and exegesis are critiqued as the experience of our communities becomes a source of rich insights into the meaning of God's revelatory activity in the world. The interpretation of traditional Christian doctrines and symbols is enriched—not just for Latinos and Latinas, but for everyone.[178]

Conclusion

This chapter is a summary of the writings of U.S. Hispanic theologians during the period from 1972 to 1998. At first glance, the amount

176. Ibid., 17.
177. Ibid.
178. Goizueta, "*Nosotros*" (1992) 64.

of material presented seems overwhelming. Closer examination, however, reveals the existence of several common themes. Before attempting any kind of synthesis it is necessary to lay out the various pieces of this theological puzzle.

By separating the various authors into four sections, this introductory exposition has shed light on their particular focus and contribution to U.S. Hispanic theology. Virgil Elizondo's pioneering efforts provide a description of its subject and context: the *mestizo* in the United States. His further reflections provide much illumination today on the role of the *mestizo* in God's salvific plan.

The male Catholic Latino theologians who come after Elizondo and who now form part of ACHTUS are addressing the lack of Hispanic voices in a Church whose Hispanic population is quite numerous. Allan Figueroa Deck, trying to mediate theory and practice, addresses many of the concrete pastoral ramifications of ministry to Hispanics. Orlando Espín's area of concentration is on popular religiosity as a means of understanding the *sensus fidelium*. Roberto Goizueta, the Latino theologian most in dialogue with prevailing theological currents, is providing some insights into the theological method operative in U.S. Hispanic theology. Like Deck, he examines the relationship between theory and practice, at the same time adding another dimension, the aesthetic. Jaime Vidal's work is similar to Espín's in that they both explore popular religiosity. Vidal's focus, however, has tended to be more pastoral, while Espín's concerns are more in the lines of theological method. Alex García-Rivera, through the use of semiotics, is bringing the voice of the popular folk to our theological discourse.

Among the women theologians in ACHTUS, two who were featured in this summary are Ada María Isasi-Díaz and María Pilar Aquino. Isasi-Díaz has come the furthest in articulating a *mujerista* theology that is distinct from North American feminist theology. Her research tool, known as ethnomethodology, is providing a platform for Latinas, particularly grass-roots Latinas, whose voices have not been heard in theological circles. At the core of Aquino's work is a critique of some of the dominant theological methods employed today, including that of some of the Latin American liberation and U.S. Hispanic male theologians.

The final two sections introduced Latino Protestants whose offerings are similar to that of Latino Catholics, yet different. Aside from his revealing work on the theological education of U.S. Hispanics, González has convincingly demonstrated the importance of taking perspective into account when doing theology. Using numerous historical examples of how sacred Scripture and ecclesial tradition were interpreted over the centuries, he reveals that theological doctrines were not formulated in a sociohistorical vacuum. Context is therefore extremely important. He is making a plea for the expansion of perspectival horizons.

Orlando Costas emphatically stresses the crucial stamp that context leaves on our theologizing. In the case of the poor and oppressed, their context is an invaluable key to understanding much of what is written in sacred Scripture, hence his insistence that the good news be communicated from the margins. Harold Recinos, also very concerned about the people at the margins, bemoans the mainline churches' disregard of the Latino poor who inhabit the inner cities. He purports that mainline churches will only become revitalized when they respond to the suffering Christ in the world today.

Eldin Villafañe and Samuel Solivan, both coming from the Pentecostal experience, highlight the importance of the experiential aspects of faith and how Pentecostal Christians offer an alternative to an excessively rational approach to divine mysteries. Both explicate a Pentecostal theology that needs to be challenged to a greater social awareness, yet also supplies a much needed expression of passion for worship and life in the Spirit. Villafañe decries a false dualism often found in Pentecostalism, and Solivan criticizes both Catholics and mainline Protestants for too easily acquiescing in the status quo. He maintains that Pentecostals exhibit a stronger existential link to the poor. Like Villafañe, Ismael García centers his work around ethics and the Latino community. His concludes that for Latinas and Latinos, the interpersonal overrides the rational.

Despite the great diversity manifested in these pages, there are some commonalities worth mentioning. To begin with, all of these Latino theologians are reflecting on their own experience of living between two very different worlds, the North American and the Latin American. They are theologizing, therefore, from a unique cultural perspective, more concretely, from the position within which they, as members of an oppressed people, experience God. This new group of theologians, of which a certain number are women, seems intuitively aware of the need to stay in touch with the faith environment that gave them birth. At the same time, however, they are responding to the challenge to dialogue with the tradition as presented today by mainstream theologians.

This self-perception on the part of Latino theologians, in many ways a product of theology's shift to the human person, has prompted recourse to the social sciences. All of these writers, in some form or other, are in dialogue with history, sociology, economics, social philosophy, and anthropology.

Another point of convergence is their search for a theology that is holistic, one that not only incorporates the rational but also the emotive and the aesthetic—this has been their religious experience among their people, an experience often embodied in both Catholic and Protestant forms of popular religiosity. Finally, in one form or another all are concerned about developing a theology that goes much further than defending the rights of Latinos or seeing that the Church caters to their needs. These pioneer theologians are convinced that U.S. Hispanic theology is revealing certain values and experiences that are essential components of the great tradition that has been handed down over the centuries. The result, undoubtedly, will be a significant contribution to a new hermeneutic of the tradition, a tradition much wider than the Hispanic experience yet deficient without it. We now turn our attention back to the wider ecclesial body, a Church that is growing in the awareness that, in a sense, all theology is contextual.

3

The Emergence of Contextual
Theology in the Church

I recall a dinner conversation among Jesuits in one of the Roman houses of study. After a rather heated debate over the validity of the theologies of liberation, my Jesuit brother from Colombia, the main advocate of this recent theological current, turned toward another brother from Zaire and asked him, "How do they feel about the theology of liberation in Africa?" He answered, "Our main concern currently is with the issue of inculturation, not liberation."

The previous anecdote illustrates well the observation made recently by a scholar of the theology of world religions in his book, *Jesus Christ at the Encounter of World Religions*.[1] Its author, Jacques Dupuis, a Belgian Jesuit who labored many years in India, accents two main current theological trends: liberation and inculturation:

> Two debates hold center stage in theology today that seem assured of a position of importance in the years to come. They are the discussions concerning liberation theology, whose particular currency is in the countries of the third world, and secondly, discussions on a Christian theology of the religious traditions of humanity, in which the Asian and African continents are particularly involved. The scenario of theological debate has considerably evolved, then, in these last years. The burning issues now touch first and foremost the life of the continents and churches of the third world. The rapid geopolitical evolution of the planet, characterized by what has been called, correctly enough, the "irruption" of the third

1. Dupuis, *Encounter of World Religions* (1991).

95

world and the "third church," is not without its repercussions on
the theological agenda of the churches.[2]

In many ways, as illustrated in the previous chapter, the writings of
U.S. Hispanic theologians draw from both currents. While theologians
such as Costas, Goizueta, Isasi-Díaz, and Aquino dialogue with Latin
American liberation thought, others such as Elizondo, Deck, and Espín
have focused their energies more on the inculturation aspects. To a
large degree, however, all of these U.S. Hispanic theologians are consciously theologizing from a certain context. In this manner, they are
part of a theological movement toward contextualization.

The purpose of this chapter is to describe this trend toward contextual theology. Later chapters will establish aspects of U.S. Hispanic theology within this general movement. We began our study in chapter 1
by situating Hispanics within American culture and Church. Its method
was basically historical and sociological. The history of Latinas and
Latinos in the United States spans the period from colonial America to
the present socioeconomic reality of this diverse population, a population progressively more urban. The treatment raised some serious challenges, however, to the urban underclass model, which has often been
applied to U.S. Hispanics. We examined the role of the Catholic Church
in light of such a history, both in earlier times and in the present. Chapter 2 presented an overview of the writings of fourteen U.S. Hispanic
theologians, both Catholic and Protestant. Its goal was to surface some
of the basic issues surrounding its evolution. By presenting highlights
of what these Latino and Latina theologians have written in the last
thirty years, the chapter gave many examples of theology done per-
spectively, thus its focus was more specific. It remains for this chapter
to examine once again the broader context, most specifically, the operative theological framework.

This chapter is divided into two parts. The first describes the contextual trend in theology. Of great importance here are some current major
thinkers and their methodological innovations in doing theology. The
second part describes some models of contextual theology proposed by
the latest person to synthesize the trend, Stephen B. Bevans.

A Growing Trend Toward Contextualization

A Methodological Shift to Human Experience

Maintaining that the study of theology has now shifted from seminaries to universities, Thomas H. Groome and Robert P. Imbelli depict

2. Ibid., 1.

a particular "turn to the subject" in our current method of theologizing.[3] Karl Rahner and Bernard Lonergan are credited for initiating this shift, which Groome and Imbelli describe as an attempt to attend not only to Scripture and tradition but also to "the life and mind, the context and interests, of the persons doing theology."[4] This approach, a methodological shift characterized by a stronger focus on the human person, is particularly attuned to human experience and historical praxis as indispensable sources for doing theology.[5]

Other authors, similarly responding to Vatican II's "signs of the times," view the starting point of theology as dipolar. Our contemporary experience is at one end and at the other, sacred Scripture. These texts of the past embody the unique revelation and lived experience of early Christians. Crucial in this perspective is the notion that experience is always interpreted experience and therefore subject to human categories.[6]

Unfortunately, in the past, particularly in Roman Catholic methodology, theology and scriptural exegesis became increasingly more separated. Theological method was often more characterized by an appeal to reason than to Scripture. Recent developments have restored Scripture to its unique status, viewing it "not as a deposit of truths but as a culturally conditioned witness and interpretation of God's proffer of salvation in the historical Christ event."[7] With Scripture assuming a privileged status, tradition is not another font of truth but, in the words of B. van Iersel, "the history of the effects of scripture."[8] Within this unification of Scripture and tradition one can begin to understand the role of theology: to serve as a hermeneutic of the tradition it confesses. Mention has already been made of the dipolar starting point for doing theology, mainly that of experience and sacred Scripture. Drawing from de Mesa and Wostyn,[9] Bevans describes the dialectic at work as it relates to contextual theology:

> Contextual theology's addition of culture and social change to the traditional loci of scripture and tradition in itself marks a revolution in the theological method when compared to traditional ways of doing theology. As José de Mesa and Lode Wostyn point out, no longer do we speak of culture and world events as areas to which

3. Groome and Imbelli, "Signposts Towards a Pastoral Theology," 127.
4. Ibid.
5. Ibid.
6. Hill, "Theology," 1013.
7. Ibid., 1014.
8. Ibid.
9. de Mesa and Wostyn, *Doing Theology*, 14–18.

theology is adapted and applied; culture and world events become the very sources of the theological enterprise, along with and equal to scripture and tradition. Both poles—human experience and the Christian tradition—are to be read together dialectically.[10]

Vatican II's injunction that we read the "signs of the times" in many ways opens the door for the emergence of contextual theology. Groome and Imbelli claim, for example, that *Gaudium et spes* is looked upon by various theologies of liberation as their Magna Carta. In its spirit,

they pursue a theological reflection that pays careful heed to the social and historical contexts in which Christians are called to live out the full responsibilities of their faith. They speak of "reading the signs of the times in light of the Gospel and the Gospel in light of the signs of the times."[11]

Much has happened in the theological world since the council fathers wrote these words. For instance, an increasing historical consciousness and the development of contextual theologies are demonstrating that all theologizing, in fact, is done from a certain social and historical context. In a sense, therefore, all theology is contextual. There is a specific thrust today, nonetheless, to consciously theologize within a specific context. There are many reasons for this move to a contextual or local theology.

Why a Concern for a Local Theology?

A good way to approach the development of a contextual method to doing theology is to examine Robert J. Schreiter's work, *Constructing Local Theologies*.[12] The value of his book is that it not only summarizes well the various issues relating to the problem of inculturation, but it also is a ray of hope in terms of pastoral directions to pursue. This quality makes for an excellent bridge between academic and pastoral perspectives. Schreiter avoids making absolute judgments. Rather, he assembles the evidence and then presents some observations and pastoral considerations to further the discussion. His attitude is one of listening and love for both the local ecclesial body and the central, hierarchical authority.

In his foreword, Edward Schillebeeckx highlights Schreiter's use of the social sciences to explore the relation between theology and its cultural context. Schillebeeckx defends the author's method:

10. Bevans, *Models of Contextual Theology* (1992) 11.
11. Groome and Imbelli, "Signposts Towards a Pastoral Theology," 128.
12. Schreiter, *Constructing Local Theologies* (1985).

> For such a manner of theologizing, the input of the social sciences, and especially the study of cultures and their significant (and economic) nodal points, is necessary. For the analysis of culture, the author makes special use of semiotics, albeit (and rightly so) with some reservation.[13]

More will be said on Schreiter's method later in this chapter.

Schreiter describes the task of his book in a nutshell: it is to discuss the topic of local theology or, in his words, to tackle the issue of "how to be faithful both to the contemporary experience of the gospel and to the tradition of Christian life that has been received."[14] His aim is to bring together the old and the new. Basically, how can we reconcile a Christian heritage and a new environment in which cultures vary greatly from those of earlier centuries or from those of other continents?

Schreiter's method is a collaborative one, not only because its inspiration was born in a seminar involving people from different countries but also because he dialogues extensively with the social sciences. Grateful for the feedback he received from his colleagues, he nonetheless stresses that his reflections are provisional and incomplete, since many of these problems have rarely been discussed extensively in Church circles. Schreiter thinks that at this point it is more important to examine the issues than to seek simplistic answers to complex theological problems.

In the opening chapter of the book Schreiter describes what has led to a concern for the creation of localized theology. Among the creative factors have been the emergence of new churches in Africa and Asia, Vatican II's Decree on the Church's Missionary Activity (*Ad gentes divinitus*), Pope Paul VI's *Evangelii nuntiandi* in 1975, and the appearance of the theology of liberation in the late 1960s which continues to the present.

These developments brought about new questions, many of them pastoral ones, for example, the requirement of celibacy for the clergy and the prohibition of polygamy. Others were more political, such as "How was one to understand church-state conflict in the repressive regimes of parts of Latin America, where the church was not a power equal to the state, but was now a church of the poor?"[15]

New churches started to feel the paternalism of the old. While these "mother churches" were often the source of financial support, they also tended to impose their own problems and solutions upon the younger

13. Ibid., ix.
14. Ibid., xi.
15. Ibid., 2.

ones, whose situations were very different. Schreiter presents a concrete example:

> As recently as the Sixth General Assembly of the World Council of
> Churches at Vancouver in 1983 this was again evident: the North
> Atlantic churches' agenda was dominated by the question of peace
> and nuclear war, while that of the rest of churches had to do with
> hunger, poverty, and political repression. Despite honest efforts to
> accommodate the agenda of the southern hemisphere, the agenda
> of the North Atlantic churches continued to have the upper hand
> in the proceedings.[16]

Even within the North Atlantic churches such minority groups as
Blacks, Hispanics, and women complained that their problems were
being met with "old answers" that were not adequate for their needs.
Moreover, in the case of Roman Catholics, the tension between that
which was perceived as necessary to maintain unity, a central authority
in Rome, and the needs and perspectives of the local church, became
more pronounced.

A New *Locus Theologicus*

A further force behind the emergence of local theology was the contribution of the social sciences. In terms of how "context" is generally
accepted, Schreiter points out that all theologies are developed within a
certain ambiance, one marked by certain interests or relationships of
power.[17] In a similar fashion, some theologians who favor a theology of
liberation note that the poor, because of their condition, are capable of
having, though do not necessarily have, a clearer vision of biblical theology.[18]

With the increased use of the social sciences in theologizing has come
a certain hermeneutic of suspicion, which calls for a rigorous examination of the terms we use. The result is a greater realization of the need
to clarify terms. We often throw words around as if we all agreed on
their meaning. Further investigation of their significance, however,
proves the contrary.

A case in point, demonstrating why he chose the term "local theology" over other common ones such as "indigenous," "ethnotheology,"
or "inculturation," Schreiter discusses the pros and cons of each term.
"Indigenous theology," while calling attention to the "integrity and

16. Ibid., 3.
17. Ibid., 4.
18. See González, *Mañana* (1990) 129.

identity of the enterprise," in some parts of the world still harkens back to the tactic of replacing British personnel in colonial government with local leadership. "Ethnotheology" also speaks of a specific people's theologizing but carries with it a certain condescending hue, as if "'sociology' were done in theologically advanced cultures, while only 'cultural anthropology' were done in less advanced cultures."[19]

"Inculturation" is used widely among Roman Catholics to speak of the combination of incarnation and acculturation but is criticized for being vague in terms of social science terminology. "Contextual theology" is another widely used term, which Schreiter accepts because of its focus on the individual context. His solution, however, is to opt for "local theology," a term which points to Vatican Council II's *ecclesia particularis*, or "local church."[20]

The same year Schreiter published *Constructing Local Theologies*, Stephen Bevans wrote an article on models of contextual theology, which contains the seeds for his book by the same name. This further development of his thought appeared in 1992, seven years later.[21] More will be said in the second part of this chapter about Bevans' work.

Schreiter outlines different approaches to doing local theology. Some of his approaches focus more on social change than others. The difficulty in speaking of adapting the gospel to a certain culture arises when we realize the ambiguity of what constitutes a certain culture. Culture is not static but rather quite dynamic. He argues that urban migrations and a younger population are factors that cannot be overlooked. "The median age of the Third World Population is less than twenty. These two factors of urbanization and youthful population indicate that much of that traditional religion and culture is being forgotten or not even learned."[22]

It is within this new context, hoping to describe what is known as the *locus theologicus*, that Schreiter presents his definition of local theology, namely, "the interaction among gospel, church, and culture." He adds, "That dynamic interaction . . . is a dialectical one, moving back and

---

19. Schreiter, *Constructing Local Theologies* (1985) 5–6.

20. Ibid. Schreiter justifies his choice: "Throughout this book the term 'local theology' will be the one used most commonly. While this does present certain problems in translation, there are advantages to recommend it. First, it allows the overtone of the 'local church' to be sounded. Second, as we shall see, not all attempts in theology are equally sensitive to the context; indeed, they can take quite different approaches to it. This allows keeping the term 'contextual' for those theologies that show greater sensitivity to context. And finally, it avoids undue use of neologisms" (p. 6).

21. Bevans, "Models of Contextual Theology," (1985) 185–202.

22. Schreiter, *Constructing Local Theologies* (1985) 13.

forth among the various aspects of gospel, church, and culture."[23] It is this very interaction that the Hispanic theologians are trying to address.

Learning to Listen to Culture

Vatican II's *Gaudium et spes* defined culture in the following manner:

> The word "culture" in its general sense indicates all those factors by which man refines and unfolds his manifold spiritual and bodily qualities. It means his effort to bring the world itself under his control by his knowledge and his labor. It includes the fact that by improving customs and institutions he renders social life more human both within the family and in the civic community. Finally, it is a feature of culture that throughout the course of time man expresses, communicates, and conserves in his works great spiritual experiences and desires, so that these may be of advantage to the progress of many, even of the whole human family.[24]

Such a positive assessment of culture on the part of the Church was not typical during the previous hundred years. Bevans speaks of a certain "cultural conscientization," which had been developing during the pontificates of Leo XIII, Pius XI, and Pius XII:

> There can be no doubt that the Roman Catholic Church in our century has witnessed a growing sense of the centrality and importance of human culture for genuine Christian existence and theological expression. . . . [In retrospect] one considers the rather anticultural and ahistorical approach of Pius IX in the "Syllabus of Errors" in the last half of the nineteenth century . . . and Pius X's condemnation of "modernism" at the beginning of the twentieth.[25]

Until this point, the word "culture" has been used without much nuancing. As Arij Roest Crollius, S.J., notes, the word's definition is often taken for granted, even by specialists.[26] Even the description of "culture" given by *Gaudium et spes,* above, seems rather general.[27] The Dutch theologian's aim is to provide a type of working understanding

---

23. Ibid., 22.

24. No. 53, as translated in Walter M. Abbot, *The Documents of Vatican II* (New York: Guild Press, 1966) 259.

25. Bevans, *Models of Contextual Theology* (1992) 42.

26. Roest Crollius, "Inculturation and the Meaning of Culture," *What Is So New About Inculturation?* ed. Roest Crollius and T. Nkéramihigo, 33–4.

27. Ibid.

of the term, especially as it relates to "inculturation." A key to his nuanced understanding is analogical thinking, a point that will be expanded later.

> Well aware, therefore, of exposing ourselves to the wrath of more disciplined specialists, we will nevertheless try to formulate at least the requirements which an adequate concept of culture should fulfill in order, precisely, to be practicable in an inter-disciplinary discussion on inculturation. In a further explicitation of a philosophical concept of culture, we hope to show how the various moments which constitute the cultural reality, on the one hand, explain the existence of the many acceptations of the term "culture," and, on the other hand, render possible an analogical understanding of the diversity of cultures. This analogical understanding serves to clarify the relation between inculturation and the dialogue among cultures.[28]

Already in the first part of this germinal work, which laid an important foundation for later discussions of the relation between culture and inculturation, Roest Crollius has typified the Church's acceptance of a definition of culture more in tune with developments in the social sciences:

> Instead of a more deductive, philosophical concept of culture, we now often encounter a more descriptive notion of it, which takes into account the investigations of cultural anthropology, sociology and ethnology.[29]

Notable is the fact that such a development in the ecclesial use of the concept of culture reflects a whole new way of doing theology. New is the shift from a deductive to an empirical method of theologizing.[30]

---

28. Ibid., 34.

29. Ibid., 16.

30. Bevans gives references for substantiating this point in *Models of Contextual Theology* (1992) 137: "See Tracy, *The Achievement of Bernard Lonergan* (New York: Herder & Herder, 1970), 80. In his essay 'Theology in Its New Context,' Lonergan speaks of how contemporary theology has undergone a shift from being a deductive to an empirical science. What this means is that 'where before the step from premises to conclusions was brief, simple, and certain, today the steps from data to interpretation are long, arduous, and at best, probable. An empirical science does not demonstrate. It accumulates information, develops understanding . . .' (p. 38). One of Lonergan's more eminent and creative disciples, J. S. Dunne, often speaks of the importance of moving from a search for certitude to a search for understanding. On this, see especially J. Nilson, 'Doing Theology by Heart: John S. Dunne's Theological Method,' *Theological Studies* 48 (1987) 71."

Before examining Schreiter's approach to studying culture, we turn to Roest Crollius' monograph for further clarification on the meaning of culture. Drawing from the thought of Karl Rahner and A. van Leeuwen, he examines how culture is a product of the relationship between the human person and his or her world. Taking this relationship a step further, culture becomes not only the means by which the *world* is humanized but also the means by which the *person* is humanized:

> Concretely, this means that, on the one hand, man develops himself and acquires his perfection by means of his activity in the external world. By developing techniques of agriculture and building, by conquering the world in his knowledge, by the exercise of arts, by devising means of organizing and shaping his environment, man develops his talents, brings to fulfillment his potentialities, in one word, becomes more human. This aspect of the self-realization of man in the world could be called "culture as the refinement of man." It would cover that aspect of culture which "consists of learned behavior patterns." On the other hand, in and through this manifold human activity, the world is "humanized." This means: it is re-shaped according to the image of man. Fields and gardens, huts and houses, roads and harbours make the pristine world into a human landscape. In this sense, anthropologists speak of culture as "the man-made part of the environment."[31]

Roest Crollius makes an analogy between cultivation and the formation of culture. Just as the human person tills the soil and through this process fruits are created, so through this activity a new way of life, a sedentary culture, in fact, is created.[32] Once again, it is clear that culture is both subject and object. It not only is the result or the end product of human behavior but also the shaper of it. In some ways, this understanding of culture does not lend itself easily to definition, a point Roest Crollius argues convincingly. At the same time, the nuancing of the concept opens the door to a fuller understanding of the complexity being dealt with.

In chapter 3 of *Constructing Local Theologies* Schreiter proposes some tools for studying culture, especially those that will produce a more attentive listening by the investigator. It is within this chapter that he introduces semiotics, the study of signs. According to his definition, semiotics "sees culture as a vast communication network, whereby both verbal and nonverbal messages are circulated along elaborate,

---

31. Roest Crollius, "Inculturation and the Meaning of Culture," *What Is So New About Inculturation?* (1991) 40.

32. Ibid.

interconnected pathways, which, together create the systems of meaning."[33] These signs are not always perceptible. In describing the complexity of such a system of meaning, he suggests the example of the experience of Roman Catholic converts:

> While they may be more conversant with the doctrines of Roman Catholicism than many who have been Roman Catholic from birth, there is something of an ethos of nonformalized rules that still govern Roman Catholic behavior, and which any experienced Roman Catholic can recognize. But most Roman Catholics would not be able to give an explicit account of what these rules are.[34]

He closes the chapter showing how a careful reading of culture can be a very important first step in bringing together inner and outer perspectives in order to construct local theology:

> In concluding, it must be stressed again that no culture is ever so simple that a comprehensive explanation and description can be given. Nor is it ever so static that all is entirely cohesive and consistent. Yet by concentrating on culture texts and various semiotic domains, an understanding of the culture can emerge, which can give new voice to the members of that culture from an inner perspective, and capacities for dealing with change and intercultural communication from the outer perspective. It can provide a way for coming to understand the sign system of a culture, and something of the metaphors that collect and guide the signs in a cultural system.[35]

The Interaction of Culture and Theology

How are these cultural symbols articulated in theological language? Both the sociology of knowledge and an ancient understanding of theology are particularly useful for this analysis. Using the classical definition of theology as "faith seeking understanding," Schreiter shows the tremendous complexity behind the terms and the extent to which Greek and Roman philosophy have left their mark on Christianity. He argues that our aim in the process of evangelization should be to try to

---

33. Schreiter, *Constructing Local Theologies* (1985) 49. On page 53, Schreiter quotes the American anthropologist Clifford Geertz's definition: "The concept of culture I espouse . . . is essentially a semiotic one. Believing, with Max Weber, that man is an animal suspended in webs of significance he himself has spun, I take culture to be those webs, and the analysis of it to be therefore not an experimental science in search of law but an interpretive one in search of meaning."

34. Ibid., 50.

35. Ibid., 73.

get back to the Christian tradition and see how that tradition interacts with local culture.

Various ways of attempting this interaction are then highlighted. These approaches, such as going back to the Church found in the New Testament or grappling with the great recurring themes in theology from a local perspective (for example, sin, grace, and salvation), together with the method of addressing the problem of terminology more directly, all present ways of bringing together the old and the new, the tradition and the new context for evangelization. He suggests some creative vehicles for incarnating the Christian tradition:

> So perhaps theology in African villages could best be expressed in proverbs rather than in Bantu philosophy. Perhaps theology could be done in poetry in Japan or in the form of sutra and commentary in South Asia. Melanesian theology might be done in songs and oratory, and United States black theology in the dialogue of gospel preaching. We need to locate those paradigms of thought in a culture which shape meaning and affirm it in the culture. Until that is done, the tradition is used naively or even paternalistically.[36]

His whole point is that even the vehicle we use for expressing theological thought in a different cultural context ought to reflect that culture's particular way of expressing itself. In the case of constructing a local Hispanic theology, for instance, one must consider the role that oral tradition and popular theology have played and continue to play in such a culture.[37]

The Role of Tradition

In chapter 5 of his book, "Tradition and Christian Identity," Schreiter brings together the different elements he has been developing throughout his presentation. Many of the difficulties that arise out of an attempt to integrate creatively the gospel, Church, and local culture are presented and discussed. This part of the book, which makes excellent use of Church history, argues for the need to see tradition as something positive:

36. Ibid., 77–8.
37. Deck applies the theories of Walter Ong and Milman Parry to the Mexican and Mexican American reality. See *Second Wave* (1989) 43–4. Ana María Pineda, similarly drawing from Ong, discusses the early evangelization in colonial Mexico from the point of view of the Aztec-Nahuatl world. She illustrates the problems that resulted when the Spanish evangelizers, a literate culture, attempted to bring the gospel to a culture whose complex system of communication was orally based. See Pineda, "Evangelization of the 'New World'" (1992) 151–61.

Tradition contributes three things to the development of human community: it provides resources for identity; it is a communication system providing cohesion and continuity in the community; it provides resources for incorporating innovative aspects into a community.[38]

Partly because of the Enlightenment, which gradually brought with it the enthronement of progress and rationality, the role of tradition gradually waned in Western culture, especially during the nineteenth century and the first half of the twentieth. Yet as this technological society found itself restricted by the limits of natural resources, to say nothing of the proliferation of nuclear weapons, it began to question itself. "Because it was possible, did it have to be done?" The Marxist state, similarly, with its scientific materialism, seemed less and less attractive as a form of human society.

Christianity has much to offer the modern world. Here Schreiter considers, for example, Christianity's sense of authority and ritual:

Christians believe that Christianity is not just a set of ethical principles; it is based upon a long history of revelation by God, culminating in the revelation of Jesus Christ. These great myths need to be recounted, especially in ritual situations where they can be reaffirmed and invite the allegiance of the adherents once again. A tradition that is not celebrated is a tradition that is dying.[39]

The above discussion takes place in the context of the relationship between older and younger churches. He stresses continuously that each needs the other. He presents, finally, some specific criteria for determining how faithful local theology is to the gospel.[40]

Inculturation? Local Theology? or Contextual Theology?

As previously mentioned, there are several terms currently in use to describe the dynamic interrelationship between culture, gospel, and tradition. Several of these expressions, in fact, are often employed inter-

38. Schreiter, *Constructing Local Theologies* (1985) 105.
39. Ibid., 107.
40. Schreiter's five criteria for establishing a communal Christian identity are as follows: (1) the cohesiveness of Christian performance, a cohesiveness between doctrines and symbols, (2) the worshiping context and Christian performance, (3) the praxis of the community and Christian performance, (4) the judgment of other churches and Christian performance, and (5) the challenge to other churches and Christian performance. Among other things, Schreiter is calling attention to the relationship between the local church and the universal. See *Constructing Local Theologies* (1985) 117–21.

changeably. One of the earliest used is "inculturation." Roest Crollius traces its origin.[41] Using material from the social sciences and ecclesial documents, he guides the reader through the labyrinth of its use both by anthropological sciences and theology. Unlike some who would find the term unusable because of a lack of precision in meaning, he defines inculturation as a theological term that describes a process of integration:

> Recapitulating, we can describe the process of inculturation in the following way: the inculturation of the Church is the integration of the Christian experience of a local Church into the culture of its people, in such a way that this experience not only expresses itself in elements of this culture, but becomes a force that animates, orients and innovates this culture so as to create a new unity and communion, not only within the culture in question but also as an enrichment of the Church universal.[42]

Highlighted in this definition are the importance of the local church, the dynamism of culture, the stress on experience, and the connectedness with the universal Church. This definition is reminiscent of Schreiter's "local theology" (i.e., "the interaction among gospel, church, and culture, . . . That dynamic interaction . . . is a dialectical one, moving back and forth among the various aspects of gospel, church, and culture"[43]).

Neither Roest Crollius nor Schreiter favors the use of the term "indigenous theology" to describe what is being called above either inculturation or local theology.[44] Schreiter critiques the use of "inculturation":

41. Roest Crollius, "Inculturation and the Meaning of Culture," *What Is So New About Culture* (1991) 1–18. Carl F. Starkloff, relying on Clifford Geertz's study of "cultural systems," suggests a method of deepening our understanding of inculturation. See Starkloff, "Inculturation and Cultural Systems—Part 1," 66–81.

42. Roest Crollius, "Inculturation and the Meaning of Culture," 15.

43. Schreiter, *Constructing Local Theologies* (1985) 22.

44. Roest Crollius writes, "For some people, 'indigenous' and 'natives' can be found in exotic countries, or everywhere except where they themselves come from." See "Inculturation and the Meaning of Culture," 4. Schreiter notes, "The difficulty with this term [indigenous theology], at least in some places, is the history of the word 'indigenous.' In those parts of the world that once made up the British empire, 'indigenous' connotes the old policy of replacing British personnel in colonial government with local leadership. The term, therefore, has a distinctively colonialist ring in East Africa and India and is unsuited to the new perspective in theology. The term continues to be used in other parts of the world, however" (*Constructing Local Theologies*, 5).

Inculturation, as a noun, is often used of this shift in theological process as well. A combination of the theological principle of incarnation with the social-science concept of acculturation (adapting oneself to a culture), the term has come to be used widely in Roman Catholic circles and appears in many documents of congresses and episcopal conferences. It refers to the wider process of which theology is an expression. While widely accepted in church circles, it causes some difficulties in dialogue with social scientists in that it seems to be a dilettantish kind of neologism on the part of non-scientists.[45]

In a footnote, however, Schreiter mentions that the Australian anthropologist Clement Godwin has made a case for the term's use in the social sciences.[46] Other authors, besides Roest Crollius, have opted for its use; among them are Peter Schineller and Aylward Shorter.[47]

Schreiter mentions "contextual theology" only in passing, noting that "as a neologism, it has the advantage of not having many previous associations and of being readily used in translation into a wide variety of languages."[48] Bevans, on the contrary, demonstrates his preference for the term, entitling his book *Models of Contextual Theology.*[49] He gives the reasons for his choice, drawing from the insights of the Asian bishops:

> All three aspects—cultural identity, social change, and popular religiosity—have to be taken into consideration when one develops a truly contextual theology. This need to include and balance each of these elements, along with the elements of scripture and tradition, is why the word *contextualization* might be considered the best way of describing the process that has also been called inculturation, indigenization, or incarnation of the gospel. As the members of the Theological Education Fund wrote when the term was introduced in 1972, the term contextualization includes all that is implied in the older indigenization or inculturation, but seeks also to include the realities of contemporary secularity, technology, and the struggle for human justice. One could also say that it includes the need to respect and deal with previous forms of theology and Christian practice that, while not native to a culture, have over the years become part of it. Although not all theologians have accepted

45. Schreiter, *Constructing Local Theologies* (1985) 5.

46. Ibid., 159. Here Schreiter refers the reader to Clement Godwin's *Spend and Be Spent* (Bangalore: Asian Trading Corporation, 1977).

47. Schineller, *Handbook of Inculturation;* Shorter, *Toward a Theology of Inculturation.*

48. Schreiter, *Constructing Local Theologies* (1985) 6.

49. Bevans, *Models of Contextual Theology* (1992).

the terminology of contextualization, the term does seem to have several advantages over the other terms that have been used in the past. As the Asian bishops pointed out in 1979, contextualization both extends and corrects the older terminology. As the Asian bishops express it, indigenization focused on the purely cultural dimension of human experience, while contextualization broadens the understanding of culture to include social, political, and economic questions. In this way, culture is understood in more dynamic, flexible ways and is seen not as closed and self-contained, but as open and able to be enriched by an encounter with other cultures and movements. While indigenization "tended to see both the home culture and the culture 'out there' as good," contextualization "tends to be more critical of both cultures."[50]

Louis J. Luzbetak, in a revision of what is now considered to be a classic text in missionary anthropology, seems to favor the term "contextualization." His definition of the term reminds us of Roest Crollius' meaning of inculturation.

Luzbetak describes contextualization as "the process by which a local Christian community integrates the Gospel message (the 'text') with the real-life context, blending text and context into that single, God-intended reality called 'Christian living.'"[51] The missiologist, trained in anthropology and linguistics, contrasts a new ecclesial attitude, contextualization, with an older one, accommodation:

> There are a number of major differences between the new contextual approach to mission and the traditional accommodational approach . . . (1) *the primary agents* involved in incarnating the Gospel are the *local* Christian community and the Holy Spirit—not the sending church or the universal Church; (2) as important as church planting and the institutional Church may be, *the direct concern of mission* is to proclaim the Kingdom of God and salvation; (3) *the ultimate goal* of incarnating the Gospel is *mutual* enrichment, one that benefits not only the local Christian community but the universal Church and the sending church as well; (4) *the depth* of cultural penetration and identification with the Gospel is incomparably greater in contextualization than in traditional accommodation; (5) as important as the primary processes may be, the chief processes in inculturation are those connected with *integration.*[52]

It is obvious by this point that what is being presented are not really divergent viewpoints but, rather, complementary ones. Each nuances the

---

50. Ibid., 21.
51. Luzbetak, *Church and Cultures*, 133.
52. Ibid., 70.

argument and attempts to describe a very complex reality. Whether we use the term "inculturation," "local theology," or "contextual theology," what is being implied is a dynamic relationship between gospel, Church, and culture. Bevans has benefited from previous articulations of these trends and has provided a framework for classifying them. Before outlining the various models he proposes, it is helpful to mention some of the areas of concern raised by this recent trend toward contextualization in the Church. Equally helpful are a few comments about method.

New Questions from a New Missiological Approach

It is clear that the study of missiology after Vatican II is no longer limited to the study of the Church's "missions" in non-Christian countries.[53] The whole tone of *Gaudium et spes* reflects a dialogical interaction with the modern world. This dialogue has brought into the discussion whole new partners, among which the most important are the social sciences. The fruits from this conversation are now being seen in a concern for a political theology, new questions about a pastoral theology, and a rethinking of certain parts of our dogmatic theology.

Issues of political theology, or "Christian life in the *polis*," are actively being pursued, as evidenced by the rise of the theology of liberation, the development of social ethics, and a general concern to recapture the prophetic element in Judeo-Christian tradition.[54] Inculturation issues are most often concretely dealt with in pastoral theology. Such topics as liturgical inculturation,[55] popular religiosity, and incorporation of sacred Scripture in local catechetics are quite relevant today. An engaging development is the combination of pastoral theology and popular religiosity as they relate to ecumenism.[56] Dogmatic theology, finally, is being reexamined in light of the development of historical and cultural consciousness. The way the tradition has been interpreted, for example, is now suspected of bearing Western biases.[57]

---

53. See Roest Crollius, "Inculturation and the Meaning of Culture," *What Is So New About Inculturation* (1991) 2, n. 2.

54. Among the many works available in this area are the writings of Gutierrez, especially *Theology of Liberation* (1971); Haughey, *Faith That Does Justice* (1977); Buhlmann, *Coming of the Third Church* (1976); Buhlmann, *With Eyes to See* (1990); Maldonado, *Introducción*; Scherer and Bevans, *New Directions*.

55. See Chupungco, *Liturgies of the Future* (1989); also see his *Liturgical Inculturation* (1992).

56. See chapter 2, "Approaches to Popular Religion," Amaladoss, *Making All Things New.*

57. See Shorter, *Toward a Theology of Inculturation*; Luzbetak, *Church and Cultures*; Schineller, *Handbook of Inculturation*; Donovan, *Christianity Rediscovered.*

All in all, this development reflects many changes in terms of theology's concerns and methods in our present time. The above describes numerous concerns, some of which reflect a desire to see theology become more "public."[58] In order for theology to dialogue with the modern world, it has had to employ a more modern way of thinking. A good example from post-Vatican II theology is its process orientation. Amidst such descriptions as "dynamic," "developing," and "emerging," one cannot help but identify a more empirical, "process way" of proceeding versus a more traditional, substance approach. Michael Amaladoss writes that "we must accustom ourselves to a new way of thinking from below, reflecting from experience and reality and not from above, deductively."[59] Implicit in this trend toward contextualization is a revolution in a theological method that is more process oriented.

This is not to say that more modern ways of doing theology must necessarily pursue a "cold, detached, rational, scientific" way of proceeding. Quite the contrary, after having described this trend in theology from a deductive to an empirical method, Avery Dulles calls attention to new "signs of the times." The U.S. theologian is referring to the emergence of postcritical thinking, which does not "reject criticism but carries it to new lengths, scrutinizing the presuppositions and methods of the critical program itself."[60] He elaborates on his use of the term as it relates to theology:

> Postcritical theology, as I use the term, begins with a presupposition of prejudice in favor of faith. Its fundamental attitude is a hermeneutics of trust, not of suspicion. Its purpose is constructive, not destructive. This is not to deny that people are entitled to doubt what they have reason to regard as false or unfounded. The doubter can be a serious thinker, candidly examining the claims

58. See Tracy, "Uneasy Alliance Reconceived" (1989) 548–70. Tracy raises the question of whether theological debate should be correlational to modern thought or more apart from it. Michael Amaladoss brings an Asian perspective to the discussion. In *Making All Things New*, the Indian theologian stresses that theology should aim to be public because the Church should not exist for itself but for the sake of India. Because it is one of the best organized institutions, it should serve as an instrument of peace, of dialogue, amidst India's great ethnic and religious diversity (See his introduction, pp. 1–8). Amaladoss writes, "I think that it is time that the Asian Churches took a clear option for understanding themselves as being on mission in the world, not primarily to build the Church up, but to build up the Reign of God. In this context let us accept that we are numerically small but ready to transform the world from within us as leaven, free from temptations to power that come from numbers" (p. 120).

59. Amaladoss, *Making All Things New*, 60.

60. Dulles, *Craft of Theology* (1992) 5.

made for religion. But theology, as commonly understood, is the kind of inquiry that takes place from within a religious commitment. Drawing on the convictions instilled by faith, the theologian uses them as resources for the proper task of theology, which is the understanding of faith.[61]

Dulles' whole point is that theological method should proceed from a position of faith, not doubt.[62]

Other Methodological Concerns

In addition to a shift from "sure knowledge" to "process thought," current developments in theology are more conscious of the role of perspective. Both the writings of Lonergan and those of the theology of liberation have been very influential in this regard. While Lonergan developed further the idea of a historical consciousness as it relates to theological method,[63] the theology of liberation has demonstrated that the world does not look the same from all social and economic levels.[64] Paul G. Hiebert notes that we are even selective in how we view certain kinds of sins. For the Western mind, sexual sins seem somehow more evil:

> The question of sin in the life of the missionary is complicated by the fact that many cultures put great emphasis on sins that we tend to ignore. For example, our Western church has a great preoccupation with sexual sins. Although we usually reinstate pastors who commit theft or lose their tempers, after they have confessed their sin, we rarely do so if they commit adultery. In India, on the other hand, the cardinal sin is anger. Yet all too frequently missionaries get angry and think nothing of it. Loewen (1975:59) tells of an African houseboy whose "mama-boss" always lost her temper over his mistakes. After listening to his stories, the group concluded that since she always got "mad as the devil," she probably was not a Christian.[65]

61. Ibid., 7.

62. At the same time, as James Nickoloff commented to me, "But can't one be 'constructively suspicious' precisely *because of* one's faith commitment? In other words, loyalty to the deeper truth of the Christian tradition can make one alert to distortion which has been uncritically accepted and promoted (or perverted?), especially distortions which are oppressive."

63. See Tracy, *Achievement of Bernard Lonergan* (1970).

64. See Haight, *Alternate Vision.*

65. Hiebert, *Anthropological Insights for Missionaries*, 267.

Already mentioned is the fact that the means of doing theology influences the content, for example, whether our theologizing is done in the atmosphere of an oral or a literate culture.[66] One's worldview, similarly, also plays a decisive role.[67] This mentality affects how one deals with such realities as analogy, symbol, and myth, topics current theologians are rediscovering. Roest Crollius, in defining inculturation, makes reference to analogical thinking. He acknowledges the work of David Tracy, who is without doubt one of the leading thinkers on the use of the analogical imagination in theology.[68] Tracy is convinced that what is most needed today to do systematic theology in the context of plurality of religious traditions and cultures is an "analogical imagination." In the following excerpt from his 1977 presidential address to the Catholic Theological Society of America he describes what he takes to be the heart of the Catholic vision of reality:

> Do you believe, with Albert Camus, that there is more to admire in human beings than to despise? Do you find with Erasmus and Francis of Assisi that in spite of folly, stupidity, illusion, and even sin, reality at its final moment is trustworthy? Do you find in yourself a belief with Aquinas and Thomas More that reason is to be trusted for finding the order of things; that faith transforms but does not destroy reason? Is your final image of God one like John's gospel of love, not fear; of Christ as fundamentally a community of hope, not a ghetto of escape and fear? Does your image of society include a trust that it can be somehow ordered short of radical disjunction? Does your image of the cosmos itself include a trust that it too is somehow ordered by relationships established by God for all reality; and that reality itself—in spite of all serious, sometimes overwhelming evidence to the contrary—is finally benign? Then you possess, I believe, a Catholic analogical imagination.[69]

One of the key components of this analogical imagination is the ability to use negations in theology. Tracy describes analogy as the "lan-

---

66. A. M. Pineda, "Evangelization of the 'New World.'"

67. Louis J. Luzbetak provides a concrete example in terms of East and West: "Looking at the cognitive process itself, one is struck by the emphasis placed by the Western mind on reasoning, rather than, say, on analogy, association, emotion, intuition, and mysticism to arrive at knowledge as does the Eastern mind. Actually, all minds use these various ways of thinking; however, depending on the world view, there is a fundamental difference in emphasis" (*Church and Cultures*, 255ff.).

68. Roest Crollius, "Inculturation and the Meaning of Culture," *What Is So New About Inculturation?* (1991) 52. David Tracy's work is quite substantial and one can easily get lost in reading it. An excellent "guide for the perplexed Tracy reader" is Sanks, "David Tracy's Theological Project," 698–727.

69. This excerpt is taken from Sanks, "David Tracy's Theological Project," 712ff.

guage of ordered relationships articulating similarity-in-difference. The order among the relationships is constituted by the distinct but similar relationships of each analogue to some primary focal meaning, some prime analogue."[70] He illustrates how noting this similarity-in-difference can help create a visualization of the whole of reality with the examples of the relationship between self, others, world, and God. For the Christian the primary analogue, or the focal meaning by which all these elements are ordered, is the event of Jesus Christ. "That focal meaning *as event* will prove the primary analogue for the interpretation of the whole of reality."[71] Tracy elaborates:

> Because an analogical, not univocal, imagination is the need of our radically pluralistic moment, the dissimilarities are as important as the similarities-in-difference, the ordered relationships will emerge from distinct, sometimes mutually exclusive, focal responses of the different traditions and the focal questions in the situation. Each of us understands each other through analogy or not at all.[72]

Tracy is trying to get us to expand our imagination, to move away from using only deductive reasoning, thus inviting us to embrace a wider vision, a more inclusive form of understanding.[73]

The ecumenist Leonard Swidler, similarly interested in probing symbolic reality, uses examples of what he calls "mythic language." Commenting on Paul's idea of "reconciling the world to God through Christ" (2 Cor 5:19ff.; cf. Rom 5:10f.), he writes:

> Although Paul necessarily used everyday language, he sometimes used it in a way that was quite common in his time in order to convey meanings that went far beyond our everyday experience of

70. Tracy, *Analogical Imagination* (1981) 408.
71. Ibid., 408.
72. Ibid., 447.
73. For example, Tracy speaks of how ethnic theology, together with an attentiveness to experience, is a good way of recovering historical consciousness: "When this same appeal to experience is made by systematic and practical theologians the referent is ordinarily an explicit and specific set of religious experiences of a particular Christian tradition. From this point of view, ethnic experience can serve as a summary expression for an historically conscious retrieval of a particular cultural and religious heritage. In sum, the two constants of most forms of contemporary theology (vis. some appeal to 'experience' and an explicit affirmation of modern historical consciousness) are both present in the more recent appeal to one's ethnic experience as a source of theology. For an appeal to ethnic experience is a heightening of consciousness of one's own relationship to a particular cultural apprehension of values, including religious values." "Ethnic Pluralism and Systematic Theology: Reflections," (1977) 93.

things. Such use of language very often is called *mythic, that is, the use of a connected set of images that points to a meaning beyond the sur-face meaning—like a metaphor.* And that is what Paul is doing here. That means that his language will *sound* as if he were describing in a very empirical, perhaps even physical and ontological, manner what he understood *really* to have happened on a different level in the relationship between the world and God in the Christ event.[74]

Swidler notes that what he labels above as mythic language, Tracy, writing in *Blessed Rage for Order,* refers to as "limit language."[75]

Once we start talking about pluralism, we are obviously referring to differences, whether they be in terms of religious traditions or ethnicity. Tracy is proposing "similarity-in-difference" as key to a Christian understanding of pluralism. Other contemporary theologians, such as Amaladoss and Shea, are also beginning to speak of pluralism in rela-tion to a broader use of the imagination in our theologizing, for ex-ample, in relation to symbol.[76] Amaladoss explains:

> In a situation of religious pluralism, we were first accustomed to speak in terms of true/false or presence/absence. Then we began speaking in terms of more/less, perfect/imperfect, or prepara-tion/fulfillment. These approaches do not really take into account all the facts. I am suggesting the category of symbol. Taken in purely objective, physical sense, the concept of symbol is empty and can be of no use in this context. But understood in a human and personal way as symbolic action, it seems to suggest a new way of posing the problem and of looking for a solution. I think that the term symbolic action translates into contemporary termi-nology the idea of first fruits in the Bible.[77]

Amaladoss speaks of the value of symbolic action in achieving a more humanistic understanding in a situation of religious pluralism. Shea, similarly, highlights the mutuality between ethnic consciousness and Christian symbols:

> In short, ethnic consciousness is a way of claiming the meaningful-ness of Christian religious symbols, and Christian religious sym-bols are a way of claiming the truthfulness of ethnic experience.

74. Swidler, *After the Absolute,* 199.

75. Ibid., 201. For a discussion of Tracy's use of "limit language," see Sanks, "David Tracy's Theological Project," 707ff.

76. John Shea laments that "supernatural positivism" has turned religious lan-guage into observational words. "Religious language is not allowed to function symbolically but is frozen into statement of facts." See Shea, "Reflections," 88.

77. Amaladoss, *Making All Things New,* 70.

The continued interaction of ethnic consciousness and Christian religious symbols is a promising endeavor.[78]

Such theologians as Tracy, Swidler, Amaladoss, and Shea are breaking new ground in how we conceive the active relationship between gospel, Church, and culture. Contextual theology is demonstrating how symbol, myth, and method all play a role in our theologizing. Undoubtedly, the means of our theologizing influences its content. New situations, new frames of reference, new ways of thinking, all demand serious attention in terms of how we perceive and act from a theological conviction. In various ways these authors want to expand our categories. Whether they speak of an "analogical imagination," "pluralism," or "mythic language," they are attempting a greater connection between these concepts as they relate to our theologizing than might have been thought previously. It is hoped that broader horizons make for better integration.

An example of a practical application of this type of thinking to sacramental theology is the recent writings that stress the anthropological dimension of these sacred rites. They function *humanly* (and what other way does God speak to us?) as rites of passage. By studying how various cultures celebrate these crucial transitions in the life cycle, insights into our need for Christian sacraments are sparked by analogy.[79]

Bevans' Models of Contextual Theology

The use of theoretical models in theology is not new. Avery Dulles' classic, *Models of the Church*, popularized their use.[80] Bevans introduces his use of models by giving a working definition:

> [A] model—in the sense that it is most often used in theology—is what is called a theoretical model. It is a "case" that is useful in simplifying a complex reality, and, although such simplification does not fully capture that reality, it does yield true knowledge of it. Theoretical models can either be exclusive or paradigmatic, or inclusive, descriptive, or complementary.[81]

78. Shea, "Reflections," 90.

79. For an example, see Couture, "Marriage as a Rite of Passage," 15–21.

80. Dulles, *Models of the Church* (Garden City, N.Y.: Doubleday Image Books, 1978). The hardcover edition was published in 1974. For an excellent history of the use of models in theology, together with a fine bibliography, see chapter 3 of Bevans, "Notion and Use of Models," *Models of Contextual Theology* (1992) 23–9.

81. Bevans, *Models of Contextual Theology* (1992) 26.

Noting that his use will be of the more inclusive or descriptive type, he explains that he will be speaking of models of operation, that is, of theological method:[82]

> Each model presents a different way of theologizing which takes a particular context seriously, and so each represents a distinct theological starting point and distinct theological presuppositions.[83]

What characterizes each distinct model is the way a theologian incorporates what Bevans has described as the four components of contextual theology: (1) the spirit of the gospel, (2) the tradition of the Christian people, (3) the culture operative, and (4) social change within that culture.[84] We note that Bevans adds a fourth element, social change, to Schreiter's triad of gospel, church, and culture (if to "church" we equate "the tradition of the Christian people"). This addition will be useful especially when dealing with the praxis model. Bevans' way of proceeding is to present five models, describe each one's method, and then to critique each one. To flesh out each methodology, he offers two examples of theologians operating from each perspective.

---

82. Clifford Geertz distinguishes between "models of" and "models for." For him, models not only demonstrate what is, reality, but also actively give meaning or shape to what we perceive. He explains, "The term 'model' has . . . two senses—an 'of' sense and a 'for' sense—and though these are but aspects of the same basic concept they are very much worth distinguishing for analytical purposes. In the first, what is stressed is the manipulation of symbol structures so as to bring them, more or less closely, into parallel with the pre-established nonsymbolic system as when we grasp how dams work by developing a theory of hydraulics or constructing a flow chart. The theory or chart models physical relationships in such a way—that is, by expressing their structure in synoptic form—as to render them apprehensible; it is a model of 'reality.' In the second, what is stressed is the manipulation of the nonsymbolic systems in terms of the relationships expressed in the symbolic, as when we construct a dam according to the specifications implied in an hydraulic theory or the conclusions drawn from a flow chart. Here, the theory is a model under whose guidance physical relationships are organized: it is a model for 'reality.' For psychological and social systems, and for cultural models that we would not ordinarily refer to as 'theories' but rather as 'doctrines,' 'melodies,' or 'rites,' the case is in no way different. Unlike genes, and other nonsymbolic information sources, which are only models for, not models of, culture patterns have an intrinsic double aspect: they give meaning, that is, objective conceptual form, to social and psychological reality both by shaping themselves to it and by shaping it to themselves" (See Geertz, *Interpretation of Cultures*, 93). Elsewhere, he attributes to religion both a "model of" aspect, and a "model for" aspect (p. 123). That is, religious beliefs not only determine how we see our world but also, in a sense, how we shape and are shaped by it.

83. Bevans, *Models of Contextual Theology* (1992) 27.

84. Ibid., 1.

The Translation Model

Without nuancing, we can say that the translation model assumes there is an unchanging message that must be communicated to different peoples throughout the world over the course of time. The job of the evangelizer is to take what some call the "gospel core" and somehow "translate" it or make it understandable within the context in question. Culture and the gospel message are seen as two entirely different things. The gospel is above culture and, therefore, must be adapted to or accommodated to particular cultures. Culture is at the service of the gospel. Bevans quotes Pope John XXIII's opening speech at the Second Vatican Council, which betrays this position: "The substance of the ancient doctrine of the deposit of faith is one thing, and the way in which it is presented is another."[85] Noting that there exists some room for divergence among those who practice this method, Bevans presents its theological presuppositions:

> In the first place, the emphasis on the priority of a message or gospel core points to the fact that revelation is understood as primarily, if not wholly, propositional. Revelation is conceived as a communication of certain truths or doctrines from God, and because they are from God they are wholly culturally free. The gospel may be able to be stripped down to as little as one basic idea, such as the Lordship of Christ, but that idea is a proposition that cannot be compromised. Secondly, revelation is understood as not only qualitatively different from culture, but also quantitatively different. The Christian message in an encounter with a new culture and new religion brings something that is *absolutely new* into that culture or religion. God's presence may not be wholly lacking in a non-Christian situation, but it only really becomes operative when the specifically Christian message is preached. This is why, in order to preach this message effectively, it must be clothed in language and patterns that the men and women of the new culture can understand.[86]

The missionary approach of Saints Cyril and Methodius, along with the approach used by many evangelical Christians today, are two examples of the translation model.

Some weaknesses of the model, according to Bevans, are that one cannot always assume a cultural equivalent in terms of the "gospel core" being communicated; that we overlook the fact that the message of Christianity is always inculturated; and that divine revelation,

85. Ibid., 34.
86. Ibid.

according to most contemporary theologians, is much more than pro-positions.[87] The two practitioners of this translation model given are David J. Hesselgrave, one of the major spokespersons for the evangelical tradition,[88] and Pope John Paul II.[89]

The Anthropological Model

Bevans' second model is at the opposite end of the spectrum from the translation model:

> If the primary concern of the translation model is the preservation of Christian identity while attempting to take culture, social change, and history seriously, the primary concern of the anthropological model is the establishment or preservation of cultural identity by a person of the Christian faith.[90]

In one of the previous chapters on the use of models, Bevans sets up a continuum. The two poles at each end are culture/social change (that is, a focus on the subject) and gospel message/tradition (with stress on the content). The anthropological model is situated at the culture/

---

87. Ibid., 35–7.

88. David J. Hesselgrave, "Counseling: Good Faith Not Enough," *Evangelical Missions Quarterly*, 21, 2 (April 1985) 186–8; "Culture-Sensitive Counselling and the Christian Mission," *International Bulletin of Missionary Research* 10, 3 (July 1986) 109–13; "Christian Communication and Religious Pluralism: Capitalizing on Differences," *Missiology: An International Review* 18, 2 (April 1990) 131–8; ed., *Theology and Mission* (Grand Rapids: Baker Book House, 1978); *Dynamic Religious Movements: Case Studies in Growing Religious Movements in Various Cultures* (Grand Rapids: Baker Book House, 1978); *Communicating Christ Cross-Culturally: An Introduction to Missionary Communication* (Grand Rapids: Zondervan, 1978); *Planting Churches Cross-Culturally: A Guide for Home and Foreign Missions* (Grand Rapids: Baker Book House, 1980); *Counseling Cross-Culturally: An Introduction to Theory and Practice for Christians* (Grand Rapids: Baker Book House, 1984). Also, E. Rommen, *Contextualization: Meanings, Methods, and Models* (Grand Rapids: Baker Book House, 1989).

89. On page 125 of the endnotes for *Models of Contextual Theology* (1992), Bevans, in offering pertinent works of John Paul II, makes the following observation: "The number of documents and discourses in which the pope deals with the question of culture—especially the dialogue between faith and culture—are too numerous to list here. I will cite a number of them in this brief summary of the pope's approach to contextualization, but there are many, many more. Several of the pope's writings are seminal, however, and should be mentioned: *Catechesi tradendae* (1970) 53; *Slavorum apostoli* (1985) 9–11, 18–20; and *Redemptoris missio* (1990) 52–4. For the relevant sections of these texts, see Scherer and Bevans, *New Directions*. For other citations of texts, see Carrier, *Gospel Message and Human Cultures*, 75–133; Shorter, *Toward a Theology of Inculturation*, 222–38.

90. Bevans, *Models of Contextual Theology* (1992) 47.

social change pole, while the translation model is placed at the gospel message/tradition pole.[91]

One of the key tenets of the anthropological model is that Christianity must be about the humanization of persons, since humanization, or the realization of human potential, is a gift from God to be cultivated. Culture is perceived as the vehicle of that humanization. This understanding is reminiscent of Roest Crollius' description of culture.[92] The model is labeled "anthropological" because (1) it centers on the human person (the subject of evangelization) and (2) it draws from the social science by that name.[93] More than any other contextual model, this model "focuses on the validity of the human as the place of divine revelation and as a source (locus) for theology that is equal to scripture and tradition."[94] Bevans explains further:

> The insight of the anthropological model is that the theologian must start where the faith actually lives, in the midst of people's lives. It is in the world as it is, a world bounded by history and culture and a particular language, that God speaks. To ignore this would be to ignore the living source of theology. But to listen only to the present and not to the past as recorded in scripture and tradition would be like listening to a symphony in monaural when, by the flick of a switch, it could come alive in full stereo.[95]

In alluding to the spirit of this model, Bevans makes reference to Justin Martyr's idea that other religions and cultures contain "the seeds of the word," as well as to *Ad gentes divinitus'* acknowledgment that today's missionaries, following the example of Jesus, "can learn by sincere and patient dialogue what treasures a bountiful God has distributed among the nations of the earth. But at the same time, let them try to illumine these treasures with the light of the gospel, to set them free, and to bring them under the dominion of God their savior."[96]

The anthropological model works out of an idea of illuminating what is already there. Robert T. Rush notes that before Vatican II the missionary was seen as a "pearl merchant." The more appropriate image today is that of a "treasure hunter."[97] This model bears many similarities to those previously labeled "indigenization" and "inculturation"

91. Ibid., 27.
92. Roest Crollius, "Inculturation and the Meaning of Culture," *What Is So New About Inculturation* (1991) 40.
93. Bevans, *Models of Contextual Theology,* 47f.
94. Ibid., 48.
95. Ibid., 54.
96. Ibid., 47. Bevans is quoting from *Ad gentes divinitus,* 11.
97. Ibid., 49.

or "ethnographic" because it insists that the native people's culture must be taken seriously.[98]

Having highlighted the advantages of the anthropological model, Bevans mentions some of its shortcomings. For one, it is subject to cultural romanticism, at times failing to be critical enough of the native culture. Secondly, its application is more easily articulated than carried out. Because of the great proliferation of Western culture and ideology throughout the world, it becomes progressively more difficult to isolate native cultural traits.[99] Bevans features two proponents of the anthropological method: an African American Episcopal priest, Robert E. Hood, and Vincent J. Donovan, an American missionary who worked in East Africa.[100]

The Praxis Model

This model, the one most closely associated with the theology of liberation, takes as its mission the bringing about of social change. Its proponents are not so much concerned with "right thinking" (orthodoxy) as they are about "right acting" (orthopraxis). While the translation model seeks the adaptation of certain gospel truths and tradition to a particular cultural context, and the anthropological model functions as a discoverer of Christian elements within a culture, the praxis model's main goal is to bring about Christian behavior, which in turn informs a new understanding of Christian doctrine. Its source of knowledge, as well as its aim, is a God who is actively present in history. Bevans affirms that the praxis method represents the biblical way of proceeding. Highlighted is the prophetic tradition that challenges us to move beyond words to action and the New Testament stress on the "need to do the truth in love."[101]

Bevans describes its inspiration and epistemology:

> It is a never-ending process which gets its considerable power from the recognition that God manifests God's presence not only, or perhaps not even primarily, in the fabric of culture, but also and perhaps principally in the fabric of history. The praxis model is a way of doing theology that is formed by knowledge at its most in-

98. Ibid., 48.

99. Ibid., 53f.

100. R. E. Hood, *Contemporary Political Orders and Christ: Karl Barth's Christology and Political Praxis* (Allison Park, Pa.: Pickwick Publications, 1985); *Must God Remain Greek? Afro Cultures and God-Talk* (Minneapolis: Fortress Press, 1990); also see Donovan, *Christianity Rediscovered* (Chicago: Fides/Claretian, 1978; 2d ed., Maryknoll, N.Y.: Orbis Books, 1982); *Church in the Midst of Creation* (Maryknoll, N.Y.: Orbis Books, 1982).

101. Bevans, *Models of Contextual Theology*, 64.

tense level—the level of reflective action. It is also about discerning the meaning and contributing to the course of social change, and so takes its inspiration neither from classic texts nor classic behavior but from present realities and future possibilities.[102]

Key in his description above is "reflective action," a phrase inspired by the Brazilian educator Paolo Freire.[103] Christian behavior is instrumental in bringing about a better understanding of the Christian message, which in turn brings about more committed Christian behavior. This process is described as a never-ending cycle of (1) committed action, (2) reflection (incorporating an analysis of the situation and a rereading of Scripture and tradition), and (3) committed and intelligent action, etc.[104] In terms of traditional theology the praxis model is not "faith seeking understanding" but rather "faith seeking intelligent action."[105]

In describing why he chose the name "praxis model" over one with a more liberational ring to it, Bevans gives the following explanation:

> As closely associated as the theology of liberation is with the praxis model, I choose to continue speaking of it as a praxis model for two reasons. First of all, this way of approaching the contextualizing of theology does not necessarily have to take on liberation themes. It may well be possible, for instance, to do theology within a particular context where structural injustice is not really very rampant. In this instance, one could still theologize by acting reflectively and reflecting on one's actions. Secondly, I would like to keep the term *praxis model* because the term reveals more clearly than *liberation model* that the specificity of the model is not one of a particular theme but one of a particular *method*. As valid as liberation theology is, its revolutionary impact has come more from its method as "critical reflection on praxis."[106]

As Bevans notes, the praxis model has contributed significantly to the development of an action-oriented methodology in doing theology. Other contributions or positive aspects of the model the author mentions are its contribution to the lay movement in the Church during this century. From the 1930s to the 1960s movements such as those of the Young Christian Workers, Young Christian Students, and the Christian Family Movement took as their methodology the "see, judge, act" *modus operandi.*[107]

102. Ibid., 63.
103. Ibid., 65.
104. Ibid., 68ff.
105. Ibid., 66.
106. Ibid.
107. Ibid., 70.

> By constantly reflecting on one's daily activity in terms of scripture and tradition (and vice versa), Christianity is understood to bring much to bear on the realities of daily life, and daily life can help sharpen expressions of Christian faith.[108]

Bevans notes that the lay movement flourished in this type of context.

Quite sympathetic to this model, Bevans nonetheless notes some of the criticism it has received:

> The model has come under some criticism, however, in its concrete form of liberation theology. Some feel uncomfortable with liberation theology's use of Marxism; others point out its selectivity and even naiveté in terms of its reading of the Bible; while others criticize liberation theologians' concentration on what is negative in society and their "inability to see intermediate manifestations of grace" in society or expressions of popular religiosity.[109]

Some of the U.S. Hispanic theologians would agree with the last criticism leveled above.[110] The rapid spread of the model, nevertheless, together with the revolution it has helped bring about in theological methodology, assures its relevancy for decades to come.

As examples of theologians espousing this model, Bevans presents a summary of the work of Douglas John Hall, a minister in the United Church of Canada, and some of the Asian feminist theologians such as Virginia Fabella, a Maryknoll sister from the Philippines, and Mary John Mananzan, a Benedictine nun also from the Philippines.[111]

---

108. Ibid.

109. Ibid., 71. Bevans, in quoting Schreiter, is pointing out some of the criticism made by others of the theology of liberation. See Schreiter, *Constructing Local Theologies*, 15. Along the same lines, the Vatican issued two documents, one in 1984 (*De quibusdam rationibus "theologiae liberationis"* [see Enchiridion Vaticanum 9 (Bologna: EDB, 1985) nos. 866–987]), and another in 1986 (*De libertate christiana et liberatione* [Enchiridion Vaticanum 10, (1987) nos. 196–344]). The gist of these magisterial letters is to stress the transhistorical dimensions of liberation as well as the priority of spirituality.

110. See Deck, *Frontiers* (1992) xiii.

111. Bevans, *Models of Contextual Theology* (1992) 76–80. D. J. Hall, *Lighten Our Darkness: Toward an Indigenous Theology of the Cross* (Philadelphia: Westminster Press, 1976); *Has the Church a Future?* (Philadelphia: Westminster Press, 1980); *The Steward: A Biblical Symbol Come of Age* (New York: Friendship Press, 1982); *The Stewardship of Life in the Kingdom of Death* (Grand Rapids: Eerdmans, 1985/1988); *Imaging God: Dominion as Stewardship* (New York: Friendship Press; Grand Rapids: Eerdmans, 1986); *God and Human Suffering: An Exercise in the Theology of the Cross* (Minneapolis: 1986); *Thinking the Faith: Christian Theology in a North American Context* (Minneapolis: Augsburg/Fortress, 1989). Also, Virginia Fabella and M. A. Oduyoye, *With Passion and Compassion: Third World Women Doing Theology* (Maryknoll, N.Y.:

The Synthetic Model

This model lies somewhere midway between the two poles, culture/ social change and gospel message/tradition, on Bevans' continuum. Other appropriate names for it are "dialectical," "conversation," or "analogical."[112] Basically, it is a synthesis of the three models already described: translation, anthropological, and praxis. Bevans describes how it strives to keep the four elements of contextual theology given (culture, social change, gospel/tradition, and other thought-forms/ cultures) in a creative tension, drawing from each when necessary:

> It might rely for scriptural justification on the whole process of the formation of the various biblical books. The Bible came about gradually, through a collection of individual books, each of which was formed within the context of contemporary concerns interacting with contemporary culture, neighboring cultures, and ancient traditions. The synthetic model might also rely on some passages of the Roman magisterium that try to walk a theological path between mere adaptation on the one hand and a broad culturalism on the other.[113]

To illustrate the inclusivity of the synthesis model, Bevans quotes from *Evangelii nuntiandi*.[114] In calling for an adaptation of the gospel message to a new context, Paul VI's document reflects the translation model. Similarly, however, by recognizing the mutuality of cultural enrichment, the document also reveals an influence of the anthropological model.

Because of its flexibility, the model is able to stress both uniqueness and complementarity. Bevans' example elucidates his contention:

> [For] instance, to speak of oneself as an Indonesian is to speak with the background of being Asian, of sharing much of Malaysian culture and linguistic patterns, as being influenced by the Muslim worldview, and as having been colonized by a western culture (Holland). What it means to be an Indonesian includes much of what it means to be Asian, Malaysian, Muslim, and Dutch, and yet there is something to being Indonesian that none of these cultures

Orbis Books, 1988); V. Fabella and S. Ai Lee Park, *We Dare To Dream: Doing Theology as Asian Women* (Maryknoll, N.Y.: Orbis Books, 1990); "Christology from an Asian Perspective," *We Dare to Dream*, Fabella and Park; Mary John Mananzan, "Redefining Religious Commitment in the Philippine Context," Fabella and Park, *We Dare to Dream*.

112. Bevans, *Models of Contextual Theology* (1992) 82.
113. Ibid., 81.
114. Ibid., 82.

has, nor do they have the other four characteristics in exactly the same mixture.[115]

Unlike the anthropological model, which stresses the uniqueness of the culture in question, the synthetic model stresses not only the uniqueness but also the complementarity (or those elements that are held in common).

Among its most worthy features is its openness to dialogue. It demonstrates a willingness to learn from other cultures yet brings the wealth of the gospel message and tradition to the fore. Ideologically it fits in well with present postmodern thought. Drawing from Tracy and Shorter, Bevans explains why:

> Perhaps the strongest aspect of the synthetic model is its basic methodological attitude of openness and dialogue. In our contemporary, postmodern world so filled with what David Tracy speaks of as plurality and ambiguity, truth will not be reached by one point of view trying to convince all the others that it alone is correct. That is neither possible, nor, as the situation has revealed, even desirable. It was possible in a world that saw truth as a simple correspondence between concept and reality; but that same world was one that also prescribed one culture and one way of thinking for all. It was, as Shorter calls it, a worldview of monoculturalism. Contemporary postmodern thinking, however, is moving away from this correspondence understanding of truth and understanding truth more in terms of relation, conversation, and dialogue. It is encouraged in this regard by the radical pluralism and multicultural consciousness which is emerging, at least implicitly, everywhere. Truth, in this scheme of things, is understood not so much as something "out there," but as a reality that emerges in true conversation between authentic women and men when they "allow questions to take over."[116]

Such a dialogical approach, especially when taken by local leaders, is particularly adept at producing a contextual theology, which, in the words of Schreiter, "can quickly help achieve the twin goals of some authenticity in the local culture and respectability in Western church circles."[117]

The greatest weakness of the synthetic approach is that, in trying to be too open, it can become noncommittal, failing to articulate authentically either Christianity or culture. A true synthesis is not always the

115. Ibid., 83.
116. Ibid., 86f.
117. As quoted in Bevans, *Models of Contextual Theology* (1992) 87.

end product, and one of the dangers it runs is that the result will be a "theology that is not a true synthesis in the Hegelian sense, but a mere juxtaposition of ideas that really do not enhance each other."[118] The two examples given of theologians using the synthesis model are Kosuke Koyama, a native of Japan, and José de Mesa of the Philippines.[119]

The Transcendental Model

Bevans' fifth and final model of contextual theology, the transcendental model, does not fit neatly in the continuum he has established. In his diagram the model floats above the spectrum because it is more concerned with the subject doing the theologizing than with the theological content.[120] The formation of this model follows the thinking of such people as Immanuel Kant, Pierre Rousselot, Joseph Marechal, Karl Rahner, and Bernard Lonergan. Bevans gives a summary of the model:

> The transcendental model proposes that the task of constructing a contextualized theology is not about producing a particular body of any kind of texts; it is about attending to the affective and cognitive operations in the self-transcending subject. What is important is not so much that a particular theology is produced but that the theologian who is producing it operates as an authentic, converted subject. In the same way that Bernard Lonergan speaks of metaphysics, a contextual theology will not appear primarily in books, but in men's and women's minds.[121]

Demonstrating the shape this form of contextual theology takes, Bevans suggests what type of questions practitioners might ask themselves as they try to live a Christian life:

118. Ibid., 88.
119. Kosuke Koyama, *Waterbuffalo Theology* (London: SCM Press; Maryknoll, N.Y.: Orbis Books, 1974); *No Handle on the Cross: An Asian Meditation on the Crucified Mind* (London: SCM Press, 1976; Maryknoll, N.Y.: Orbis Books, 1977); *50 Meditations* (Belfast: Christian Journals Limited, 1975; Maryknoll, N.Y.: Orbis Books, 1979); *Three Mile an Hour God: Biblical Reflections* (London: SCM Press, 1979; Maryknoll, N.Y.: Orbis Books, 1980). Bevans notes that José de Mesa has contributed to journals such as *Witness, UST Journal of Theology,* and *East Asian Pastoral Review.* He has also published in the following books: *And God Said, "Bahala Na!": The Theme of Providence in the Lowland Filipino Context,* Maryhill Studies 2 (Quezon City: Maryhill School of Theology, 1979); *Isang Maiksing Katesismo Para Sa Mga Bata: A Study in Indigenous Catechesis* (Quezon City: CSP Bookshop, 1984); *In Solidarity with the Culture: Studies in Theological Re-Rooting,* Maryhill Studies 4 (Quezon City: Maryhill School of Theology, 1987). With L. Wostyn: *Doing Theology: Basic Realities and Processes* (Manila: Wellspring Books, 1982); *Doing Christology: The Re-Appropriation of a Tradition* (Quezon City: Claretian Publications, 1989).
120. Bevans, *Models of Contextual Theology* (1992) 27f.
121. Ibid., 97.

> "How well do I know myself? How genuine is the religious experi-
> ence I am trying to interpret? How well does my language express
> this experience? How free of biases am I? Do I feel comfortable
> with a particular expression of my religious experience? Why or
> why not? Do I really understand what I am trying to articulate?"[122]

Such concerns reveal a desire to identify one's worldview, an attempt
to understand how one is historically and culturally conditioned. It is
within this context, this human experience, that God's self-revelation
becomes known:

> The only place God can reveal Godself truly and effectively is
> within human experience, as a human person is open to the words
> of scripture as read or proclaimed, open to events in daily life, and
> open to the values embodied in a cultural tradition.[123]

According to this model, theology is that which happens in the
struggle to relate to the divine. "Revelation is understood as an event,
not as a content; it is something that happens when a person opens
himself or herself to reality."[124] Since experience is key to this method,
its theological method does not limit itself to discursive means. Doing
theology is not limited to the professional theologian, since any person,
by virtue of trying to deepen her or his faith, is involved in the theological process. "To the extent that a person does this as an authentic
human subject conditioned by history, geography, culture, and so forth,
he or she is doing genuine contextual theology."[125] Nondiscursive
means of doing theology, such as artistic ones, are also seen as valid
and important.[126]

The advantage of the transcendental model is that it strives for
understanding rather than certitude. It is similar to the anthropological
model in that both value people's aesthetic concerns, which are often
expressed in stories or other art forms. Noting Anselm of Canterbury's
definition of theology as faith seeking understanding, we are comfortable with its emphasis on process. The method is very helpful in identifying the context of the person who is theologizing. Thus the emphasis
is on identifying how God is revealing Godself through human beings
and events within a specific cultural context. Another positive aspect is
that because it is based on experience it will be more attuned to a local

122. Ibid., 99.
123. Ibid.
124. Ibid.
125. Ibid., 100.
126. Ibid., 101.

context. At the same time, as Bevans notes, "because of the transcultural nature of the human mind, conversations with persons of other cultures or other periods of time (e.g., with the classics of Christian tradition or members of other cultures working in one's own) are not excluded."[127] All of the above are advantages of the transcendental model of contextual theology. The author also notes some problematic aspects. For example, its method is perceived by some to be too abstract, too complex. The shift from theology as content to be taught, to theology as a process carried out by a believer in a given cultural context seeking understanding, is not an easy one to grasp.[128]

Another criticism leveled against this model is that what it presents as universal, the process by which the human person comes to know, is not really universal at all. These critics insist that this method is more a reflection of "western, male-dominated cultural thought forms."[129] Is there not more than one way of knowing? Bevans' references here provide sources that support or dismiss Lonergan's method. Bevans notes, finally, the difficulty of achieving the type of authenticity the model calls for:

> [S]ince it is so hard to be an authentic human being, it might seem that a theology that depends on these criteria would never get started. The transcendental model might simply be too ideal, or at best only a "meta-model" that lays down the condition for the possibility of any contextual theological training.[130]

Bevans' two examples of theologians working out of the transcendental model are Sallie McFague, a U.S. theologian, and Justo L. González, also a U.S. theologian, but born in Cuba.[131]

Conclusion

Just as in the study of a painting it is important to alternate between detail and background in order to appreciate the whole, this chapter

127. Ibid., 100.
128. Ibid., 102.
129. Ibid.
130. Ibid.
131. Sallie McFague, *Speaking in Parables: A Study in Metaphor and Theology* (Philadelphia: Fortress Press, 1975); *Metaphorical Theology: Models of God in Religious Language* (Philadelphia: Fortress Press, 1982 [second printing, with an additional preface, 1985]); *Models of God: Theology for an Ecological, Nuclear Age* (Philadelphia: Fortress Press, 1987). Because he is one of the eight U.S. Hispanic theologians I analyze more specifically, Justo González' major works are mentioned elsewhere in this book. See especially chapters 2 and 4.

has provided a background for understanding the examples of U.S. Hispanic theology given in the previous chapter. Its goal has been to trace the development of contextual theology and to present some concrete models that are acknowledged to be operative.

The shift to the human person in theological method yielded a renewed attentiveness to experience as a valid and necessary source for theological reflection. The years after Vatican II have witnessed a greater integration of sacred Scripture and tradition. This unity manifests itself in a view of tradition as being both the divine force behind the formulation of Scripture and, at the same time, the history of the effects of that Scripture on humankind. The revitalized importance given to the human as manifestations of the divine, therefore, provides an ample stage for new theological developments.

A key element in the formation of a contextual theology was the Second Vatican Council's attentiveness to culture. This chapter has explored some of the thought surrounding the relationship between theology and culture. The theologians writing in this area, through their quest for more precise terminology and a clearer understanding of how contextualization works, have achieved a greater clarity than might have been possible fifty years ago. The chapter concluded with a brief exposition of the five models proposed by the latest theologian to synthesize contextual theologies, Steven B. Bevans.

The next chapter focuses on eight of the fourteen Latino theologians presented thus far. Since much of the theological apparatus invoked has been Roman Catholic, although after Vatican II this denominational gap has been significantly narrowed, seven of the eight are Catholic. Having gotten a general sense of the contextual theological movement, we are now in a position to examine their methodologies in light of Bevans' models. The task here is to determine which model or models each theologian is using. Thus the alternation between detail and background continues.

4

U.S. Hispanic Theology as a Contextual Theology

The previous chapter has provided ample evidence for substantiating the view that theologians writing today are much more attentive to the *locus theologicus* than they were before the Second Vatican Council. In describing this period Bevans remarks that during the pre–Vatican II era, a time characterized by a certain "unity of theology," "theological students from Manila, Chicago, Sao Paolo, and Accra all studied the same theology out of pretty much the same books—Ott or Tanquerey or van Noort were all cut from the same theological cloth."[1] The more recent developments described in chapter 3 are today marking a trend toward contextualization. U.S. Hispanics are part of a larger group of theologians whose content and method reflect the great diversity of cultures that provides the context for evangelization. The work of Latino theologians is a clear North American example of local theology.[2] Having established this fact, I now explore how one might classify these types of contextual theology.

The goal of this chapter, therefore, is to situate the writings of eight U.S. Latino theologians within this trend. After a summary of their thought, the next pertinent question is "Why do they say what they say?" or "What process do they use to arrive at their conclusions?" Since Bevans' schema is primarily methodological, the strongest emphasis will be placed on classifying the various writings in terms of their methodologies.

1. Bevans, *Models of Contextual Theology* (1992) 112.
2. This is one of the major conclusions of my bibliographic study in 1992 of U.S. Hispanic theology. See E. C. Fernández, "Towards a U.S. Hispanic Theology."

Classification of Eight Latino Theologians
by Operative Model

Some Preliminary Points

Before actually naming what model is characteristic of each Latino theologian it will be beneficial to keep several things in mind. For one, the models Bevans presents are imaginary constructs designed to highlight certain major qualities about a particular way of thinking or proceeding. It is important, therefore, to retain some flexibility in assigning categories. Drawing from Sallie McFague's definition, Bevans speaks of this flexibility:

> A model, as Sallie McFague points out, partakes in the metaphorical nature of all language, and so while it certainly affirms something real, it never really captures that reality. One can say that "the key to the proper use of models is . . . to remember always the metaphorical tensions—the 'is and is not'—in all our thinking and interpreting."[3]

One is reminded of the analogical thinking Tracy and others are trying to foster in our theologizing. Far from pigeonholing the methodology of certain theologians, our process should be dialogical and descriptive, not absolutist and reductionistic. To the extent that all theologians somehow work from their own experience of conversion, all models are transcendental. Similarly, since two of the key fonts of our theological method are sacred Scripture and tradition, elements of the translation model are always operative. The same ambiguities are found in the use of other models. What is important to keep in mind is the innovative aspect of Bevans' work. In *Models of Contextual Theology,* he has attempted to tease out five strands of thought in the vast field of various contextual theologies now being produced. His aim is to facilitate an awareness of difference in method, an awareness that necessarily includes certain ambiguities. Not to be overlooked is the fact that the models are basically complementary. Bevans concludes:

> To summarize, a model—in the sense that it is most often used in theology—is what is called a theoretical model. It is a "case" that is useful in simplifying a complex reality, and although such simplification does not fully capture that reality, it does yield true knowledge of it.[4]

3. As quoted in Bevans, *Models of Contextual Theology* (1992) 25.
4. Ibid., 26.

Another factor to keep in mind is the role of the theologian. How the theologian perceives her or his role will determine the dialogical partners in the conversation. Bevans explains one of the views of the role of the theologian, mainly, as someone who articulates the voice of the people:

> A number of contextual theologians insist that theology is not really done by experts (like Rahner, Lonergan, or Gutiérrez) and then "trickled down" to the people for their consumption. If theology is truly to take culture and cultural change seriously, it must be understood as being done most fully by the subjects and agents of culture and cultural change. The process of contextualization, says Peter Schineller, is too complex and important to be left to professional theologians. The role of the trained theologian (the minister, the theology teacher) is that of articulating more clearly what the people are generally or vaguely expressing, deepening their ideas by providing them with the wealth of the Christian tradition, and challenging them to broaden their horizons by presenting them with the whole of Christian theological expression. As Filipino theologian Leonard Mercado puts it, "the people are the best contextualizers," and the role of the theologian is to function as a midwife to the people as they give birth to a theology that is truly rooted in a culture and moment of history. Krikor Haleblian says much the same thing when he says that "the believing community in each culture must take ultimate responsibility for contextualizing the gospel, but there is a place and a need for professionals who can act as 'brokers' in this difficult and ongoing task."[5]

Two Latina feminists, Ada María Isasi-Díaz and Yolanda Tarango, adopt the same position, appropriating for themselves Carlos H. Abesamis' term, "theological technicians":

> "Theological technicians" are those who are "in possession of certain technical competences in exegesis, social sciences, languages, archaeology, or history and who offer(s) these findings in these different fields to the real theologians to help them in the act of interpreting reality from . . . (their) perspective.[6]

Isasi-Díaz and Tarango add, "Theological technicians likewise need competence in process design and group process facilitation. Because they are part of the community, theological technicians are 'real theologians.'"[7] According to these thinkers, therefore, the job of the theolo-

---

5. Ibid., 13.
6. As quoted in Isasi-Díaz and Tarango, *Hispanic Women*, 106.
7. Isasi-Díaz and Tarango, *Hispanic Women*, 123, n. 9.

gian is to facilitate or serve as a type of midwife in a community's formulation of its theology.

A final caveat concerns the use of certain terms such as "anthropology" or "praxis." At first glance their meaning may seem obvious, but a closer examination of their employment by Hispanic theologians displays a significant amount of ambiguity. For example, by "anthropological" one can simply be referring to a contextual way of doing theology, that is, a theological method that is cognizant of its *locus theologicus* and similar to Vatican II's "signs of the times." On the other hand, "anthropological" is sometimes used in a more explicitly theological way, as, for example, in describing a "seeds of the Word" approach, as employed by Bevans. This approach delves into how God, even before the arrival of Christianity, has been working with and through a certain people to illuminate them with religious values.

A similar ambiguity is found in how "praxis" is used. In many ways some theologians equate praxis with human experience. Thus a theology from praxis is simply one that takes human experience seriously. Others link praxis specifically with action for liberation. A praxis approach in theological method, according to this perspective, is one whose primary goal is to bring about change or action on behalf of justice. The confusion with this use of the terms stems from its temporal occurrence. Is it a "one-time" phenomenon that is then reflected upon theologically, or is it more of a cyclical method, which, in the words of Bevans, is "reflection upon reflected-upon action"?

There is a great deal of difference between this cyclical method of doing praxis theology and praxis theology as "reflection on reflection." While the difference may not seem important at this point, later examples from the various writings of U.S. Hispanic theologians will elucidate the lack of uniformity in the use of such terms as praxis or anthropology. The schema for my classifications here will be Bevans' categorizations. As the argument unfolds, it will be up to the reader to determine the adequacy of these models for understanding Hispanic theology. For now, this standardization provides a common frame of reference, one that will help to eventually develop a common understanding in our use of terms. These preliminary remarks now give way to a categorization of eight Latina and Latino theologians in light of Bevans' models.

Virgil P. Elizondo

This Mexican American theologian's project over the years has been to examine the relationship between Christianity and culture, which, by the way, is the title of his first book. Because he has developed his thought along the lines of identity, in this case, that of the *mestizo*, one immediately thinks of the anthropological model. He views culture and cultural pluralism positively as vehicles of humanization and, therefore, is in favor of their preservation, despite the melting-pot mentality that has been quite strong in the United States over the last century. By making the situation of the *mestizo* the *locus theologicus*, Elizondo has focused more on the subject of evangelization than on the content or message. This approach certainly characterizes Bevans' anthropological model. Moreover, Elizondo's recourse to the science that bears that name, as in his delineation of the role of marginal persons in the construction of social reality, would further strengthen the argument that his method is basically anthropological. His attempt to locate "seeds of the Word" in pre-Christian Aztec culture, finally, might seal the verdict on his predominant methodology.

But his case gets more complex as other models are considered. For example, Elizondo is very concerned about social change. His focus is certainly more orthopraxis than orthodoxy. According to him, God affirms the *mestizo* in his or her identity in order to challenge this person to help transform unjust social, political, and economic institutions. The challenge for the *mestizo* remains clear: not to seek power for the sake of personal gain but power for the sake of all the oppressed.

Elizondo draws extensively from history, trying to discern how God has been working through people and events, such as the great Guadalupe event. Again, the goal here is to look back so as to be able to go forward in action. In referring to this praxis model, Bevans cites the notion of prophecy in the Hebrew Scriptures, which calls for action beyond simple words, and the New Testament emphasis on the "need to do the truth in love."[8] Elizondo's mention of such actions for justice as the formation of community organizations in poor neighborhoods in the United States or that of *comunidades eclesiales de base* in Latin America, together with the work of the United Farm Workers, illustrates his praxis concerns. Perhaps where the praxis bent, as described by Bevans (i.e., "reflection upon reflected upon action"), is not as obvious is in the lack of a strong cyclical dimension. In comparison to theologizing from concrete work for justice, which in turn informs one's theology and spurs persons on to further action, Elizondo's thought seems to emerge more from a less cyclical "event" such as Guadalupe or *mestizaje*. Of course, Guadalupe and *mestizaje* are "events" only in a special sense. Undoubtedly, we must remain flexible in forming our categories and keep in mind that the models are meant to be complementary, not exclusive of each other.

8. Bevans, *Models of Contextual Theology* (1992) 64.

In the same vein, one can identify in Elizondo's thought some elements of the transcendental model. Like Justo Gonzalez, whom Bevans gives as an example of a Latino theologian using this model,[9] Elizondo draws from his own experience of conversion to write a theology reflective of a very unique context. In the words of Bevans, this model "is about attending to the affective and cognitive operations in the self-transcending subject."[10] Of course, to the extent that all theologians possess some degree of self-awareness and are involved in a process of conversion, all show a trace of the transcendental model.

As if to muddle distinctions even further, Elizondo's work certainly bears some marks of the translational model. In comparing Christianity to pre-Columbian Aztec religion, he calls attention to certain parallel rites involving initiation and marriage.[11] His approach to popular piety, likewise, is to demonstrate how it fits in with orthodoxy. Non-Christian elements found there are rarely, if ever, treated or commented upon.[12]

The discussion concerning which of Bevans' models best describes Elizondo's work has revealed both the complementary aspects of the models yet, at the same time, Elizondo's own synthetic approach. All the contextualists, of course, incorporate some aspect of each of the five models to one degree or another. The purpose of making the classifications, however, is to focus on the overriding methodological approach of the theologian. For this reason, I would argue that Elizondo is primarily operating within the synthetic model. As was previously mentioned, this model is a synthesis of three of the four specified above: the translation, the anthropological, and the praxis.[13]

---

9. Later in this chapter I will elaborate on González' reaction to Bevans' categorization of his method as transcendental.

10. Bevans, *Models of Contextual Theology* (1992) 97. When asked how, in terms of his transcendental model, he distinguished between Elizondo's and González' thought, Bevans replied that Elizondo is very conscious that he is starting from *mestizaje*. González, on the other hand, approaches theology from a perspective more integrated with the tradition. As an example, he referred to González' reflections on the natures of Christ (from an interview with Bevans on March 22, 1994, in Berkeley, California).

11. Elizondo, *La Morenita*, (1980) 21.

12. See Isasi-Díaz and Tarango, *Hispanic Women*, 67–70. Some of Elizondo's work, relative to this point, is mentioned in one of their footnotes (n. 22). The anthropological model's bias is to overlook the negative in its search for "the seeds of the word." In this sense, it is less critical than some of the other models.

13. In the case of Elizondo, Bevans feels that a case can be made for either an anthropological or synthetic classification. He leans towards the anthropological model, however, because Elizondo's starting point is much more the notion of *mestizaje* than anything else. "It is his reflection on his own liminality of being mestizo

Allan Figueroa Deck

The *modus operandi* of this Mexican American theologian, like that of Elizondo, seems to be very much a synthetic approach. In Deck's case, the weakest of the three models that Bevans fuses to describe the synthetic (translation, anthropological, and praxis) is probably translation. One gets the impression from reading Deck that his main concern is not getting across a certain content but rather creating an environment where people can discover a way of proceeding that is consistent with gospel values. Thus his stress seems to be on process, not content.

For the time being, let us put aside the translation model in the case of Deck and focus instead on two other ones, namely, the anthropological and the praxis. In some ways his method is characterized by both. Once again, however, the problem of vocabulary surfaces. Deck claims that Latin America's theology of liberation has stressed a praxis approach, one more committed to social change, over an anthropological one. Deck seems to associate praxis more with socioeconomic change while thinking of anthropology more in terms of cultural analysis. Although these associations are not explicitly made, they do seem to bear some validity if we read between the lines. The following passage might reveal a different slant on praxis and anthropology from Bevans' understanding:

> A third way in which U.S. Hispanic theology manifests its bridge character and originality is more implicit than explicit. It has to do with (1) the importance given to certain elements of Marxist analysis and (2) the explicit call for radical change that at times was quite influential in Latin American theology. While seldom if ever critiquing the emphasis on economic, structural, and social class analysis of their Latin American counterparts and their passionate calls for socio-economic and political transformation, U.S. Hispanic theologians have gravitated toward *cultural* analysis, especially to popular culture as epitomized by popular religiosity. Such a tendency has a muting effect, at least in the short term, on the urgent calls for radical change.[14]

In the same place, Deck points out that María Pilar Aquino, in her article in the same collection, "critiques this approach and warns us about its pitfalls and inadequacies."[15]

---

that opens up the perspective of how Galileans, and then Jesus, hold a place of particular ripeness for receiving God's revelation" (interview previously cited, see n. 10, above).

14. Deck, *Frontiers* (1992) xviii.

15. Ibid. Deck likewise refers to Elizondo and Espín: "The thought of Elizondo certainly moves with the cultural, anthropological reality more than with any other,

For Bevans, praxis has to do not so much with liberation themes or with the desire for social change but with a certain way of doing theology, since his models are methodological.[16] True, according to Bevans the aim of the praxis model is to bring about Christian behavior, but it does not stop there. This Christian behavior then informs a new understanding of Christian doctrine. That is why it is a theological method. In the words of Bevans, "The praxis model is a way of doing theology that is formed by knowledge at its most intense level—the level of reflective action."[17]

In light of Bevans' description of the praxis model, the case can be made that Deck's primary theological method is praxis oriented. The majority of his reflections reveal a strong familiarity with pastoral realities and a desire to bring about a change for the better. Segovia notes that this perspective is certainly a transformative one, noting even Deck's use of the term.[18] Deck's insistence on the relevance of pastoral theology to the entire theological enterprise betrays a conviction that true theology must be practical, that is, it must come from and be directed to action (Bevans' "reflective action"). The cyclical movement here is obvious. Deck's contribution of describing Hispanic ministry and what gifts Hispanics bring to the U.S. Church are two examples of how faith is nurtured by behavior and vice versa. Although he uses the Bible and tradition to inform his theology, his focus remains on the practical effects of these sources on present realities and on future possibilities for Hispanic ministry. Deck's pastoral experience generates a certain criteria, which informs further action.

Although I have put Deck's methodology in the "praxis camp," some mention should be made of his ample use of the science of anthropology. I believe that this use is not the same as that implied in Bevans' anthropological model. Bevans is referring to a methodological approach that

---

and therefore may be viewed as somewhat more 'culturalist' than 'liberationist.' Orlando Espín, as cogently demonstrated in chapter 4 of this book [*Frontiers* (1992)] and in much of his other writings, has insisted, however, on the value of popular religiosity as the least invaded or colonized source for the doing of a U.S. Hispanic theology. In his view it can and must be linked to the liberation struggle. For popular religiosity is a special instance of a first moment, a response, precisely to the initial oppression of indigenous and African cultures in the Americas" (ibid., xix).

16. For an explanation of this point see Bevans, *Models of Contextual Theology* (1992) 66.

17. Ibid., 63.

18. Segovia, "New Manifest Destiny" (1991) 105. Segovia adds in note 10: "This methodology—characterized as 'investigation-action'—is based on the work of Orlando Fals Borda ('El problema de como investigar la realidad para transformarla' in *Crítica y Política en Ciencias Sociales*, Tomo I (Bógota: Punta de Lanza, 1978) 209–49; *Conocimiento y Poder Popular* (México, D. F.: Siglo Veintiuno Editores, 1985)."

takes as a given that God is already working in people's lives, the basis of this work being manifested in the human person and culture. In his approach to evangelization, Deck looks to anthropology as a resource, as manifested, for example, in his writings on Hispanic worldviews, his use of history, and his concern for popular religiosity. This use, however, is more geared toward understanding the context of evangelization, not the way of proceeding. It is Deck's way of broadening horizons to include the whole person. Deck's functional model is more praxis oriented because his frame of reference as well as his aims are primarily pastoral.

Orlando O. Espín

Of the eight Latino theologians being discussed, probably one of the clearest examples of the use of the anthropological model is found in the work of Espín. As previously stated, a key tenet of this model is that Christianity is about the humanization of persons, since humanization, or the realization of human potential, is a gift from God to be cultivated. According to this thinking culture is perceived as the vehicle of that humanization. This respect for God's gift as manifested in culture is clear in the words of the Cuban American theologian:

> If the ultimate will of God for us is that we become that which we are from creation (that is, truly human, images of the God who is love), then this divine will must include our cultural dimension, since we cannot be human without culture. Or put another way, it must be the will of God that each of us humanize him or herself in the manner in which we are human, and that manner is specifically cultural. To trample on the culture of a human group, therefore, cannot be justified in the name of the Christian God, because it would imply a denial of the incarnation of grace. Furthermore, it would reject the possibility that the trampled-on human group might have of perceiving and responding to the love of the God-for-them.[19]

From the start, in the tradition of St. Ireneus and Karl Rahner, Espín opts for a positive view of human nature, seeing human persons as a manifestation of God:

> Paraphrasing Karl Rahner, it can be said that human beings are that which God is when God expresses God's self outside of the sphere of the divine. And if it is true that God is love, then that understanding of humanness is extremely important.[20]

19. Espín, "Grace and Humanness" (1992) 147.
20. Ibid., 138. Espín gives the source of Rahner's thought: "Concepción teológica del hombre," *Sacramentum Mundi*, ed. Karl Rahner et al., (Barcelona: Herder, 1976)

Having drawn on the tradition of the Church as expressed in the *sensus fidelium*, Espín extends this reverence to the believing community. Within this understanding, Espín argues that because it is "the least 'invaded' cultural creation of our peoples, and a locus for our most authentic self disclosure,"[21] popular piety is a privileged means of understanding this *sensus fidelium*. He feels that it is a key source for constructing a theology of grace and providence.

In Bevans' scheme the anthropological model focuses on "where the faith actually lives, in the midst of people's lives."[22] Theology, then, seeks to illuminate what is already there. Such a procedure seems to describe Espín's methodology well. He defines popular religiosity as the faith as it is lived by the people; in his words, "it's people's Catholicism."[23] As far as elucidating what is already there, Espín singles out two key symbols found in Hispanic popular religiosity: the crucified Christ and Mary. These two he identifies as "bearers of the Christian gospel."[24]

To summarize, Espín's contextual theology is anthropological because it "focuses on the validity of the human as the place of divine revelation and as a source (locus) for theology that is equal to scripture and tradition."[25]

Roberto S. Goizueta

Goizueta's methodological approach, which, using Bevans' models, I characterize as synthetic, is certainly the most dialogical of the eight U.S. Hispanic theologians. As stated previously, Goizueta's early work reveals a willingness to engage Latin American theology, especially the theology of liberation, with other theological and philosophical currents. His more recent writing incorporates the insights of such diverse thinkers as Aristotle, Marx, Lonergan, Habermas, Vasconcelos, and Tracy.[26] Deck presents a summary of what has distinguished Goizueta's project:

---

vol. 3, 493–504; Rahner, *Foundations of Christian Faith* (New York: Crossroad, 1985) 26–42, 75–81, 117–33.

21. Espín, "Grace and Humanness" (1992) 148.

22. Bevans, *Models of Contextual Theology* (1992) 54.

23. *National Catholic Reporter*, September 11, 1992.

24. Espín, "Tradition and Popular Religion" (1992) 69–75.

25. Bevans, *Models of Contexual Theology* (1992) 48. Bevans himself says that Espín is working out of the anthropological model. He elaborated: "For him (Espín) the starting point of theology needs to be the reality of popular religiosity—looking at the people's faith is what determines for him how their faith is to be articulated in theological formulae" (interview previously cited, see n. 10, above).

26. For example, see Goizueta, "La Raza Cósmica?" (1994) 5–27.

His theological writings focus on issues of method and hermeneutics. He deals with the epistemological suppositions of the dominant North American theological milieu, Roman Catholic and Protestant, and the interface of that epistemology with that of U.S. Hispanic theologians. Goizueta pursues the issues of ontological individualism and pluralism as they are understood and sometimes reflected by mainstream theologians. He critiques these conceptions and values from the vantage point of a committed U.S. Hispanic.[27]

The last sentence hints of the transcendent qualities from Bevans' model found in Goizueta. Similarly, his own journey to find his identity has already been alluded to.[28]

Before examining how his *modo de proceder* reflects a synthesis of the translation, anthropological, and praxis models, more need be said concerning the dialogical character of his work. In describing the synthetic model Bevans elaborates on other terms that designate the same type of approach:

> [S]ince this model involves constant dialogue and employment of what David Tracy has named the analogical imagination, the model might also be spoken of as the "dialogical model," the "conversation model," or even the "analogical model." This is the model that theologians such as Aylward Shorter mean when they speak of the inculturation or interculturation of theology as "the ongoing dialogue between faith and culture or cultures . . . the creative and dynamic relationship between the Christian message and a culture or cultures."[29]

As Shorter explains, the term "interculturation," coined by Bishop Joseph Blomjous in 1980, is meant to accent the reciprocal nature of inculturation. To some, the term "inculturation" means simply the transfer of faith from one culture to another; this transfer is often seen as a one-directional reality. Blomjous' point is that "the process of inculturation must be lived in partnership and mutuality,"[30] not in a nondialogical fashion.

As evidenced by his dialogue with other theologies, Goizueta is convinced that the U.S. Hispanic theologian must, for the sake of both the Latino peoples and the mainstream theological academy, be true to the

27. Deck, *Frontiers* (1992) xvi.
28. *National Catholic Reporter,* September 11, 1992.
29. Bevans, *Models of Contextual Theology* (1992) 83. The quote from Aylward Shorter is taken from his book *Toward a Theology of Inculturation,* 11.
30. Shorter, *Toward a Theology of Inculturation,* 13.

creative tension characteristic of such a discourse. He claims, for example, that one of the major ways Latino theologians contribute to the development and living out of theology is by bringing the U.S. Hispanic experience of community to the theological enterprise. This unique type of praxis, explained more in detail below, is a constant challenge to Latino theologians.

> The ontological priority of community revealed in U.S. Hispanic praxis suggests, as we have seen, that all of us are particular manifestations of an organic whole before we are individual entities: community—ultimately, the entire human community—is mediated by the particularity of individual identity. This fact anticipates, as we have also seen, both the possibility of ethical-political action and the possibility of rational discourse. The ontological priority of community implies that the theological reflection of U.S. Hispanics is important, not only because there happen to be Hispanics in our churches, our seminaries, or our universities, but also because, inasmuch as every culture and every individual is a unique and particular manifestation of the whole human community, the theology of Hispanics has significance for the whole theological community. It is by being self-consciously faithful to the particularity of our own experience as U.S. Hispanics that we are faithful to the larger human community. Consequently, it is by being faithful to our identity as U.S. Hispanic theologians that we are faithful to the larger theological community.[31]

Thus Goizueta is convinced that Latino theologians must not only listen to what other, more mainstream theologians have to say but also that they are in a position to make a significant and unique contribution. One is reminded here of Tracy's discussion concerning the function of the "classic": a term to designate something that is both specific and concrete and yet at the same time quite universal.[32]

31. Goizueta, "Rediscovering Praxis" (1992) 77.
32. See Tracy, "Ethnic Pluralism and Systematic Theology" (1977) 94. Here Tracy notes that "the emergence of 'ethnic theologies' (such as black theology or Italian-American theology) is not a plea for particularism or private language. Indeed ethnic theology can occasion further reflections upon the fuller meanings of public language itself. As a single example of that fuller meaning, one must reflect upon the phenomenon of the 'classic.' Intuitively we all recognize that the great classics of our heritage, including our religious heritage, are both deeply particular in origin and expression, yet genuinely public in disclosive and transformative power. Indeed, any classic involves a significant paradox: precisely an artist's or thinker's fidelity to his/her own concrete and particular personal, social, cultural, and religious heritage occasions the emergence of a public form of discourse. Any classic, however particular its origins and form, bears publicly disclosive and transformative power for all human beings."

Naturally, as in any true discussion, it is important that the dialogue partners understand each other. This understanding is important not only in terms of the present but also in terms of the past, more specifically, the sources of sacred Scripture and tradition. As Bevans notes, all of the models, to one degree or another, have a translation component. The translation model's primary methodology, however, is one-directional. As has been noted, this model assumes that there is an unchanging message that must be relayed to different peoples in different cultural situations throughout the world over time. It is the job of the evangelizer to "translate" this message in a way that is understandable.

The reason Goizueta's methodology does not follow the translation model is that it is dialogical. Only through dialogue, a dialogue based on praxis, are persons able to discern and live out gospel values. His work bears the mark of what has been described as *teología de conjunto*. The result of his conversation with modern currents in theological method has been a questioning, from the perspective of Hispanic culture, of the basic paradigms this theological method is using. One of Goizueta's main concerns is that Cartesian and Kantian epistemological paradigms have tended to create false dichotomies, such as that between praxis and theory or that between mind and body. As a corrective, he calls for a more integrative approach, one that distinguishes itself by a "holistic anthropology," that is, one that does not separate theory and praxis, mind and body. He maintains that U.S. Hispanic theology can be of great help here:

> There is no pure praxis any more than there is pure theory. U.S. Hispanic theology does not reject reason, rather it rejects the dominant culture's conceptualist and instrumentalist *models* of reason and criteria of reasonableness. U.S. Hispanic theology seeks to uncover the irrationality of what the dominant society calls reason.[33]

As mentioned above, Goizueta points out that the aesthetic epistemological paradigm, as an alternative to the Cartesian, has played an important role in the history of Latin American philosophy.[34] This heritage has clearly marked the worldview of Hispanics in the United States:

> From the perspective of the U.S. Hispanic experience praxis is revealed as not only inherently communal but also inherently celebratory, or aesthetic. The centrality of music, dance, and ritual in Hispanic life reveals the aesthetic sense underlying that life. Insofar as praxis is an affirmation of community, it is an affirmation of

33. Goizueta, "Challenge of Pluralism" (1992) 18.
34. See Goizueta, "Rediscovering Praxis" (1992) 67.

community as the highest form of beauty. Popular religiosity reveals praxis as communal, aesthetic performance.[35]

Goizueta conceives praxis as reflection on the lived experience of the people. It is a praxis that is itself dialogic because it seeks to critique supposedly contradictory propositions. In this sense it is closer to the Hegelian dialectic of a synthesis of opposites than to Bevans' methodological notion of praxis as "reflection upon reflected upon action."

> U.S. Hispanic theology finds its roots in the praxis of U.S. Hispanic communities. That praxis reflects an instinctive and implicit repudiation of the conceptualist dichotomies underlying modern, Western anthropologies and epistemologies, whether dichotomies of mind-body, intellect-affect, or individual identity–communal identity. As the praxis of whole human persons, hearts and minds, spirits and bodies, it has a reflective moment. The task of U.S. Hispanic theology is to bear witness to the significance of that moment *within* the socio-historical struggles of U.S. Hispanic communities.[36]

Once again, the same term "praxis" has been shown to signify many things. In Goizueta it has a more synthetic sense than in someone like Deck, whose praxis is more methodological. It is for all these reasons that I chose to classify Goizueta's methodology as synthetic.

Jaime R. Vidal

This Puerto Rican theologian's ethnographic focus, especially in terms of popular piety among Latinos, makes his work a prime candidate for Bevans' anthropological model. Given such an ethnographic thrust, some might question whether his writings should in fact be called, strictly speaking, theology. It is important to keep in mind that in his early writings Vidal is building an anthropological foundation for his evolving theological positions.[37] At the same time, by exploring the theological issues behind popular religion, he is already making a significant contribution not only to pastoral but also to systematic theology.[38] While he is naturally concerned about educating pastoral agents

---

35. Ibid., 67.

36. Goizueta, "Challenge of Pluralism" (1992) 18.

37. See, for example, Vidal, "Understanding of Synthesis" (1994) 69–95. In a letter to me dated July 11, 1994, he describes his theology as "a theology which is basically Bonaventurian rather than either Thomistic or contemporary, and owes very much to Jung and to Ewert Cousins."

38. Vidal, "Popular Religion in the Lands of the Origin of New York's Hispanic Population" (1982); "Popular Religion Among the Hispanics in the General Area of

in being sensitive to Latinos in the United States, especially the immigrant population, he also believes, as do other Latino theologians, that U.S. Hispanic theology has much to contribute to mainline theology.

His concern for holistic spirituality is very similar to Goizueta's call for a holistic anthropology. Also, like Goizueta, Vidal believes that more attention needs to be paid to aesthetic experience on the part of theologians. His work, which basically views popular religiosity positively, delves into how God is present there. Thus, by focusing on popular religiosity, he starts at the level of lived faith for many Hispanics in the United States. Secondly, to use an earlier example, Vidal acts more like a "treasure hunter" than a "pearl merchant"[39] by seeking to demonstrate how popular religiosity is well within the Hispanic faith tradition. He insists that it is precisely through popular religiosity that Latinos integrate into their lives who God is for them. For these reasons, I characterize his method, using Bevans' schema, as anthropological.[40]

---

the Archdiocese of Newark" (1988) 235–352; "American Church and the Puerto Rican People" (1990).

39. See Bevans, *Models of Contextual Theology* (1992) 49.

40. Vidal had this to say about my classification: "As for where I would fit in Bevans' models, it's hard to say; I have some points of identification with each, but none of them feels like my home. I suspect that I come from a model he doesn't include, which I would call the Coincidence of Opposites Model, which is based on the total opposition between the Transcendent, Wholly Other God of Israel and the Immanent, Great-All God of World Religions, except that in the Incarnation the Wholly Other becomes a Man like us in all things but sin, thus revealing the Immanence of the Utterly Transcendent (with no toning down of the Utter Transcendence, mind you).

"This at once postulates the uniqueness of Christianity as *the* One True Religion, and the truth of both Biblical Revelation and the insights of World Religions—except that each of these is true in what it says, but false in its denial of its opposite's truth, and therefore the truth of other religions is only true when they are subsumed into the Revelation of Christ. This includes the Old Testament; it is only really true when read in the context of Christ. And at the same time Christianity is the One True Religion *precisely* because it is only in the Incarnate Christ of Orthodox Christianity that the incompatible Truths of the other religions are shown to be both true.

"This would also apply to the Faith/Culture issue; there is a core of Christianity which is non-negotiable, and which is expressed (in terms of one culture) in things like the Nicene Creed and the Chalcedonian definition, and this *must* be faithfully expressed in terms of whatever culture. In fact no culture really has the terms for it, and cultural terms must be stretched and modified to accommodate this; things like *ousía* or *hypostasis* did not mean in Greek culture what we made them mean in the search for a vocabulary for the inexpressible. But what must be expressed in terms of each culture is not a bunch of definitions but a world-view/outlook on reality which is there, unexpressed in jargon, just as much in Teilhard as in the *viejitas*. And which comes from experiencing the God of Israel, the God of the Burning Bush and of Ezekiel's theophany, as one Person with our Brother Jesus, the baby of Bethlehem

Ada María Isasi-Díaz

In her 1993 book, *En la Lucha/In the Struggle: A Hispanic Women's Theology*,[41] Isasi-Díaz uses the same methodology she and Yolanda Tarango developed in writing *Hispanic Women: Prophetic Voice in the Church.*[42] The ideas that appeared in her earlier writings, those describing what she terms "a Hispanic women's theology of liberation," take a more concrete form as she expounds further on what she means by activism, praxis, perspective, *mestizaje*, and community.

Which of Bevans' five models best characterizes her work? Here is an instance where his models shed light on a person's method but do not necessarily describe it. I believe, for example, that a case can be made for classifying Isasi-Díaz's work as being both anthropological and praxeological.

Insofar as Tarango has collaborated with Isasi-Díaz in the writing of *Hispanic Women: Prophetic Voice in the Church*, the latter's thought is reflected in this approach. One of the major reasons for saying that this methodology is partly anthropological has to do with her method of collecting data. As previously described, this "ethnomethodology," which was pioneered by social psychologist Harold Garfinkel, uses personal faith histories to arrive at an understanding of how people perceive themselves and their situation in everyday life.[43] In order to accent emotive and ethical aspects of religion, Isasi-Díaz and Tarango applied anthropologist Clifford Geertz' definition of religion, which includes people's "moods and motivations."[44]

Besides using anthropological methods, Isasi-Díaz's work can be located in Bevans' anthropological category because, in the continuum he has set up, it focuses not on the message or tradition (content) but on

---

and victim of Calvary; from looking at this broken victim of abuse and oppression and singing 'Holy God, Holy Mighty One, Holy Immortal One' as we used to do on Good Friday, or calling him *el Señor del Gran Poder*. You simply can not be Christian, in any culture, without cultural creativity; you have to do to the language of your culture what Gerard Manley Hopkins did to English.

"But the point is that anyone who has the Faith; who has experienced God in Christ, already *knows* this implicitly; the problem is finding the cultural/verbal/iconic expression for the inexpressible we have 'seen with our eyes and handled with our hands.' *That* is the job of the theologian in each culture, and the job of the misnamed 'magisterium' is to check my attempts at expressing it and see if they in fact *do* express the Coincidence of Opposites, or if they have somehow explained it away (as both Nestorius and Eutyches did) by explaining one of the Opposites away" (in Vidal letter previously cited; see n. 37, above).

41. Isasi-Díaz, *En la Lucha* (1993).

42. Isasi-Díaz and Tarango, *Hispanic Women* (1988).

43. See Isasi-Díaz, "*Mujerista* Theology's Method" (1992) 42.

44. See Geertz, *Interpretation of Cultures*, 90.

the culture or social change (subject).[45] As others in the Christian tradition before her have done, she underscores the importance of the human as the place of divine revelation. It is within a given culture, namely that of oppressed Latinas who struggle to survive, that God becomes manifest. The source of a Hispanic women's theology of liberation is said to be the lived experience of the Hispanic woman. This experience is analyzed from three perspectives: cultural, religious, and existential. These three elements are intrinsically related and together form one reality.[46] Isasi-Díaz explains what she means by "lived-experience":

> Though the expression "lived-experience" might seem tautological to some, in the context of *mujerista* theology it refers not only to what has happened—what a person has endured or made happen—but also to that experience upon which she reflects in order to understand its significance and to value it accordingly.[47]

In asking how she goes about doing theology contextually, we see that her primary source is not sacred Scripture or ecclesial tradition but "lived-experience."[48] Her goal, as she perceives it, is to bring to light, to articulate, a theology already present among Latinas:

> Mujerista theologians do not deny that the Bible and Church teaching are also a source of our theology. Undoubtedly certain aspects of them have become an intrinsic part of our culture and, as such, they are part of the lived experience of Latinas. Besides, there is a current of struggle and liberation to be found in both the Bible and Church teaching which we consider to be the best of the tradition and one of the bases for our own liberation perspective and understandings. But we make it very clear at all times that our lens is a liberative one and that the lived experience of Hispanic Women, our religious understandings and practices, are the primary source of *mujerista* theology, making it a tool for survival. Because it takes

45. Isasi-Díaz had this to say about my statement: "My point is precisely that. It is time we pay attention to the message of Hispanic women—how we understand and live our understanding of Christianity . . . and that is a repressed/ignored strand of the tradition" (in a letter to me dated July 1994).

46. Isasi-Díaz and Tarango, *Hispanic Women* (1988) 74–6.

47. Isasi-Díaz, "*Mujerista* Theology's Method" (1992) 49.

48. She gives her reasons for not making Scripture or Church teaching her primary source: "Those who claim the Bible or Church teaching as the source of their theology are glossing over the fact that the real source of their theology is *their* understanding of the Bible and of Church teaching. Furthermore, theologians often ignore the fact that both these sources are conditioned by the socio-economic-political realities of the period in which they were written or formulated" (Isasi-Díaz, "Praxis" [1993] 48).

the lived experience of Latinas seriously, *mujerista* theology helps
us to find meaning in our lives despite the alienation we suffer.
That is why to do *mujerista* theology is a liberative praxis.[49]

As demonstrated above, Isasi-Díaz is examining certain religious and
cultural values in Latina experience, studying how Latinas understand
and explain these values. Thus the anthropological model's *modus
operandi*, that is, approaching contextualization from the idea of illuminating the Christian as well as the religious African and Amerindian
elements present, seems operative.

Having said all of the above, however, one detects a clear inclination
to action or, stated in a more systematic way, to a praxis mode. For
Isasi-Díaz what is most critical is the "lived experience," or reflected-
upon experience, of ordinary Hispanic women. She is not so much reflecting upon the culture as she is about women's experience. Her role
is to articulate and systematize this experience as, in the words of Carlos
H. Abesamis, a "theological technician"[50] and in this way to effect
social change. In fact, from the start Isasi-Díaz and Tarango identify
themselves as activists:

> First and foremost we are activists—Hispanic Women committed
> to the struggle for justice and peace. Our lived experience has
> pointed us in the direction of being theologians. We see no conflict
> in being both theologians and activists; this follows our under-
> standing of the intrinsic unity between what has been classically
> referred to as systematic theology and moral theology or ethics.
> This will become obvious as we clarify what it means for us to *do*
> theology.[51]

Isasi-Díaz specifically describes her method as the "praxis of Hispanic
women."[52] Acknowledging the influence of Leonardo Boff, José Míguez
Bonino, and Paulo Friere, she presents her understanding of praxis:

> In *mujerista* theology praxis refers to a conscious human action, a
> political action which seeks to change the oppressive economic-
> socio-cultural structures of society. Praxis, therefore, requires
> human agency, intentionality, political commitment to change the
> infrastructure while understanding its relationship to the supra-
> structures, and a keen awareness that how we go about changing
> structures is a key element in what we will accomplish. *Mujerista*

49. Ibid., 49.
50. Isasi-Díaz and Tarango, *Hispanic Women* (1988) 110.
51. Ibid., ix.
52. Isasi-Díaz, "Praxis" (1993) 49.

theology defines praxis as critical reflective action, as opposed to mechanical routine. The reflection part of praxis does not follow action nor is it "at the service of action." In praxis action and reflection become inseparable moments. Praxis "combines reflection with action to create the human world of ideas, symbols, language, science, religion, art, and production."[53]

It seems from the above that for Isasi-Díaz praxis is more concerned with intentionality than with methodology. It is what these women are doing in their daily lives, the stuff from which we make theology, that is a true praxis. Therefore, praxis is that "lived-experience" which, using her understanding, implies a combination of reflection with action.[54]

True, she acknowledges the strong interconnection between action and reflection in a praxis mode, and she is well within the Marxian tradition of praxis as a desire to "change the world," not "understand it,"[55] yet in terms of Bevans' categories, praxis is more about one's methodology than about one's aim.[56] For Bevans, who chose not to call this model "liberative" even though it is the liberation theologians who are

<hr>

53. Ibid. She cites three thinkers: L. Boff, "Qué es hacer teología desde América Latina?" *Liberación y Cautiverio. Encuentro Latinoamericano de Teología* (Mexico, 1975) 144; J. Míguez Bonino, *Doing Theology in a Revolutionary Situation* (Philadelphia: Fortress Press, 1975) 72; D. E. Collins, *Paulo Freire: His Life, Works, and Thought* (New York: Paulist Press, 1977) 49.

54. Isasi-Díaz disagrees with me: "I repeatedly say that mujerista theology is praxis. Never do I say praxis has to do with intentionality—as a matter of fact, I repeatedly say it is action, reflective action . . . praxis is not what motivates me. My method is praxical. I gather Hispanic women to do theology with them because theology is a liberative praxis" (from her letter; see n. 45, above).

55. See Bevans, *Models of Contextual Theology* (1992) 64–6.

56. Bevans explains (note the emphasis on the continual dialogue between gospel, tradition, culture, and social change): "When we speak of the praxis model of contextual theology, we are speaking about a model, the central insight of which is that theology is done not simply by providing relevant expressions of Christian faith but also by commitment to Christian action. But even more than this, theology is understood as the product of the continual dialogue of these two aspects of Christian life. The praxis model employs a method which 'in its most profound sense is understood as the unity of knowledge as activity and knowledge as content.' It works on the conviction that 'truth is at the level of history, not in the realm of ideas.' As Philip Berryman characterized it by referring to its use by Paolo Freire, praxis is 'action with reflection.' It is reflected-upon action and acted-upon reflection—both rolled into one" (ibid., 65). Here he gives the following citations to reference his quotes (in order): (1) Sobrino, "El conocimiento," 93, quoted in Hennelly, "Theological Method," 721; (2) J. Miguez Bonino, *Doing Theology in a Revolutionary Situation* (Philadelphia: Fortress Press, 1975) 72; (3), Philip Berryman, *Liberation Theology,* 86. To the previous quote, Isasi-Díaz, making reference to the final chapter of *Hispanic Women* (1988), comments, "This is a pretty good description of how I understand mujerista theology" (letter; see n. 45).

most responsible for its use and development, "praxis" refers more to how one proceeds than to what motivates one.

María Pilar Aquino

In many ways Aquino's approach to doing theology is similar to Isasi-Díaz's. Both are attempting to develop a theology of liberation from the perspective of Latinas. Having seen that perspective overlooked, they are critical of much of the work being done in the field of theology today, even that of some of the Latin American liberationists, First World feminists, and U.S. Hispanics. Despite this criticism they both define themselves as liberation theologians and, therefore, use what has been generally accepted as a praxis method of doing theology. In answering a criticism made by First World feminist theologians of feminist Latin American theology, Aquino summarizes their method, and in this way describes her idea of praxis:

> [First World feminists] cannot accuse feminist Latin American theology of methodological *under-development,* as its results clearly show otherwise. On the contrary, this theology demands a knowledge of its own channels to formulate an understanding of faith in terms of our own situation and as a response to it. Latin American women theologians are aware of the need to advance toward a way of thinking in line with women's vision. We recognize the gaps and realize that the internal methodological unity of our theology needs work, but we understand that this unity will not come as a result of intellectual activity alone. It is the fruit of a collective process of dialogue, consultation, and exchange among professional, pastoral, and popular theologians in order to agree about how to move forward. This process is slower than the process followed in the First World, which mainly advances in an academic environment. In the long run, however, it is much more effective because the feminist vision grows in breadth and depth.[57]

Indirectly, she is detailing above the elements that have gone into the formulation of her theology. The various "channels" that have fed into "an understanding of faith in terms of our own situation and as a response to it," sources she has alluded to in her book, are sacred Scripture, systematic theology, anthropology, and current economic realities as seen today from the emerging perspective of women, particularly poor women in Latin America. Moreover, because of her desire to further the cause of women, especially that of poor women, she includes pastoral and popular theologians.

57. Aquino, *Our Cry for Life* (1993) 196.

Again, as in the case of other theologians, it is not clear how her methodology would fit into Bevans' categories. She explicitly supports both feminist theology and the theology of liberation. In fact, the goal of her book seems to be to engage and critique both, of course not ignoring more traditional theology. It is her conviction that women, particularly from their position and labors in causes on behalf of justice, can discover truth not visible from other vantage points. She describes the aim of her work:

> I hope to show that theology done by Latin American women has special features that distinguish it from the theology done by men and women in other latitudes. This does not mean, however, that we distance ourselves from our common commitment to liberation. On the contrary, it highlights our originality and particular identity. It invites male theologians to overcome their androcentric systems and it stresses our links with other feminists. No liberating theology can set itself up in opposition to other women, and our theological work must emphasize our solidarity with the liberating experiences and hopes of men and other women. We share a hermeneutic position that bases the process of knowledge and consequently our understanding of faith on *actual human life* as it is lived by both men and women.[58]

Although there is a dialogical, synthetic tone to her work, the main goal is clear: true liberation. As she states elsewhere, "in accordance with the core of the liberating biblical vision, this aim [of theology from the point of view of women] is on the path toward the attainment of the fullness of life, human integrity, shared solidarity, complete liberation, and common enjoyment of the goods of the earth."[59] Since true liberation is clearly the goal of her theology, as it is for Isasi-Díaz, this liberation theme is consistent with the notion of praxis as "not faith seeking understanding but rather intelligent action."[60] Bevans makes it clear, however, that this aim, which characterizes the praxis model, does not necessarily describe its methodology. As previously stated, he has refrained from calling his model liberational (preferring "praxis") because the term "praxis model" reveals "more clearly than *liberation model* that the specificity of the model is not one of a particular theme but one of a particular *method.*"[61]

Which of Bevans' models, then, most accurately describes Aquino's methodology? Like that of Isasi-Díaz, her work reflects many of the

58. Ibid., 3.
59. Aquino, "Perspectives" (1992) 24.
60. Bevans, *Models of Contextual Theology* (1992) 66.
61. Ibid., 66.

characteristics of both the praxis and the anthropological model.[62] There are significant differences, however, between Aquino's and Isasi-Díaz' methodologies. While Isasi-Díaz has focused more on a small, specific group, Aquino does a much broader historical and theological sweep of the situation of women in the Church and in Latin America. Isasi-Díaz's interlocutors tend to be women in the United States, while Aquino's are Latin American. Aquino is looking at the history of philosophy and history through the eyes of a women's liberative praxis, while Isasi-Díaz' praxis emerges from the lived experience of the specific women she has engaged in dialogue. All in all, despite their differences, both Latinas, when measured by Bevans' categories, seem to share a similar understanding of praxis. Therefore, although somewhat hesitatingly, I would say that Aquino's method is more anthropological (as Bevans would define it) than it is praxeological.

The present discussion of praxis is a clear sign that our terminology still needs to be refined. Is praxis, for example, an ongoing cycle involving reflection and action, similar to community organizing in which what is learned is clearly the result of certain action and, therefore, influences further action for justice? Or, is it, as Isasi-Díaz and Aquino seem to be saying, reflection based on lived experience (either historical or in the present)? Of course, this distinction may not be an important one, and in fact, as we have seen, the term "praxis" has been described in both ways.

This discussion may also shed some light on the ambiguity found in Bevans' models, which, as I have argued, provides the flexibility needed at this stage for an adequate understanding of contextualization. The workability of models only becomes obvious in their use. Perhaps new operative models will emerge as the dialogue continues. Bevans elaborates on the compatibility of models, as opposed to their exclusivity:

> Though each model is distinct, each can be used in conjunction with others. A particular use of the translation model may have several aspects of the praxis model within it; a version of what is basically an anthropological model may be much more cognizant of the importance of the traditional content of Christian message than another version. In the same way, no one model can be used exclusively; exclusive use will distort the theological enterprise.

---

62. Aquino's basic point seems to be that the way women do theology can serve as a corrective to the type of theology that has been done for centuries. As an oppressed group, their perspective and their approach are going to be very different. This openness to enriching and illuminating the tradition, at times calling it into question from their perspective, that is, as members of a type of subculture, "womanhood," marks one of the key tenets of the anthropological model.

While every one of these models is in some sense a translation of a message, an adequate theology cannot be reduced to a mere application or adaptation of a changeless body of truths. Even the biblical message was developed in dialogue with culture and cultural and social change, and a theology that neither issues forth in action nor takes account of the way one lives one's life can hardly be a theology with much worth. Finally, a theology that is not the activity of a faithful integrated subject cannot claim to be an adequate expression of Christian faith.[63]

The unique contribution that both Aquino and Isasi-Díaz make is that they take contextualization to a deeper level. Their treatment of the situation and the contribution of the Latina is actually a contextualization within a contextualization. The fact remains that Latinas are one of the poorest segments of the Latino population, and to ignore their perspective would undoubtedly bring about disastrous results.

Justo L. González

Of the eight Latino theologians being considered, González is the only one Bevans explicitly categorizes. According to Bevans, the Cuban-born theologian's methodology follows the transcendental model.[64] The task of this model is to create a contextual theology by "attending to the affective and cognitive operations in the self-transcending subject."[65] Its theological presupposition is that it is precisely through the human that God chooses to be revealed. The role of the subject is to be aware of one's own

63. Bevans, *Models of Contextual Theology* (1992) 28.
64. When asked how he felt about this categorization of his theological method, González responded, "I am not certain I would agree with Bevans' understanding of my work, unless one widens his understanding of the 'subject' and its experience to include the entire church and its tradition. I certainly am not 'more concerned with the subject who is doing the theologizing than with the theological content.' My concern is rather for all the subjects doing the theologizing, all within a Christian catholic tradition broadly construed, to help illumine that tradition. Thus the content is central. It is true that, because so much of traditional theology has thought that the content could be approached and defined apart from the subject, much of what I have done is a corrective to that position. But I would be even more uncomfortable with a theology based solely on the subject's experience. Perhaps this is why I tend to use the word "perspective"—as in the subtitle of *Mañana*. A perspective requires something one is looking at. That something is not entirely at the mercy of the observer, even though one's point of vantage does affect how one sees and describes it. Using the understanding of catholicity in *Out of Every Tribe* [González, 1992], I would say that a theology based solely on Hispanic experience would be sectarian. And also that traditional theology, inasmuch as it does not recognize that it is based on a particular, partial experience, is equally sectarian" (letter dated July 11, 1994).
65. Bevans, *Models of Contextual Theology* (1992) 44.

worldview and in this manner to understand how one is historically and culturally conditioned. This awareness is the means to true conversion. Taken together, this human experience of having our horizons broadened forms the basis of our *locus theologicus*. As stated previously, theology is that which happens in the struggle to relate to the divine.

It is precisely because he is attentive to his own traditions, whether as a Christian heir to a rich biblical and doctrinal tradition or as a Hispanic in the United States, that González can embrace his identity and see it as an important component of God's self-revelation. Having given numerous examples of how González exemplifies this way of proceeding, Bevans explains why he chooses to call González' methodology transcendental:

> Reading González, one is not confronted at every turn with what it means to be Hispanic; nor is one reminded frequently that the Christian message has to be preserved as one speaks of God in a Hispanic context. What does become clear is that theology is done out of a deep conviction of the value of Hispanic identity, as well as of the Christian tradition. González might well be an example of the praxis model; nevertheless, what seems even more evident is a commitment not to a particular method or model, but to being faithful to history: his history as a Hispanic and the history of the Christian church, which he also cherishes as his own.[66]

According to González, one of the most important contributions that Hispanics can make to theology, for example, is to insist on its fundamentally and irreducibly communal dimension. In a country of entrenched individualism, the Latino gift for forming community can be a great blessing and a sign of a more evangelical direction. His plea for communality and inclusivity in our theologizing was mentioned in detailing what he means by "*Fuenteovejuna* theology."[67] In his words, "The best theology is a communal enterprise."[68]

His discussions of other doctrinal areas such as christology or the foundations of a theology of liberation reveal the richness a diverse background can bring to the theological enterprise, especially in a country such as the United States, which, because of its powerful position in the world, can easily suffer from myopia. Latinos, together with other minorities, for example, can serve as a powerful reminder that U.S. domestic and foreign policy has not always been the most enlightened.[69] The fact is that at times our interpretation of Scripture or the tra-

66. Ibid., 110.
67. J. L. González, *Mañana* (1990).
68. Ibid.
69. Ibid., 79–80.

dition has been tainted by social and economic interests that, in reality, are incompatible with gospel values. The more attentive we are to our own biases, the more receptive we can be to God's salvific plan.[70]

To a certain degree, all contextual theologians use the transcendental method to the extent that they are acting as faithful, integrated subjects, sensitive to the experience of God in their group histories and personal lives. Thus they all work from their own experience of conversion. This use of the transcendental method is obvious in the eight Hispanic theologians being discussed. Their theologizing stems from living between two very different realities: the North American and the Latin American. It is within this context that they relate (both as individuals and as members of a group) to the divine.

Conclusion

This chapter has situated eight U.S. Hispanic theologians within the general theological trend toward contextualization. Having identified their work as local theology, we looked to a categorization of their methodologies. That is, the main question of this section has been "What process or method do these Latino theologians use to arrive at their conclusions?" Because Stephen Bevans' models are primarily methodological, they furnished a frame of reference for comparing the works of these various authors.

What resulted from such an analysis was greater clarity in terms of the different shades that words such as "praxis" and "anthropology" take in the literature. It is hoped that, along with such general words as "inculturation" and "evangelization," these terms will gradually take on a more precise signification so that the dialogue can become more precise. Overall, it seems that we are developing a more sophisticated vocabulary as well as expanding it. This is not the first time this has happened in our Christian history. For example, *homousia* was not just a translation of a biblical notion for the more Hellenic mind; rather, it put Greek concepts at the service of a gospel reality. Today, Elizondo, for example, is helping us discern new insights about the gospel from his own experience of being a *mestizo*.

Let me close this chapter with a few words about the suitability of particular models in various contexts.[71] As my Asian colleagues have often pointed out to me, in the area of evangelization there is a world of difference between a Christian and a non-Christian context. How

---

70. Ibid., 75–87.
71. On this point especially, I am indebted to Stephen Bevans (interview previously cited; see n. 10, above).

appropriate is it to use these models to analyze the process of contextualization in traditionally Christian cultures such as the Filipino or the Mexican?

In effect I have been using the same set of models to deal with both Christian and non-Christian settings. This use may not necessarily be flawed if we keep in mind a certain flexibility in terms of ambiance and time period. True, some models are more appropriate than others, such as the anthropological for a non-Christian context (which would look to such religions as Buddhism, ancient Aztec, or Native American to find the "seeds of the Word" in them). However, we must not forget that there are certain "pagan elements" in Christianity that have never been integrated. These pagan elements may not necessarily be "bad." There are many examples early Christianity of taking a pagan idea, such as the winter solstice, to illuminate Christian reality. It is not simply a translation. Rather, these pagan elements illuminate a Christian reality and thus is created a new, yet still Christian, reality. To fail to recognize this is to view Christianity and Judaism as something that can exist apart from human culture.

A final point regarding the use of models has to do with the question as to which might be best suited for the creation of a U.S. Hispanic theology. Given the diversity of Latinos in the United States, might some models be better suited to certain contexts than others? As stated previously, Hispanics now can be found in all social classes. As some observers have commented, there is a tendency in the U.S. Catholic Church to see Hispanics as being only immigrants. Second-generation or professional Latinos have often been ignored despite the fact that they are struggling with identity issues. Andrew Greeley bemoans their abandonment of the Church.[72]

Deck has commented that because of the dire socioeconomic situation of the poor in Latin America, liberation theologians have chosen a more explicitly liberation-oriented mode. However, in the United States, as previously stated, Deck concludes that "Hispanic theologians have gravitated toward *cultural* analysis, especially to popular culture as epitomized by popular religiosity. Such a tendency has a muting effect, at least in the short term, on the urgent calls for radical change."[73] He proceeds to note that Aquino's article in the same collection critiques this approach, warning of its hazards.[74] The focus he is referring

---

72. Greeley, "Defection Among Hispanics" (1988).

73. Deck, *Frontiers* (1992) xix.

74. See Aquino, "Perspectives" (1992) 23–40. Isasi-Díaz disagrees with Deck's "way of seemingly dichotomizing Hispanic culture from the socio-economic reality of our people." She adds, "In *En la Lucha*, I talk about Hispanic ethnicity as a social

to, therefore, is more anthropological, or in Deck's words previously cited, who uses Elizondo as an example, "[Elizondo's thought] certainly moves with the cultural, anthropological reality more than with any other, and therefore may be viewed as somewhat more 'culturalist' than 'liberationist.'"[75]

Perhaps then, judging from the presence of both the cultural and the liberation perspectives operative today in Hispanic theology, the best model or models would be both the anthropological and the praxis models. The good news is that life and theology are much more complex than models. It is with hopeful anticipation that we now look toward the future.

---

construct (I think this applies also to culture of course) and one of the key elements of Hispanic culture/ethnicity is 'poverty'" (in letter previously cited; see n. 45, above).

75. Deck, *Frontiers* (1992) xvii–xix.

5

Toward the Future

Someone once said "anything worth doing is worth doing at least halfway." One reason we fail to execute badly needed projects is the fear that we will not be able to give them adequate attention. Yet the need remains. The presence of Hispanics in the United States, for example, is hardly a new phenomenon. In fact, they are the oldest of the European groups who settled in this enormous territory. A new tide of Hispanic immigration during the second part of this century, however, has brought with it a challenge that Hispanic theologians are now trying to address. Their conviction, moreover, is that the development of Latino theology will benefit the entire Church. This study has centered on that conviction. The context and the methodology involved in the writings of Hispanic scholars during the last thirty years or so has been the focus of this work.

Given the great number of writings, especially those published during the period from 1991 to 1998, some generalizations are now possible. Of course, within these wide parameters my conclusions, especially in regard to the use of contextual models, are tentative. The models themselves, as devised by Stephen Bevans, are designed to be generally illustrative of methodology, not rigid and absolute. At this initial stage I am convinced that these paradigms, despite their limitations, are helpful in identifying methodologies and will ultimately help us to be more precise about our terminology. Before discussing these observations, a summary of what we have seen is in order.

Summary

One view that surfaced from an examination of the situation of the Latino population in the United States and Church was that of a young, nationally diverse, poor, and often undereducated people, or communities of people, who are very much in need of the Church's assistance. In many ways this is how Hispanics are often viewed in the United States. In fact, until recently sociologists quickly resorted to the urban underclass model to understand poor Hispanics.

In light of more recent socioeconomic analysis, for example, that of California sociologist David E. Hayes-Bautista and others, these communities are exhibiting in some cases a greater quality of life in regard to overall family, work, health, and community values than does mainstream culture. The application of the urban underclass model to U.S. Hispanics, therefore, is now being seriously attacked by some social scientists. The failure of this model to adequately explain Latino poverty and marginalization has prompted a search for new categories that will take into account the world of meaning, inherent standards, and beliefs, or in the words of one social worker, "entrenched family values," ones that are not so easily quantifiable.[1] This realization has opened the door to the role other intervening factors, such as religion, play in Hispanic culture.

The U.S. Bishops, in their 1987 *Pastoral Plan,* acknowledged the strength of Latino communities and described their presence in the U.S. Church as a prophetic one. Praising the culture's great sense of religion, family, and community, the hierarchy praised these values as a solution to rampant materialism and individualism. They concluded that "since the majority of Hispanics are Catholic, their presence can be a source of renewal within the Catholic Church in North America."[2]

Two current demographic trends in regard to Catholic Hispanics are simultaneously present and therefore warrant more investigation: first, there is a significant number leaving the Catholic Church, and second, by the year 2010 many estimate that they will comprise more than 50 percent of the total U.S. Catholic population. A review of the history of the Catholic Church in the United States revealed an earlier situation where the Church came to the defense of its largely European immigrant population. What remains to be seen is whether it will do so again in the case of poor Latinos in the United States or new immigrants of the "second wave." In the 1990s Los Angeles Cardinal Roger Mahoney's explicit stance against Proposition 187 in California, a law designed to seriously curtail social services to immigrants, was a step in the right direction.

---

1. *New York Times,* September 11, 1995, "Hispanic Gang Members Keep Strong Family Ties," by Seth Mydans.
2. National Conference of Catholic Bishops, "Pastoral Plan" (1987) no. 5.

The next task was to examine the writings of specific Latino and Latina theologians, eight Catholic and six Protestant, covering the period from 1972 to 1998. This survey rendered a picture of what is now being called U.S. Hispanic or Latino theology. Several building blocks of this distinctive theology are now discernible. Among the major accomplishments in this period is a much more precise description of the subject, Latinos in the United States church, and of the wider theological context, a post-Vatican II resurgence of contextual theology in the modern world. These Latino theologians are attempting to integrate theory and practice, though they employ various notions of praxis. Another development is an increasing acknowledgement of the theological method operative in each of their works. Popular religiosity is receiving more careful treatment, as some are describing it as a primary indicator of the *sensus fidelium* and one of the least invaded manifestations of Hispanic culture.

Also noteworthy is the birth of a Latina feminist theology, sometimes called *"mujerista* theology." Different from North American feminist theology, it is more conscious of the role socioeconomic factors play in the oppression of women. Its liberative praxis is engaging creative methodologies to help surface the voice of women, especially those whose lived experience embodies gospel values.

The contributions of these Latina theologians extend beyond national borders. María Pilar Aquino, who chooses not to call herself a *mujerista,* was the first to systematically compile Latin American theological thought developed from the perspective of women. Similarly, Ada María Isasi-Díaz has breached racial barriers by dialoguing extensively with African American Womanists. In describing the emergence of contextual theology, the role of perspective has been highlighted as the social sciences have helped reveal how sacred Scripture and tradition were formed within particular contexts. More precise knowledge of these historical and philosophical contexts, particularly how they betray certain biases, is seen as crucial. The formulation of a theology from the perspective of an oppressed group, moreover, helps to guarantee broader horizons. The Hispanic theologians' interests go far beyond a translation of the Christian message for Latinas and Latinos; they ask how they can contribute to building up the kingdom.

Thus there is a strong prophetic tone in much of what they have written. This tone signals a move beyond mere adaptation. It dynamically brings into creative tension gospel values, Church, and culture. There is the growing sense that there are some genuinely Christian values in Hispanic culture previously ignored, which are God's gift not only to the rest of the Church but to society. Within the context of a local church, that of the United States, Latino culture is a window on a global reality markedly different from life in the First World. The many parallels between local theology in Asia or Latin America and that which is emerging in the United States are striking. What immediately comes to mind are the dramatic shifts from traditional to modern societies all within a few years. What important Christian values are being lost in often chaotic transitions?

It is partly because of the writings of these Hispanic theologians that we can now begin to understand some of the dynamics of these cultural shifts and how these changes affect our "God-talk."[3] The theologians are demonstrating why a clear understanding and sensitivity to any given culture is essential, not only for our pastoral work but also because it challenges and critiques our own growth as human beings.

A key element in the formation of a contextual theology was the Second Vatican Council's attentiveness to culture. This historic gathering of bishops, the most "ecumenical," that is, the most internationally representative the Church had ever sponsored, signaled a new era for Christianity in the modern world.[4] Theological developments after the council bear the distinctive mark of a greater contextualization as demonstrated by the inclusion of social, economic, and political concerns in our theologizing. In addition, the shift of attention to the human person in theological method yielded a fresh awareness of experience as a valid and necessary source for theological reflection.

Other significant developments after the council included a greater integration of sacred Scripture and tradition. This wholeness manifests itself in a view of tradition as being the divine force behind the formulation of Scripture and, at the same time, as the history of the impact of that Scripture on humankind. The renewed emphasis given to the human as a manifestation of the divine, therefore, provides great hope for the integration of both. In fact, this underscoring is a reflection of the mystery of the incarnation.

Such an integrated approach to the human and the divine in theological method generated a renewed interest in process, or methodology. Among the most recent scholars to synthesize the current status of contextual theology is Stephen B. Bevans. His models provide a way of analyzing the *modus operandi* animating various projects of contextualization. These models, together with some insights from other theologians, provided an analytical apparatus for studying the writings of

3. See G. Gutiérrez, *On Job* (1987). In this work Gutiérrez refers to theology as discussion about God.

4. Rahner, "Fundamental Interpretation of Vatican II" (1980) 323–34. For an illustration of how this universalization of the Church was also taking place outside the Roman Catholic Church, see J. L. González, *Christian Thought Revisited* (1989) 141–3.

eight among the Hispanic theologians. By categorizing these eight thinkers according to Bevans' models, that is, by providing a common frame of reference, several strands became more obvious. The need for common terminology remains. For instance, words such as "praxis" and "anthropology" take on different meanings in these writings. At the same time, a more sophisticated vocabulary should be and is being developed as the dialogue continues.

On the other hand, my use of Bevans' models did not go uncriticized by several of the theologians whose work I studied. As I mentioned earlier, several of them felt that their method could not be easily categorized according to Bevans' schema. Some preferred that comparisons be made among the various Hispanic theologians' work, not to models formulated by a non-Hispanic. Moreover, some did not favor my designation of their work as "contextual theology," asking if "we do not have a right to name our own work."

Nevertheless, I maintain that given his usage, Bevans' label, which highlights perspective, is applicable. I am convinced that Bevans' models are useful at this pioneering phase of Latina and Latino theology because he engages theologians within and outside of the U.S. milieu. The nature of this comparative task, dealing as it does with the confluence of U.S. and Latin American culture, is moreover intercultural and therefore lends itself to such an analysis.

Having said this, I now realize how complex the methodologies of the various persons I studied are. In addition, we should not overlook Clifford Geertz' insight that models not only demonstrate what is (reality) but also help shape our view or perception of it, hence the need for Latino models.[5] Just as the urban underclass model is proving to be inadequate in reference to Latinos, Bevans' models may need to be revisited.[6]

Ada María Isasi-Díaz suggested other possible ways of proceeding to me, for example, critiquing his models in light of U. S. Hispanic theology, noting what Latinas and Latino theologians can contribute to them. Another valuable recommendation of hers was that I demonstrate the U. S. Hispanic theologians' contribution to the ongoing discussion of local and contextual theology, or analogical method. To a

5. Geertz, *Interpretation of Cultures*, 93, 123.

6. Vidal, in attempting to situate Hispanic popular religiosity within Avery Dulles' *Models of the Church* (1974), similarly found them inadequate. He writes, "I am not sure if our *religiosidad popular* fits comfortably into *any* of Dulles' models; it may be a very modified hybrid of the 'Church as sacrament' and 'Church as mystical communion.' But it certainly is too independent of the clergy to fit the institutional model, and too centered on the Sacred to fit the servant model" (Vidal, "Understanding of Synthesis" [1994] 83–4).

certain extent I feel that I have initiated the latter. Tackling the first remains a possibility for the future.

We should not overlook the fact that models point to realities that "are and are not," to use Sallie McFague's expression.[7] Time will tell whether Bevans' models appropriately describe what is going on in contextual theology today. Similarly, perhaps the number of these categories may increase or decrease as a clearer delineation surfaces. Bevans' aim was to get a discussion going, and that he has certainly achieved!

A meeting held in New York in the summer of 1995 between members of ACHTUS and BCTS (Black Catholic Theological Symposium) revealed many similarities in their theologizing. For instance, as evidenced by a concern for current cultural, racial, and class oppression, there is a common inspiration in Latin American liberation theology. In addition, both are turning to *la base* (the grass-roots folk culture) for exploring the epistemology of suffering. And finally, both have the vivid sense that these theologies have as their goal the betterment of the whole Church, not simply one ethnic group.[8]

Differences between the two groups also emerged and have to do with the sources for doing theology. A key divergence is seen also in the prominent role Protestants have played in the formation of U.S. Black theology.[9] The encounter between the two groups proved to be a great blessing. After all, the search for identity in an environment of plurality is a transforming process. In the words of Alejandro García-Rivera, who was present at the meeting, "If we have trouble with our own identity, then we cannot cross over to that of others. On the other hand, it is by crossing boundaries that we come to know ourselves."

Some Growing Edges

Most of this study has been devoted to discussing the emergence, contents, and methodology of U.S. Hispanic theology. By way of con-

---

7. McFague, *Metaphorical Theology*, 74–5.

8. See the February 1996 issue (vol. 3, no. 3) of the *Journal of Hispanic Latino Theology*, which contains articles based on the presentations given at this meeting of ACHTUS and the Black Catholic Theological Symposium in Douglaston, N.Y., June 12–13, 1995. The contributors are M. Shawn Copeland, Roberto S. Goizueta, Ana María Pineda, and Jamie T. Phelps.

9. See G. S. Wilmore and J. H. Cone, eds. *Black Theology: A Documentary History, 1966–1979* (Maryknoll, N.Y.: Orbis Books, 1979); Cyprian Davis, *The History of Black Catholics in the United States,* (New York: Crossroad, 1990). As I have demonstrated, Latino Protestants are quickly making their contribution in their increasing number of publications. I am sure that Latina Protestants will soon start putting out major works, given that several are now finishing doctorates in theology.

clusion, I wish to make some remarks regarding this theology's future direction. As with any human endeavor, it has its blind spots, or lacunae. What might some of these be? If in fact Latino theology is praxis-based, in this case in the lived experience of Hispanics, given its complexity there may be some aspects of this experience that have been ignored in the writings.

One of the most serious omissions, or near omissions, is the lack of serious thought given to the situation of Latino youth, particularly how they figure into our theologizing.[10] The sociological consequences of having a population whose average age is about seven years younger than the general one are enormous. This gap will only become wider in the future as many Hispanic females reach childbearing age. What does the phrase "Hispanic traditions" mean when the primary socializer is the mass media and not the *abuelita,* as some Hispanic theologians would have us think? The impact of the media is not to be underestimated. Living in a world where the cartoon character Bart Simpson is more well known than the Hispanic legend of *La Llorona,* Latino youth today live in an environment where the media, not oral tradition, is one of the primary, if not *the* primary socializer.[11] Given that socialization, how comfortable will they be at a Sunday liturgy, for example, that is in Spanish and geared to a large group of immigrants? Even language can quickly become a barrier within just two generations.

10. A ray of hope in this area is two volumes issued in Spanish and English on Hispanic youth under the general editorship of Carmen María Cervantes (Prophets of Hope Pastoral Team, *Hispanic Young People and the Church's Pastoral Response,* Prophets of Hope, vol. 1, and vol. 2, *Evangelization of Hispanic Young People* [Winona, Minn.: Saint Mary's Press, 1994]). Coming from a pastoral perspective, they provide a general view of current Hispanic youth ministry in the United States as well as present concrete methods and strategies for future evangelization. The editorial team, in explicitating some of the lights and shadows of Hispanic culture, have demonstrated their familiarity with the reality they are writing about. Moreover, their inclusion of the role of Mary and popular religion as a means of evangelization is noteworthy. One deficiency, however, is the lack of attention given to more assimilated U.S. Hispanics, if, in fact, the book is about ministry to youth and young adult Hispanics in the United States. Perhaps this oversight stems from the fact that most Hispanic youth groups in the country are made up of recent immigrants. In making such statements as "only a small number of Hispanic young people enter universities" (p. 222 of vol. 2 in English), once again, the existence of the middle class is overlooked. I doubt that this statement is accurate in speaking of the southwestern part of the country.

11. I am not saying that Hispanic elders, such as child caretakers, still do not play a role in their formation. With the advent of more mothers working out of the home, immigrant women often are the ones who care for their children, thereby passing on certain values and traditions. I merely wish to point out the media's prominent role in children's socialization process.

Furthermore, our cities are full of youths facing terrible violence, often related to gangs, inferior education, unemployment, and drug addiction. As previously stated, a recent study by the United Nations Children's Fund found the murder rate for young people in the United States to be the highest in the industrialized world.[12] The question of Latino youth's cultural identity given their position between two very different worlds, the Anglo-American and the Latin American, is one these Latino theologians have surfaced, much to their credit, but much remains to be explored. Might the children of recent immigrants, for example, be the new *mestizos*, especially because they are often marginalized by both earlier immigrant generations and mainstream U.S. culture?[13]

In many ways this generation is the product of two cultures and, therefore, has the potential to be important bridges between them, as when young children are called upon to translate between their school teachers and their immigrant parents.[14] What remains to be done in our theologizing, at least from a praxis perspective, is further reflection on how our speculations are affected and can affect this situation, since we believe that Jesus is the way, the truth, and the life.[15]

---

12. *San Francisco Chronicle,* September 23, 1993.

13. Shreiter's discussion of "hybridity" and "third cultures" is applicable here (see Schreiter, *New Catholicity* [1997]).

14. Another way of viewing these children caught between two very different cultures is to see them as "culture brokers" or "marginal people." Although he is referring to the children of foreign missionaries, Paul G. Hiebert's term is applicable here. He describes their situation and their potential contribution: "Culture brokers are often lonely because they are caught between two worlds. The people in each world have only vague and often strange notions about one another. Moreover, each group expects the culture broker to be loyal to its interests and becomes suspicious when the missionary sides with the other. For example, many missionaries have been unable to convince Americans that much of other cultures in the world is good, or to persuade the people among whom they work that not everyone in the West is fantastically wealthy (p. 229). On page 230 he writes, "Marginal people have a significant contribution to make to any group. In a sense they are prophets who speak from outside. Missionaries, for example, represent the worldwide fellowship of the church. They make visible the ties of the local church to the church in other parts of the world. They also provide the broad perspective and critique that can help a young church struggle with its identity within a non-Christian setting" (see Hiebert, *Anthropological Insights for Missionaries*).

15. Of course, some of what I am suggesting might be taken to belong more to the area of pastoral theology. But if my understanding is correct, part of the project of U.S. Hispanic theologians who claim to use a praxis methodology is to bring the fields of dogmatic and pastoral theology more into dialogue. A discussion with José de León a few years ago helped me to appreciate more this need for their integration. He pointed out that much of the material written by Hispanic theologians

The material for theologizing from the perspective of youth is not difficult to find. Why is it, for example, that despite the violence displayed among Hispanic gangs in Los Angeles, family ties, even once the person is in prison, remain strong?[16] In that subculture, for instance, shooting a rival gang member is not allowed if that young male is in the presence of his mother. As Seth Mydans concludes, "In the struggle between the home and the streets, the mothers—and the girlfriends—wage a fierce battle."[17] How might this positive family value counteract the forces of death? What kind of moral discourse has to take place here? Or put theologically, what do these Latinas and Latinos reveal about a God who defies death against seemingly invincible odds?

Understanding this reality is crucial for theologians' "God-talk" today. If not, they will be working out of the fallacy that culture and religion are static realities that are passed down unaltered to later generations. This romantic notion, which is heavily folkloristic in tone, ignores the dynamics of culture. Almost all cultures in the world undergo continuing social change. Among the most visible is the world trend toward urbanization. Schreiter writes, "The median age of the Third World population is less than twenty. These two factors of urbanization and youthful population indicate that much of that traditional religion and culture is being forgotten or not even learned."[18] The importance of these trends to the young U.S. Hispanic population is obvious.

Another example of a reality that is quickly changing is the role of Latinas. Other responsibilities, such as being one of the primary breadwinners, if not the *only* breadwinner, are being added to their many traditional roles as the primary caregiver, especially as daughter, wife, and mother. What does theology say about struggles against *machismo*

---

had been somewhat defensive or apologetic, in the sense that they have tried to explain the Hispanic reality to non-Hispanics in the Church. One of the effects of that stance is that they have tended to stress the positive over the negative in the culture. His position was that we have to quit apologizing for who we are and start examining what is happening with our own people. Among the most serious problems today is the breakdown of the family. In their writings Latino theologians have had to be more descriptive (because, to a large extent, their audience has been non-Hispanic). While he feels this descriptive stage has been a valuable one, he maintains that it is now time to move into a more analytical mode. I agree and see this trend actually taking place.

16. Gahisi Sowande, a Black man who has been in prison for almost twenty years, had this to say about the loyalty of Hispanic family members: "What I notice about the Mexican prisoners is that no matter if they are in prison for a year or 20 years, their family unit is going to close ranks around them and visit them no matter what" (*New York Times*, September 11, 1995).

17. Ibid.

18. Schreiter, *New Catholicity* (1997) 13.

and/or the woman as martyr, especially in situations where she is destroying herself? The question of how to pass on the religious values of traditional Hispanic culture is a real one, especially in an environment that is indifferent, if not hostile, to them.

The gradual emergence of the Latino middle class, often the place where traditional values are challenged cannot be overlooked here. Latina theologians will continue to add much depth as they formulate and enhance a theological perspective that acknowledges the important role of that gender, which is probably the culture's most important religious socializer.

Another example of what might be an unconsciously static view of culture is the lack of serious attention devoted to the situation of the middle class. Is it taken for granted that it is now assimilated and therefore part of the general U.S. culture, perhaps a "minority" no longer?

A few years ago at a meeting of Hispanic seminarians in California, I was surprised to discover that the majority of these seminarians had not been born in the United States. "What about second- and third-generation Hispanics," I asked myself. Why are there so few Hispanic priests today in comparison with Hispanics in other professions? In many places, Hispanic pastoral agents tend to be immigrants, not those who are native born.

If about 25 percent of Hispanics live under the poverty level, then that means that 75 percent are at least middle class. Yet our pastoral vision has tended to ignore this group, which in many ways seems to be drifting away from the Catholic Church. Indeed, many middle-class Hispanics no longer feel welcome in a Church that is either tailored to "Anglos" (i.e., non-Hispanics) or to recently arrived immigrants.

Another Hispanic group that has not been adequately attended to is composed of immigrants who have no intention of staying in the United States; rather, they intend to return to Latin America after a period of work. The early U.S. European immigrant Church model does not apply here because the intention is not to seek permanent residency. Recent efforts by both the U.S. and the Mexican bishops to collaborate on the catechesis of a large border region in the Southwest could prove to be quite valuable, especially for this transitory population.[19]

The arts comprise another field that has not been explored a great deal by Hispanic theologians. Several of their African American counterparts have mined this great resource, especially in the form of the

19. See *Sin Fronteras: Lineamientos para una Catequesis Evangelizadora*, Comité Episcopal de Baja y Alta California, Sonora y Arizona (México: Librería Parroquial de Clavería, 1993).

novel. Dwight N. Hopkins describes the contribution of one Black writer:

> In Toni Morrison's novels poor black women's spirituality—an immortal, thus divine, spirit of liberation incarnated in poor African American women's values and traditions—teaches a constructive black theology of liberation that God is a holistic divinity, whose power of liberation manifests throughout the African American church and community. God's power of loving the poor through justice and freedom knows no boundaries. Consequently, a black theology of liberation must open its heart and mind, ears and eyes to wider resources in the total African American spiritual experience. The novels of Toni Morrison, then, provide one source for broadening our openness to God's spiritual involvement in human affairs.[20]

African American theologians have not overlooked this rich source for "God-talk."[21]

Given the recent harvest of popular Hispanic novels as well as several films, it is surprising not to see some treatment of the religious themes inevitably raised in them. Another artistic source, sayings and stories *(dichos y cuentos)*, is found in Latino folk culture. Hopkins, using the Black American experience, suggests a vast array of religious wisdom and where it may be found.

> Like a natural spring in the rich soil of the Black Belt South, theology in African American folk culture gushes forth in all directions. Waters of self-identity and self-affirmation spew out and blanket the black earth. Poetry, plays, work songs, folk tales, blues, short stories, autobiographies, sermons, toasts, ballads, personal narratives, and protest literature blossom. Here, showered with "a wealth of colorful, distinctive material," a poor people name and claim themselves with the flowers of new definitions and positive assertions.[22]

U.S. Hispanic theology has also been sounding such notes of self-affirmation and appreciation of how God has been present in Latino culture over the centuries.

---

20. Hopkins, *Shoes That Fit Our Feet*, 82.
21. Ismael García's book, *Dignidad*, which uses the film *Mi Familia* as a case study, is a fine example of the kind of art works involving Latinos that can provide sources for theologizing.
22. Hopkins, *Shoes That Fit Our Feet*, 84.

In the field of visual art, murals, especially those springing up in poor Hispanic neighborhoods, provide much from which to theologize. Church architecture and music, in the case of this population whose past was heavily influenced by the baroque as well as by strong religious elements in Indian and African religions, are other topics not yet being addressed. A comparison of themes in older liturgical hymns with those of the music being sung today, for example, would make a useful study.

Some have commented that the work of U.S. Hispanic theologians is overly represented in the insertion model and that it therefore lacks theoretical depth. There are numerous philosophical, anthropological, and psychological realities behind their theologizing, which only now are beginning to be explored. Aquino, Goizueta, Villafañe, García, Espín, and García-Rivera are addressing this dearth. This academic profundity is necessary not only for self-criticism but also for furthering dialogue with other branches of theology as well as with the human sciences. The recent increase in the number of trained Hispanic theologians, both men and women, will contribute much to this exchange.

Another factor strongly influencing the development of Latino theology is the number of lay theologians. Indeed, part of the whole explosion of modern theology is a direct result of the inclusion of this group, which makes up the majority of the Church. Their perspective, according to some, reveals a distinctive difference.[23]

One of the questions that U.S. Hispanic theology is facing is whether it will continue to reflect on living communities, as its theologians claim, or whether it will become more and more abstract.[24] The areas

23. John C. Haughey, S.J., discusses this difference. "If social location means anything, it means that theologians theologize within their situations. Consequently, lay Catholics tend to approach theology from a different angle of vision than their clerical counterparts since the laity's social location gives its members a different relationship to the Church and the world than their clergy colleagues. The vocation of the laity is very much in the world of the temporal order, as Church documents like to call it. Furthermore, lay theologians will speak for themselves and not for or as the Church. Experiencing church in a different way than clergy do, lay theologians are likely to claim more from experience than the clergy who are held to more of the discipline required for those whose training has them act in the name of the Church" ("Theology and the Mission" [1994] 7).

24. In "Directions and Foundations of Hispanic/Latino Theology: Toward a *Mestiza* Theology of Liberation," María Pilar Aquino, in referring to the relationship between theology and pastoral action, writes: "In my view, the basic concern is not so much how we address the methodological relation between theology and pastoral ministry, but rather how each of us establishes an active relationship with concrete pastoral projects as trained theologians" (p. 20).

mentioned above—youth, women, social class, and the influence of lay theologians—reflect a desire for a fuller praxis. The same can be said about the need to develop an authentic Latino christology. Latin America's theology of liberation has struggled in the last few years to do just that. Michael L. Cook's question will also soon be asked of the U.S. Hispanic theological context: "Does the actual state of Christology in Latin America show it to be truly different from Western progressive theology or is it too dependent on European theology and method?"[25] Cook is concerned that liberation theologians have not produced results comparable with their methodological claims in the christologies so far constructed. To attempt to speak for those "who have no voice in history" is not an easy matter. Once again, the question remains, to what extent will Latino theologians remain rooted in the experience of living communities? Samuel Solivan's criticism of the mainline churches for their lack of existential link to the poor is quite pertinent here.

One of the signs that Hispanic theologians have kept their ear close to the ground is the emphasis now being given to popular religiosity. The methodologies being suggested by the work of Espín and Goizueta are providing a good foundation for future work in this key area. It is encouraging to see such writers as Jeanette Rodríguez now addressing the role of Mary in the Hispanic community.[26] I hope some significant studies on the role of saints in Latino spirituality will be undertaken. Alejandro García Rivera's work on San Martín de Porres will certainly expand this horizon.[27] Latino Protestants are demonstrating that their communities also draw from the rich spirituality found in popular religiosity. The works of Recinos, Villafañe, and Solivan exhibit such a "grass-roots feel."

Some consideration should be given to applying the type of methodology Don S. Browning describes as "strategic practical theology"[28] to

---

25. Cook, "Jesus From the Other Side of History," 258–87. Cook adds on the same page (267), "To put it another way, are the Christologies that have been produced so far truly reinterpretations in the light of historical praxis or are they merely applications of traditional theology to the Latin American situation?"

26. J. Rodríguez, *Our Lady of Guadalupe* (1994).

27. García-Rivera, *St. Martín de Porres* (1995).

28. Browning, *Fundamental Practical Theology*, 55. "I use the phrase strategic practical theology to convey the complex, multidimensional character of this movement of theology. This is where ministers and lay persons who think about the practical life of the church really function. Here they make incredibly complex judgments of the most remarkable kind. If they are good political thinkers, the richness and virtuosity of their work can contribute greatly to both the life of the church and the common good beyond it. Such persons are worth studying, understanding, and emulating."

the Hispanic reality in the United States. Certain exemplary Hispanic ministries, such as key parishes, youth ministries, vibrant movements, and theological training centers, could provide crucial insights not only to pastoral theology but also to a praxis methodology. Worthy of mention is Gary Riebe-Estrella's recent study of Latinos in Catholic seminary formation.[29] Recinos' and Solivan's descriptions of certain faith communities could be taken as recipes for the type of church growth that needs to take place if the Church is to remain credible.

Another topic worth exploring, given the significant exodus of Hispanic Catholics from the Church in the last twenty-five years or so, is a systematic comparison between Catholic and Protestant, especially fundamentalistic, methods of evangelization. Many have commented that the key to the success of these groups is a closer adherence to methods of inculturation than those practiced by the Catholic Church in the United States, for example, in terms of language, music, and small-community orientation. Some theologians are now suggesting, for example, that there exists a strong parallel between Hispanic popular Catholicism and evangelical/Pentecostal Christianity.[30] The fact that Latino Protestants and Catholics are starting to read each other's works is one of the reasons for being hopeful about what some are calling a "new ecumenism."[31]

A final point worth mentioning is U.S. Hispanic theology's need to stay in dialogue with other contextual theologies, especially liberation theologies now being put forth from different perspectives and which, until recently, had gone unacknowledged. Whether coming from African Americans, Native Americans, Asian Americans, Latinas or Latinos, or more recently, from gay and lesbian persons, there is a need to tell one's own story.[32] This "drinking from our own

---

29. G. Riebe-Estrella, "Formación" (1992).

30. See Deck, "Challenge of Evangelical/Pentecostal Christianity to Hispanic Catholicism," *Hispanic Catholic Culture,* ed. Dolan and Deck (1994) 409–39; Roberto O. González, "The New Evangelization of Hispanics in the United States," *America* (October 19, 1991).

31. See the section entitled "A New Ecumenism," in J. L. Gonzalez' *Mañana* (1990) 73–4.

32. T. E. Clarke, in *Tracing the Spirit: Communities, Social Action, and Theological Reflection,* ed. James E. Hug (Mahwah, N.J.: Paulist Press, 1983) 18–50. Clarke writes, "To be deprived of one's story is the most ruthless form of oppression. Individuals, groups, peoples who society through racism, sexism, classism has denied ownership of a distinctive story will inevitably be tempted to despair of themselves" (as quoted in J. J. McNeill, *Taking a Chance on God: Liberating Theology for Gays, Lesbians, and their Lovers, Families, and Friends* (Boston: Beacon Press, 1988) 202–3. As noted in the title, McNeill applies aspects of liberation theology to the situation of gays and lesbians. For an understanding of Black Womanist theology, see the following: D. S.

well"[33] not only affirms the goodness of God's creation in all its manifestations but also contributes to the good of all, for the wells are not ours to hoard. The poor and the marginalized have an important role to fulfill, that of pointing to God's transcendence:

> The privileged position of the poor does not derive from their personal morality but from their socio-historical location outside the dominant power structures of our societies. Since, as "other" to those systems, the poor cannot be comprehended by or reduced to those systems. Like the crucified Jesus, the poor stand as the guarantee of God's transcendence. The preferential option for the poor tells us nothing about the moral quality of the poor themselves; rather, it tells us something about God.[34]

And the faces of God are many.

As I reflect on the current direction of some of these contextual theologies, I detect a growing awareness of God's grace in the history of human suffering. Earlier writings from the perspective of minority groups seem to have focused more on the dominant groups' sin of oppression.[35] Yet that is not the only reality. How is it that despite the im-

---

Williams, *Sisters in the Wilderness* (Maryknoll, N.Y.: Orbis Books, 1993); D. L. Hayes, "To Be Black, Catholic, and Female," *New Theology Review* 6, no. 2 (May 1993) 55–62; *And Still We Rise: An Introduction to Black Liberation Theology* (Mahwah, N.J.: Paulist Press, 1996); Jamie Phelps, "Providence and Histories: African American Perspectives with Emphasis on the Perspective of Black Liberation Theology," *CTSA Proceedings* 44 (1989) 12–18; "Joy Came in the Morning, Risking Death for Resurrection: Confronting the Evil of Social Sin and Socially Sinful Structures," *A Troubling in My Soul*, ed. E. Townes (Maryknoll, N.Y.: Orbis Books, 1993) 48–64; "Black Spirituality," *Spiritual Traditions of the Contemporary Church*, ed. R. Maas and G. O'Donnell (Nashville: Abingdon Press, 1990); S. Copeland, "African American Catholics and Black Theology: An Interpretation," *African American Religious Studies*, ed. G. Wilmore (Durham: Duke Univ. Press, 1989) 228–48; S. Copeland, "Wading Through Many Sorrows: Toward a Theology of Suffering in Womanist Perspective," *A Troubling in My Soul*, 109–29. For theology from an Asian perspective, see C. S. Song, *Third-Eye Theology: Theology in Formation in Asian Settings* (Maryknoll, N.Y.: Orbis Books, 1979), also his *Theology from the Womb of Asia* (Maryknoll, N.Y.: Orbis Books, 1986). Two articles about Native American (North and South) theology are C. S. Starkloff, "Religious Renewal in Native North America: The Contemporary Call to Mission," *Missiology: An International Review* 13, no. 1 (January 1985) 81–101; Judd, "From Lamentation to Project," 226–35. See also A. Peelman, *Christ Is a Native American* (Maryknoll, N.Y.: Orbis Books, 1995).

33. McNeill refers to Gustavo Gutierrez' appropriation of St. Bernard of Clairvaux's phrase (McNeill, *Taking a Chance on God*, 202 [see n. 33, above]).

34. Goizueta, "Church and Hispanics in the United States" (1991) 165.

35. In the case of the pioneers of Black theology, see Cummings, "Black Theology," 215–29.

mense burdens the poor and marginal groups have had to bear, they have been able to carry on in hope? Whether spoken of in terms of the "Hispanic epistemology of suffering,"[36] or "years of cross bearing,"[37] or of "structures that sustain hope and resistance,"[38] or the living memory of *"pueblos testigos,"*[39] or *"la lucha,"*[40] this empowering grace, as revealed through a community, is the same.[41]

Conclusion

The question is as old as theology: "Where is God in all this?" I pondered this theme as I watched the news clips of the 1992 riots in Los Angeles on television. The sight of a weeping Mexican mother, the presence of a large crucifix over the casket of her son who was killed in the rioting, and the familiar brown faces gathered round to mourn this terrible loss, made me wonder what on earth I would say had I been asked to preach at this funeral.

I am convinced that contact with the Hispanic presence in the United States is bearing and will continue to bear great fruit for the kingdom. Amidst great suffering, a spirit, a hope, live on. God is alive and well among these hurting people. It is these very Hispanic theologians who are now in a position to proclaim just that.

It is as though your *abuelita* once told you an awesome secret when you were a child, and now, years later as an adult, you long to share that secret, that touch of the sacred, we might say, with others. You hesitate at first, thinking, "What if it's just the mumbling of a pious *viejita?* Poor Grandma, what did she know about such an abstract thing as theology? She never even had a chance to go to school." But gradually as you speak, you realize that there was more to her presence, her palpable relationship with a God who is no stranger to suffering, than you ever imagined. As you begin to speak, you see that her living word possessed a power all of its own. And proclaiming this good news to a hungry world in a tangible way is what being a *cristiano* is all about.

36. Espín, "Popular Religion as an Epistemology of Suffering" (1994).

37. Hopkins, *Shoes That Fit Our Feet*, 46.

38. Cummings, "Black Theology," 225.

39. Judd, "From Lamentation to Project," 228.

40. Isasi-Díaz, *En la Lucha* (1993).

41. This enabling presence of the Spirit is one of the major themes in Solivan's *Spirit, Pathos, and Liberation*.

Bibliography

Basic Sources and Ecclesial Documents

Abbott, Walter M., ed. *The Documents of Vatican II.* New York: Guild Press, 1966.

Congregation for the Doctrine of the Faith. *De libertate christiana et liberatione. Enchiridion Vaticanum* 10. Bologna: EDB, 1987.

Congregation for the Doctrine of the Faith. *De quibusdam rationibus "theologiae liberationis." Enchiridion Vaticanum* 9. Bologna: EDB, 1985.

"Documents of Medellín." *The Church in the Present-Day Transformation of Latin America in the Light of the Council.* 2 vols. Washington, D.C.: United States Catholic Conference, Division for Latin America, 1973.

National Conference of Catholic Bishops. *Los Obispos Hablan con la Virgen: Carta Pastoral de los Obispos Hispanos de los Estados Unidos.* Maryknoll, N.Y.: Revista Maryknoll, 1981.

_____. "The Hispanic Presence: Challenge and Commitment." Washington, D.C.: United States Catholic Conference, 1984.

_____. "National Pastoral Plan for Hispanic Ministry." *Origins* 26 (December 10, 1987).

_____. *To The Ends of the Earth: A Pastoral Statement on World Mission by the Catholic Bishops of the United States.* New York: The Society for the Propagation of the Faith, 1987.

Neuner, J., and J. Dupuis. *The Christian Faith in the Documents of the Catholic Church.* Rev. ed. London: Collins Liturgical Publications, 1983.

Pope John Paul II. *Redemptoris Missio.* Washington, D.C.: United States Catholic Conference, 1991.

Pope Paul VI. *Evangeli Nuntiandi. New Directions in Mission and Evangelization 1: Basic Documents 1974–1991.* Ed. James A. Scherer and Stephen B. Bevans. Maryknoll, N.Y.: Orbis Books, 1992.

"The Puebla Final Document," *Puebla and Beyond.* Ed. John Eagleson and Philip Scharper. Maryknoll, N.Y.: Orbis Books, 1979.

"The Santo Domingo Final Document." *Santo Domingo and Beyond: Documents and Commentaries from the Historic Meeting of the Latin American Bishops Conference.* Ed. Alfred T. Hennelly. Maryknoll, N.Y.: Orbis Books, 1994.

May, Herbert G., and Bruce M. Metzger, eds. *The New Oxford Annotated Bible with the Apocrypha, Revised Standard Version.* New York: Oxford Univ. Press, 1977.

Bibliography by Authors

Abalos, David T. *Latinos in the United States: The Sacred and the Political.* Ind.: Notre Dame, 1986.

Abesamis, Carlos H. *Exploring the Core of Biblical Faith: A Catechetical Primer.* Quezon City, Philippines: Claretian Publications, 1986.

Acuña, Rodolfo. *Occupied America: A History of Chicanos.* New York: Harper-Collins, 1988.

Amaladoss, Michael. *Making All Things New: Dialogue, Pluralism, and Evangelization in Asia.* Maryknoll, N.Y.: Orbis Books, 1990.

Aquino, María Pilar. "Presencia de la mujer en la tradición profética." *Servir* 88–9 (1980) 535–58. Mexico.

_____. "El culto a María y María en el culto." *FEM Publicación Feminista* 5, no. 20 (1981–2) 41–6. Mexico.

_____. *Aportes para una Teología desde la mujer.* Madrid: Edición Biblia y Fe, 1988.

_____. "Women's Participation in the Church: A Catholic Perspective." *With Passion and Compassion: Third World Women Doing Theology.* Ed. V. Fabella and M. A. Oduyoye, 159–64. New York: Orbis Books, 1988.

_____. "Bienaventurados los perseguidos por causa de la justicia y los que buscan la paz." *Sal Terrae, Revista de Teología Pastoral* (December 12, 1989) 895–907. Santander.

_____. "Entrevista." *Las mujeres toman la palabra.* Ed. E. Tamez, 13–21. San José, Costa Rica: Ed. DEI, 1989.

_____. "¿Qué es hacer teología desde la perspectiva de la mujer?" *Iglesia y derechos humanos, IX Congreso de Teología.* Madrid: Asociación de Teólogos. Juan XXIII, 1989.

_____. "'Sin contar a las mujeres' toca su fin. La contribución de la mujer a la teología." *La situación de la mujer en America Latina.* San José, Costa Rica: Ed. DEI, 1989.

_____. "Mujer y Praxis ministerial hoy. La respuesta del Tercer Mundo." *Biblia y Fe* 46 (1990) 116–39. Madrid.

_____. "The Challenge of Hispanic Women." Missiology 20, no. 2 (April 1992) 261–8.

_____. "Doing Theology from the Perspective of Latin American Women." *We Are a People! Initiatives in Hispanic American Theology.* Ed. Roberto Goizueta, 79–105. Minneapolis: Fortress Press, 1992.

_____. "La Mujer/Women." *Prophetic Vision: Pastoral Reflections on the National Plan for Hispanic Ministry.* Ed. Soledad Galerón and others, 142–62, 316–35. Kansas City: Sheed & Ward, 1992.

_____. "Perspectives on a Latina's Feminist Liberation Theology." *Frontiers of Hispanic Theology in the United States.* Ed. Allan Figueroa Deck, 23–40. Maryknoll, N.Y.: Orbis Books, 1992.

_____. "Directions and Foundations of Hispanic/Latino Theology: Toward a *Mestiza* Theology of Liberation." *Journal of Hispanic/Latino Theology* 1, no. 1 (November 1993) 5–21.

_____. *Our Cry for Life: Feminist Theology from Latin America.* Maryknoll, N.Y.: Orbis Books, 1993.

_____. "Santo Domingo Through the Eyes of Women." *Santo Domingo and Beyond: Documents and Commentaries from the Historic Meeting of the Latin American Bishops Conference.* Ed. Alfred T. Hennelly, 212–25. Maryknoll, N.Y.: Orbis Books, 1993.

_____. *La Teología, La Iglesia y La Mujer en América Latina.* Bogotá: Indo American Press, 1994.

Aymes, María de la Cruz. "Case-Study: Catechesis of Hispanics in the United States Today." *Effective Inculturation and Ethnicity.* Ed. Arij A. Roest Crollius, 3–28. Rome: Centre Culture and Religions—Pontifical Gregorian University, 1987.

_____. "Toward the Fulfillment of a Dream." *Faith and Culture: A Multicultural Catechetical Resource,* 65–76. Washington, D.C.: United States Catholic Conference, 1987.

Bañuelas, Arturo. "U.S. Hispanic Theology." *Missiology* 20, no. 2 (1992) 275–300.

_____, ed. *Mestizo Christianity: Theology from the Latino Perspective.* Maryknoll, N.Y.: Orbis Books, 1995.

Barron, Clemente. "On My Mind: Racism and Vocations." *New Theology Review* 3, no. 4 (November 1990) 92–103.

Baum, Gregory. "Editorial Summary." *Ethnicity.* Ed. Andrew M. Greeley and Gregory Baum, 100–2. New York: Seabury Press, 1977.

Bevans, Stephen B. "Models of Contextual Theology." *Missiology* 13, no. 2 (April 1985) 185–202.

_____. *Models of Contextual Theology.* Maryknoll, N.Y.: Orbis Books, 1992.

Bokenkotter, Thomas. *A Concise History of the Catholic Church.* New York: Doubleday, 1979.

Bolton, Herbert Eugene. *The Rim of Christendom: A Biography of Eusebio Francisco Kino, Pacific Coast Pioneer.* New York: Macmillan Company, 1936.

Bridgers, Lynn. *Death's Deceiver: The Life of Joseph P. Machebeuf.* Albuquerque: Univ. of New Mexico Press, 1997.

Browning, Don S. *A Fundamental Practical Theology: Descriptive and Strategic Proposals*. Minneapolis: Fortress Press, 1991.

Buhlmann, Walbert. *The Coming of the Third Church: An Analysis of the Present and the Future of the Church*. Trans. Robert R. Barr. Slough: St. Paul Publications, 1976.

_____. *With Eyes to See: Church and World in the Third Millennium*. Trans. Robert R. Barr. Maryknoll, N.Y.: Orbis Books, 1990.

Burgaleta, Claudio M. "Can Syncretic Christianity Save? A Proposal for a Christian Recovery of the Syncretic Elements in Latin American Popular Religiosity Based on Rahner's Concept of Anonymous Christianity." S.T.L. thesis, Jesuit School of Theology at Berkeley, 1992.

_____. *José de Acosta, S.J. (1540–1600): His Life and Thought*. Chicago: Loyola University Press, 1999.

Cadena, Gilbert A. "Chicano Clergy and the Emergence of Liberation Theology." *Hispanic Journal of Behavioral Sciences* 2, no. 2 (1989) 107–21.

_____, and A. L. Pulido. "Bibliography: Chicanos and Religion." *Syllabi and Instructional Material for Chicano and Latino Studies in Sociology*. Ed. M. Romero, 254–68. American Sociological Association, 1990.

Candelaria, Michael R. *Popular Religion and Liberation: The Dilemma of Liberation Theology*. Albany: State Univ. of New York Press, 1990.

Carrier, Herve. *Gospel Message and Human Cultures: From Leo XIII to John Paul II*. Pittsburgh: Duquesne Univ. Press, 1989.

Cather, Willa. *Death Comes for the Archbishop*. New York: Vintage Books, 1971.

Chupungco, Anscar. *Liturgies of the Future: The Process and Methods of Inculturation*. New York: Paulist Press, 1989.

_____. *Liturgical Inculturation: Sacramentals, Religiosity, and Catechesis*. Collegeville, Minn.: The Liturgical Press, 1992.

Comite Episcopal de Baja y Alta California, Sonora y Arizona. *Sin Fronteras: Lineamientos para una Catequésis Evangelizadora*. Mexico: Librería de Clavería, 1993.

Cook, Michael L. "Jesus from the Other Side of History: Christology in Latin America." *Theological Studies* 44 (June 1983) 258–87.

Cortina, Rodolfo J., and Alberto Moncada. "El Sentido de la diversidad: recientes investigaciones sobra las minorías hispanas en los Estados Unidos." *Hispanos en los Estados Unidos*. Ed. Rodolfo J. Cortina and Alberto Moncada, 31–58. Madrid: Ediciones de Cultura Hispánica, 1988.

Costas, Orlando E. *The Integrity of Mission*. San Francisco: Harper & Row, 1979.

_____. *Christ Outside the Gate*. Maryknoll, N.Y., 1982.

_____. *Liberating News: A Theology of Contextual Evangelization*. Grand Rapids: William B. Eerdmans Publishing Co., 1989.

Couture, André. "Marriage as a Rite of Passage in World Religions." *Ecumenism* 108 (December 1992) 15–21.

Cummings, George C. L. "Black Theology and Latin American Liberation Theology: A Framework for Race and Class Analysis." *New Visions for the Americas: Religious Engagement and Social Transformation.* Ed. David Batstone. Minneapolis: Fortress Press, 1993.

Davis, Kenneth G. "Father, We're Not in Kansas Anymore." *The Priest* (1990).

_____. *Cuando El Tomar Ya No Es Gozar.* Los Angeles: Franciscan Communications Press, 1993. Second rev. ed. Mexico City: Editorial DABAR, 1994.

_____. *Primero Dios.* Susquehanna, Pa.: Susquehanna Univ. Press, 1994.

_____. *Misa, Mesa y Musa.* Schiller Park, Ill: J. S. Paluch, 1997. Rev. ed. 1998.

_____, and Yolanda Tarango. *Building Bridges: Hispanic Ministry in the United States.* Scranton, Pa.: Scranton Univ. Press, 2000.

Dawson, Christopher. *Religion and the Rise of Western Culture.* New York: Doubleday Image Books, 1991.

De Aragon, Ray John. *Padre Martínez and Bishop Lamy.* Las Vegas, N.Mex.: The Pan-American Publishing Co., 1978.

Deck, Allan Figueroa. "A New Vision of a Tattered Friendship." *Grito del Sol* 4, no. 1 (1974) 87–93.

_____. *Francisco Javier Alegre: A Study of Mexican Literary Criticism.* Rome: Historical Institute S.J., 1976.

_____. "Liturgy and Mexican American Culture." *Modern Liturgy* 3, no. 7 (October 1976) 24–6.

_____. "A Christian Perspective on the Reality of Illegal Immigration." *Social Thought* (fall 1978) 39–53.

_____. "Una Perspectiva Cristiana Sobre la Imigración Ilegal." *Christus* (1979).

_____. "A Hispanic Perspective on Christian Family Life." *America* (December 19, 1981) 400–2.

_____. "El Movimiento Hispano y la Iglesia Católica de los Estados Unidos." *Christus* (March 1983) 48–50.

_____. "Vida Familiar Cristiana: Perspectivas Hispanas." *Christus* (March 1983) 44–7.

_____. "The Worldview, Values, and Religion of Mexican Immigrants in Orange Today." *Second Lives,* 71–3. Santa Ana, Calif.: South Coast Repertory Publications, 1983.

_____. "Fundamentalism and the Hispanic Catholic." *America* (January 26, 1985) 64–6.

_____. "Hispanic Ministry Comes of Age." *America* (May 17, 1986) 400–2.

_____. "Hispanic Vocations: Light at the End of the Tunnel." *Call to Growth Ministry* 11, no. 2 (winter 1986) 12–8.

_____. "Hispanic Vocations: What Happens Once You've Got Them." *The Priest* (March 1986) 18–22.

_____. "Rural Hispanic Ministry." *Rural Roots* 5, no. 1 (May/June 1986).

_____. "Ministry and Vocations: Going Back to the Drawing Board." *America* (March 14, 1987) 212–8.

_____. "Multicultural Sensitivities." *Human Development* 8, no. 2 (summer 1987) 32–4.

_____. "Proselytism and the Hispanic Catholic: How Long Can We Cry Wolf?" *America* (December 10, 1988) 485–90.

_____. "The Multicultural Seminary: Need for Kenosis." *The Priest* (January 1989) 35–9.

_____. "The Pastoral Plan, Window of Opportunity." *Origins* 19, no. 12 (August 17, 1989) 198–201.

_____. *The Second Wave: Hispanic Ministry and the Evangelization of Cultures.* Mahwah, N.J.: Paulist Press, 1989.

_____. "The Hispanic Presence: A Moment of Grace." *The Critic* 45, no. 1 (fall 1990) 48–59.

_____. "Hispanic Theologians and the United States Catholic Church." *New Theology Review* 3, no. 4 (November 1990) 22–7.

_____. "The Spirituality of the United States Hispanics: An Introductory Essay." *U.S. Catholic Historian* 9, nos. 1 and 2 (winter 1990) 137–46.

_____. "Amen!" *Church* (spring 1991) 64.

_____. "The Trashing of the Fifth Centenary." *America* (December 19, 1992) 499–501.

_____. "La Raza Cósmica: Rediscovering the Hispanic Soul." *The Critic* 37, no. 3 (spring 1993) 46–53.

_____. "Hispanic Ministry: Reasons for Our Hope." *America* (April 23, 1994) 12–5.

_____, and José Armando Nuñez. "Religious Enthusiasm and Hispanic Youth." *America* (October 23, 1982) 232–4.

_____, ed. *Frontiers of Hispanic Theology in the United States.* Maryknoll, N.Y.: Orbis Books, 1992.

de Mesa, José, and L. Wostyn. *Doing Theology: Basic Realities and Processes.* Manila: Maryhill School of Theology, 1982.

Díaz-Stevens, Ana María. *Oxcart Catholicism on Fifth Avenue: The Impact of the Puerto Rican Migration upon the Archdiocese of New York.* Notre Dame, Ind.: Univ. of Notre Dame Press, 1993.

_____, and Anthony M. Stevens-Arroyo. *Recognizing the Latino Resurgence in U.S. Religion: The Emmaus Paradigm.* Boulder Colo.: Westview Press, 1998.

Dimas Soberal, José. *La Verdad Sobre Ciertos Ministerios Falsos.* Bayamón, P.R.: Grafar Arte, 1988.

_____. *La Verdad Sobre La Ex-Monja Ilduara Pabón Agudelo.* Bayamón, P.R.: Grafar Arte, 1989.

_____. *Madres Solteras.* Bayamón, P.R.: Grafar Arte, 1989.

_____. *O Ministerio Ordenado Da Mulher.* Sao Paulo, Brazil: Ediciones Paulinas, 1990.

Dolan, Jay P. *The American Catholic Experience: A History from Colonial Times to the Present.* Garden City, N.Y.: Doubleday, 1985.

_____. "Hispanic Catholics in America." *The Encyclopedia of American Catholic History.* Ed. Michael Glazier and Thomas J. Shelley, 635–42. Collegeville, Minn.: The Liturgical Press, 1998. 635–42.

_____, and Allan Figueroa Deck, eds. *Hispanic Catholic Culture in the U.S.: Issues and Concerns.* Notre Dame, Ind.: Univ. of Notre Dame Press, 1994.

_____, and Gilberto Hinojosa, eds., *Mexican Americans and the Catholic Church, 1900–1965.* Notre Dame, Ind.: Univ. of Notre Dame Press, 1994.

_____, and Jaime R. Vidal, eds. *Puerto Rican and Cuban Catholics in the U.S., 1900–1965.* Notre Dame, Ind.: Univ. of Notre Dame Press, 1994.

Donovan, Vincent J. *Christianity Rediscovered.* Maryknoll, N.Y.: Orbis Books, 1978.

Dulles, Avery. *Models of the Church.* Garden City, N.Y.: Doubleday, 1974.

_____. *The Craft of Theology: From Symbol to System.* New York: Crossroad, 1992.

Dupuis, Jacques. *Jesus Christ at the Encounter of World Religions.* Trans. Robert R. Barr. Maryknoll, N.Y.: Orbis Books, 1991.

Durkin, Mary. "The American Experience: An Irish Catholic Perspective." *Ethnicity.* Ed. Andrew M. Greeley and Gregory Baum, 36–41. New York: Seabury Press, 1977.

Dussel, Enrique D. *Historia de la Iglesia en América Latina: Coloniaje y Liberación (1492–1973).* Barcelona: Editorial Nova Terra, 1974.

Elizondo, Virgil P. "The Mystery of Human Fulfillment." *Good Tidings* 7 (September/October) Manila, 1969.

_____. "Signi dell' Autorivelazione di Dio all' Interno Iell' di Ogni Uomo." *Nuove Prospettive.* Torino, Italy, 1969.

_____. "The Crisis of our Times." *Good Tidings* 9 (July/August) Manila, 1970.

_____. "Documento Final de la Semana Internacional de Estudios sobre Medios de Comunicación Social y Catequesis." *Catequesis Latinoamericana* 2, no. 5 (enero–marzo) México (1970) 78–88.

_____. "Toward a Definition of Pastoral Theology." *Good Tidings* 9 (January/February) Manila, 1970.

_____. "Educación religiosa para el México-Norte Americano." *Catequesis Latinoamericana* 4, no. 14 (enero–marzo) México (1972) 83–86.

_____. *Mary: Prophetess and Model of Freedom for Responsibility.* San Antonio: MACC, 1972.

_____. *Anthropological and Psychological Characteristics of the Mexican American.* San Antonio: MACC, 1974.

_____. "Biblical Pedagogy of Evangelization." *American Ecclesiastical Review* 168, no. 8 (October 1974).

_____. "A Challenge to Theology: The Situation of Hispanic Americans." *Proceedings of the Catholic Theological Society of America* 30 (1975) 163–76.

_____. *Christianity and Culture.* Ind.: Our Sunday Visitor Press, 1975.

_____. "Pastoral Planning for the Spanish Speaking in the United States." *Colección Mestiza Americana.* San Antonio: MACC, 1975.

_____. "Pentecost and Pluralism." *Momentum* (October 1975) 12–5.

_____. "Politics, Catechetics, and Liturgy." *Religion Teachers' Journal* (November/December 1976) 30–2.

_____. "The San Antonio Experiment." *New Catholic World* (May/June 1976) 117–20.

_____. *The Human Quest: A Search for Meaning Through Life and Death.* Ind.: Our Sunday Visitor Press, 1977.

_____. "La Virgen de Guadalupe como símbolo: 'El Poder de los impotentes.'" Concilium. *Ediciones Cristiandad* 22 (February 1977) 149–60.

_____. "Our Lady of Guadalupe as Cultural Symbol: The Power of the Powerless." *Liturgy and Cultural Religious Traditions.* Concilium 120 (1977).

_____. "Who Is the Catechumen in the Spanish Speaking Community of the U.S.A.?" *Becoming a Catholic Christian.* New York: Sadlier, 1977.

_____. *Mestizaje: The Dialectic of Birth and Gospel.* San Antonio: MACC, 1978.

_____. "Commentary on John Paul's Opening Address at Puebla." *Puebla and Beyond.* Maryknoll, N.Y.: Orbis Books, 1979.

_____. "Theological Education and Liberation Theology, A Symposium, Response to Frederick Herzog." *Theological Education* 16, no. 1 (autumn 1979).

_____. "Identity and Mission of Hispanic (USA) Catholics." *Origins* (1980).

_____. *La Morenita: Evangelizer of the Americas.* San Antonio: Mexican American Cultural Center, 1980.

_____. "The Gospel Mandate—Implications for the Future." *Proceedings of the National Catholic Educators Association Curriculum Conference* (1981) 18–28.

_____. "The Hispanic Church in the USA: A Local Ecclesiology." *Proceedings of the Catholic Theological Society of America* 36 (1981) 155–70.

_____. "La Teología Integrada a la Vida de la Iglesia." *Páginas* 6 (December 1981) 14–6.

_____. "Thou Shalt Not Have Strange God Before Me: A Bicultural Approach to Religious Education." *Religious Education* 76 (May/June 1981).

_____. "The Language of Resistance, Survival, and Liberation." *CEP, Theological Journal of Peru.* Lima, Peru (November 1982).

_____. "By Their Fruits You Will Know Them: The Biblical Roots of Justice and Injustice." *Readings in Social Justice Education.* Ed. Padraic O'Hara. New York: Harper & Row, 1983.

_____. "A Child in a Manger: The Beginning of a New Order of Existence." *Proclaiming the Acceptable Year: Sermons from the Perspective of Liberation Theology.* Ed. Justo Gonzáles, 61–70. Valley Forge: Judson Press, 1983.

_____. "Christian Challenge and the Disadvantaged." *Linacre Quarterly* 51 (August 1983).

_____. *Galilean Journey: The Mexican American Promise.* Maryknoll, N.Y.: Orbis Books, 1983.

_____. "Le Métissage comme lieu théologique." *Spiritus* 93 (Paris, 1983).

_____. "Mary and the Poor: A Model of Evangelizing Ecumenism." *Mary and the Churches.* Ed. H. Kung and G. Multmann. Concilium, 1983.

_____. ¿Quién Eres Tu? San Antonio: MACC, 1983.

_____. "Stages of Practical Theology." *Twenty Years of Concilium: Retrospect and Prospect.* Concilium 170 (1983).

_____. "Theological and Biblical Foundations for Comunidades de Base." *Developing Basic Christian Communities.* Chicago: Federation of Priests' Councils, 1983.

_____. *Virgen y Madre: Reflexiones bíblicas sobre María de Nazaret.* San Antonio: MACC, 1983.

_____. "Religious Education in the United States." *The Transmission of the Faith to the Next Generation.* Ed. Virgil P. Elizondo and Norbert Greinacher. Concilium 174. Edinburgh: T & T Clark, 1984.

_____. "Conditions and Criteria for Authentic Intercultural Theological Dialogue." *Different Theologies, Common Responsibilities.* Concilium 194 (1985).

_____. "Self-Affirmation of the Hispanic Church." *The Ecumenist* (March/April 1985).

_____. "I Forgive, but I Do Not Forget." *Forgiveness.* Concilium 204 (1986) 87–98.

_____. "Mary in the Struggles of the Poor." *The New Catholic World* (November/December 1986).

_____. "Popular Religion as Support of Identity: A Pastoral-Psychological Case-Study Based on the Mexican American Experience in the USA." *Popular Religion.* Concilium 186 (1986).

_____. "Response to Peter Wagner, 'A Vision for Evangelizing the Real America.'" *International Bulletin of Missionary Research* 10, no. 2 (April 1986) 65–6.

_____. "Hispanic Evangelization—A Lost Cause?" *Paulist Evangelization Association.* 1987.

_____. "The Ministry of the Church and Contemporary Migration." *Social Thought: Special Papal Edition.* Washington, D.C. 1987.

_____. "America's Changing Face." *The Tablet.* London (July 23, 1988).

_____. *The Future Is Mestizo: Life Where Cultures Meet.* New York: Meyer-Stone, 1988.

_____. "Mestizaje as Locus of Theological Reflection." *The Future of Liberation Theology.* Ed. Marc Ellis and Otto Maduro. New York: Orbis Books, 1989.

_____. "A Paradigm for Cultural Study." *Journal of Catholic Education* 6, no. 3. Melbourne, Australia (1989).

_____. "Mary and the Evangelization of the Americas." *Mary: Woman of Nazareth.* Ed. Doris Donnelly, 146–60. New York: Paulist Press, 1990.

_____. "The New Humanity of the Americas." *1492–1992: The Voice of the Victims.* Concilium. Ed. Virgil P. Elizondo and Leonardo Boff, 141–7. Philadelphia: Trinity Press, 1990.

_____. "The Voice of the Victims: Who Will Listen to Them?" *1492–1992: The Voice of the Victims.* Ed. Virgil P. Elizondo and Leonardo Boff, 141–7. Concilium. Philadelphia: Trinity Press, 1990.

_____. "Analysis of Racism." *Migrants and Refugees.* Ed. Dietmar Mieth and Lisa Sowle Cahill, 52–9. Maryknoll, N.Y.: Orbis Books, 1993.

_____. *Guadalupe: Mother of the New Creation.* Maryknoll, N.Y.: Orbis Books, 1997.

_____, and Friends. *A Retreat with Our Lady of Guadalupe and Juan Diego: Heeding the Call.* Cincinnati: St. Anthony Messenger Press, 1998.

_____, and Timothy M. Matovina. *Mestizo Worship: A Pastoral Approach to Liturgical Ministry.* Collegeville, Minn.: The Liturgical Press, 1998.

_____, and Timothy M. Matovina. *San Fernando Cathedral: Soul of the City.* Maryknoll, N.Y.: Orbis Books, 1998.

_____, and Norbert Greinacher, eds. *Women in a Man's Church.* Concilium. Edinburgh: T. & T. Clark, 1980.

_____, and Norbert Greinacher, eds. *Churches in Socialist Societies of Eastern Europe.* Edinburgh: T. & T. Clark, 1982.

_____, and Norbert Greinacher, eds. *Church and Peace.* Edinburgh: T. & T. Clark, 1983.

_____, and Leonardo Boff, eds., *Theologies of the Third World: Commonalities and Differences.* Edinburgh: T. & T. Clark, 1988.

_____, ed., with Sean Freyne. *Pilgrimage.* Concilium. Maryknoll, N.Y.: Orbis Books, 1996.

Espín, Orlando. "Religiosidad Popular: Un Aporte Para Su Definición y Hermenéutica." *Estudios Sociales* 17, no. 58 (October/December 1984) 41–56.

_____. "Iroko E Ará-kolé: Comentário Exegético A Um Iorubá-Lucumí." *Perspectica Teológica* 18, no. 44 (January/April 1986) 29–61.

_____. "The God of the Vanquished: Foundations for a Latino Spirituality." *Listening: Journal of Religion and Culture* 27, no. 1 (1992) 70–83.

_____. "Grace and Humanness: A Hispanic Perspective." *We Are a People! Initiatives in Hispanic American Theology.* Ed. Roberto Goizueta, 133–64. Minneapolis: Fortress Press, 1992.

_____. "Tradition and Popular Religion: An Understanding of the *Sensus Fidelium.*" *Frontiers of Hispanic Theology in the United States.* Ed. Allan Figueroa Deck, 62–87. Maryknoll, N.Y.: Orbis Books, 1992.

_____. "Trinitarian Monotheism and the Birth of Popular Catholicism: The Case of Sixteenth-Century Mexico." *Missiology* 20, no. 2 (April 1992) 177–204.

_____. "Popular Religion as an Epistemology (of Suffering)." *Journal of Hispanic/Latino Theology* 2, no. 2 (November 1994) 55–78.

_____. *The Faith of the People: Theological Reflections on Popular Catholicism.* Maryknoll, N.Y.: Orbis Books, 1997.

_____, and Sixto J. García. "Hispanic-American Theology." *Proceedings of the Forty-Second Annual Convention, CTSA,* vol. 42, 114–9. Philadelphia, 1987.

_____, and Sixto J. García. "The Sources of Hispanic Theology." *Proceedings of the Forty-Third Annual Convention, CTSA,* vol. 43, 122–5. Toronto, 1988.

_____, and Sixto J. García. "'Lilies of the Field': A Hispanic Theology of Providence and Human Responsibility." *Proceedings of the Forty-Fourth Annual Convention, CTSA,* vol. 44, 70–90. St. Louis, 1989.

_____, and Miguel Díaz, eds. *From the Heart of Our People: Latino/a Explorations in Catholic Systematic Theology.* Maryknoll, N.Y.: Orbis Books, 1999.

Espinoza, Manuel. *Crusaders of the Río Grande.* Chicago: Institute of Jesuit History, 1942.

Estevez, Felipe J. *El Perfil Pastoral de Félix Varela.* Miami: Editorial Universal, 1989.

_____. *Felix Varela, Letters to Elpidio: A Critical Translation.* New York: Paulist Press, 1989.

Fernández, Eduardo C. "Towards a U.S. Hispanic Theology: A Study of a Current Bibliography." S.T.L. thesis, Pontificia Universitá Gregoriana, 1992.

_____. "'Reading the Bible in Spanish': U.S. Catholic Hispanic Theologians' Contributions to Systematic Theology." *Apuntes* 14, no. 3 (fall 1994) 86–90.

_____. "Reflexiones Sobre la Realidad de los Hispanos en los Estados Unidos: Sombras y Luces." *Reflexiones Catequéticas: Encuentro de San*

Antonio, Texas, Julio de 1995. Ed. Roberto Viola, 175–9. Bogotá: Ediciones Paulinas, 1996.

_____. "Seven Tips on the Pastoral Care of Catholics of Mexican Descent in the United States." *Chicago Studies,* vol. 36, no. 3 (December 1997) 255–68.

Fernández, Juanita García. "Latina Garment Workers in El Paso, Texas, Challenging the Urban Underclass Model." Master's thesis, Univ. of Texas at El Paso, 1995.

Fitzpatrick, Joseph P. *One Church, Many Cultures: Challenge of Diversity.* Kansas City, Mo.: Sheed & Ward, 1987.

_____. "The Hispanic Poor in the American Catholic Middle-Class Church." *Thought* 63 (June 1988) 189–200.

Floristán, Casiano. *Teología Práctica: Teoria y Praxis de la Acción Pastoral.* Salamanca: Ediciones Sígueme, 1991.

Friere, Paulo. *The Pedagogy of the Oppressed.* New York: Herder & Herder, 1970.

Fuentes, Carlos. *The Buried Mirror: Reflections on Spain and the New World.* New York: Houghton Mifflin, 1992.

Fung, Jojo. *Shoes-Off Barefoot We Walk: A Theology of Shoes-Off (Theologi Buka Kasut).* Kuala Lumpur: Longman Malaysia SDN. BHD, 1992.

Galerón, Soledad, Rosendo Urrabazo, and Rosa María Icaza, eds., *Prophetic Vision: Pastoral Reflections on the National Plan for Hispanic Ministry.* Kansas City: Sheed & Ward, 1992.

García, Ismael. *Dignidad: Ethics Through Hispanic Eyes.* Nashville: Abingdon Press, 1997.

García, Mario. *Desert Immigrants, The Mexicans of El Paso, 1880–1920.* New Haven, Conn.: Yale Univ. Press, 1981.

García-Rivera, Alex. *St. Martín de Porres: The "Little Stories" and the Semiotics of Culture.* Maryknoll, N.Y.: Orbis Books, 1995.

_____. *The Community of the Beautiful: A Theological Aesthetics.* Collegeville, Minn.: A Michael Glazier Book, The Liturgical Press, 1999.

Geertz, Clifford. *The Interpretation of Cultures.* San Francisco: Basic Books, 1973.

Goizueta, Roberto S. "The History of Suffering as Locus Theologicus in German Political Theology and Latin American Liberation Theology." *Proceedings of the Association of the Scientific Study of Religion: Southwest.* 1985.

_____. *Liberation, Method, and Dialogue.* Atlanta: Scholars Press, 1988.

_____. "Liberation Theology: Retrospect and Prospect." *Philosophy Theology* 3, no. 1 (fall 1988) 25–43.

_____. "The History of Suffering as *Locus Theologicus:* Implications for U.S. Hispanic Theology." *Voices from the Third World: Journal of the Ecumenical Association of Third World Theologians* 12 (December 1989) 32–47.

_____. "Liberating Creation Spirituality." *Listening: Journal of Religion and Culture* 24, no. 2 (spring 1989) 85–115.

_____. "The Church and Hispanics in the United States: From Empowerment to Solidarity." *That They May Live: Power, Empowerment, and Leadership in the Church.* Ed. Michael Downey, 160–75. New York: Crossroad, 1991.

_____. "Theology as Intellectually Vital Inquiry: The Challenge of/to U.S. Hispanics." *Proceedings of the Catholic Theological Society of America* 46 (1991) 58–69.

_____. "*Nosotros:* Toward a U.S. Hispanic Anthropology." *Listening: Journal of Religion and Culture* 27 (winter 1992) 55–69.

_____. "Rediscovering Praxis: The Significance of U.S. Hispanic Experience for Theological Method." *We Are a People! Initiatives in Hispanic American Theology.* Ed. Roberto Goizueta, 51–77. Minneapolis: Fortress Press, 1992.

_____. "U.S. Hispanic Theology and the Challenge of Pluralism." *Frontiers of Hispanic Theology in the United States.* Ed. Allan Figueroa Deck, 1–21. Maryknoll, N.Y.: Orbis Books, 1992.

_____. "U.S. Hispanic *Mestizaje* and Theological Method." Concilium. *International Review of Theology* 4 (1993) 21–30.

_____. "La Raza Cósmica? The Vision of José Vasconcelos." *Journal of Hispanic/Latino Theology* 1, no. 2 (February 1994) 5–27.

_____. *Caminemos con Jesús: Toward a Hispanic/Latino Theology of Accompaniment.* Maryknoll, N.Y.: Orbis Books, 1995.

_____, and María Pilar Aquino. *Theology: Expanding the Borders.* Mystic, Conn.: Twenty-Third Publications, 1998.

_____, ed. *We Are a People! Initiatives in Hispanic American Theology.* Minneapolis: Fortress Press, 1992.

González, Justo L. *The Development of Christianity in the Latin Caribbean.* Grand Rapids: William B. Eerdmans Publishing Co., 1969.

_____. *A History of Christian Thought.* Nashville: Abingdon Press, 1987.

_____. *The Theological Education of Hispanics.* New York: The Fund for Theological Education of Hispanics, 1988.

_____. *Christian Thought Revisited: Three Types of Theology.* Nashville: Abingdon Press, 1989.

_____. *Faith and Wealth: A History of Early Christian Ideas on the Origin, Significance, and Use of Money.* San Francisco: Harper & Row, 1990.

_____. *Mañana: Christian Theology from a Hispanic Perspective.* Nashville: Abingdon Press, 1990.

_____. *Hechos.* Miami: Editorial Caribe, 1992.

_____. *Out of Every Tribe and Nation: Christian Theology at the Ethnic Roundtable.* Nashville: Abingdon Press, 1992.

_____. *Santa Biblia: The Bible Through Hispanic Eyes.* Nashville: Abingdon Press, 1996.

_____, and Catherine G. González. *Liberation Preaching: The Pulpit and the Oppressed.* Nashville: Abingdon Press, 1980.

_____, and Catherine G. González, *The Liberating Pulpit.* Nashville: Abingdon Press, 1994.

_____, ed. *Voces: Voices from the Hispanic Church.* Nashville: Abingdon Press, 1992.

_____, ed. *Alabadle! Hispanic Christian Worship.* Nashville: Abingdon Press, 1996.

González, Roberto O., and Michael La Velle. *The Hispanic Catholic in the United States: A Socio-Cultural and Religious Profile.* New York: Northeast Catholic Pastoral, 1985.

Goodpasture, H. McKennie, ed. *Cross and Sword: An Eyewitness History of Christianity and Latin America.* Maryknoll, N.Y.: Orbis Books, 1989.

Greeley, Andrew. "Editorial Summary." *Ethnicity.* Ed. Andrew M. Greeley and Gregory Baum, 57–9. New York: Seabury Press, 1977.

_____. "Defection Among Hispanics." *America* (July 30, 1988) 61–2.

_____. *The Catholic Myth: The Behavior and Beliefs of American Catholics.* New York: Charles Scribner's Sons, 1990.

Greenleaf, Richard E. *Zumarraga and the Mexican Inquisition, 1536–1543.* Washington: Academy of American Franciscan History, 1962.

_____. *The Mexican Inquisition of the Sixteenth Century.* Albuquerque: Univ. of New Mexico Press, 1969.

_____, ed. *The Roman Catholic Church in Colonial Latin America.* Tempe: Arizona State Univ., 1977.

Griffiths, Nicholas. *The Cross and the Serpent: Religious Repression and Resurgence in Colonial Peru.* Norman: Univ. of Oklahoma Press, 1996.

Groome, Thomas H., and Robert P. Imbelli. "Signposts Towards a Pastoral Theology." *Theological Studies* 53, no. 1 (March 1992) 127–37.

Guerrero, Andrés G. *A Chicano Theology.* Maryknoll, N.Y.: Orbis Books, 1987.

Guerrero, José Luis. *Flor y canto del nacimiento de México.* Mexico: Libreria Parroquial de Clavería, 1990.

Gutiérrez, Gustavo. *On Job: God-Talk and the Suffering of the Innocent.* Trans. Matthew J. O'Connell. Maryknoll, N.Y.: Orbis Books, 1987.

_____. *A Theology of Liberation.* Maryknoll, N.Y.: Orbis Books, 1988.

_____. *Las Casas: In Search of the Poor of Jesus Christ.* Trans. Robert R. Barr. Maryknoll, N.Y.: Orbis Books, 1993.

Haight, Roger. *An Alternate Vision: An Interpretation of Liberation Theology.* New York: Paulist Press, 1985.

Haughey, John C. "Theology and the Mission of the Jesuit College and University." *Conversations* 5 (spring 1994) 5–17.

_____, ed. *The Faith That Does Justice: Examining the Christian Sources for Social Change.* New York: Paulist Press, 1977.

Hayes-Bautista, D. E., A. Hurtado, R. Burciaga Valadez, and A.C.R. Hernández. *No Longer a Minority: Latinos and Social Policy in California.* Los Angeles: UCLA Chicano Studies Research Center, 1992.

_____. *Redefining California: Latino Social Engagement in a Multicultural Society.* Los Angeles: UCLA Chicano Studies Research Center, 1992.

Hemrick, Eugene F. *Strangers and Aliens No Longer,* part 1, *The Hispanic Presence in the Church in the United States.* Washington, D.C.: United States Catholic Conference, 1993.

Herrera, Marina. "La Teología en el Mundo de Hoy." *Páginas Banilejas* (July 1974) Baní, Dominican Republic.

_____. "¿Necesitan las Mujeres Liberación?" *Listín Diario* (June 6, 1975) Santo Domingo, Dominican Republic.

_____. "La Mujer en el ministerio de la Iglesia." *Amigo del Hogar* (March/ April 1977) Santo Domingo, Dominican Republic.

_____. "Madres: Fuentes de Esperanza." *Ultima Hora* (May 28, 1977) Santo Domingo, Dominican Republic.

_____. *Compartiendo la Luz de la Fe.* Department of Education of the United States Catholic Conference, 1978.

_____. "Hispanics in the Church: Issues and Visions." *Military Chaplains' Review* (fall 1978).

_____. "Conference on Native American Catechesis." *Dimensions* (1979).

_____. "A Hispanic Catechetical Project." *Dimensions* (April 1979).

_____. "The Hispanic Challenge." *Religious Education* 74, no. 5 (September/ October 1979).

_____. *Methodology and Themes for Hispanic Catechesis.* Department of Education of the United States Catholic Conference, 1979.

_____. "Proclaiming a Fascinating God." *Dimensions* (summer 1979).

_____. "What Is Multicultural Catechesis." *Dimensions* (March 1979).

_____. "Yearly Series of Columns." *Catechist* (1979–87).

_____. "Catechetical Institutes for Lay Hispanics." *Dimensions* (May/June 1980).

_____. "Catechetics for a Multicultural Society." *Catechist* (April 1980).

_____. "Hispanic Intercultural Ministry Program." *Dimensions* (March/ April 1980).

_____. "'Hispanics' Cultural Riches and Parish Renewal." *Parish* (1980).

_____. "The Multicultural Challenge for Religious Educators." *Dimensions* (January/February 1980).

_____. "Parishes in a Multicultural Society." *Parish Ministry* (July/August 1980). Parish Project of the United States Catholic Conference.

_____. "Pastoral Care in a Multicultural Society." *Camillian, Journal of the National Association of Catholic Chaplains* 19, no. 1 (spring 1980).

_____. "The Religious Education of Hispanics in a Multicultural Church." *New Catholic World* (July/August 1980).

_____. "Vivir la Palabra de Dios." *Living the Word of God* (1980).

_____. "Series of Family Activities and Reflections in Spanish." *Catechist* (1980–82).

_____. "La Palabra de Dios es Espiritu y Vida." *Spirit and Life* (1981).

_____. "Popular Piety as a Parish Resource." *Service* 3 (1981).

_____. *Hablemos del Compadrazgo en la Familia Hispana.* Chicago: Claretian Publications, 1982.

_____. "Hispanics: How Can the Church Respond to Their Presence?" *PACE* 12 (April/May 1982).

_____. "Sharing Scripture with the Non-Print Oriented." *Liturgy* 2, no. 3 (1982).

_____. "Teresa de Avila: Mujer para todos los tiempos." *El Visitante Dominical* (7 November 1982).

_____. "Celebrations for a Multicultural Church." *Momentum Journal of the National Catholic Educational Association* (February 1983).

_____. "Multicultural Adult Catechesis: What Is It and for Whom?" *Christian Adulthood: A Catechetical Resource.* Washington, D.C.: United States Catholic Conference, 1983.

_____. "Toward Multicultural Youth Ministry." *The Journal of Youth Ministry* 1, no. 1 (spring 1983).

_____. *Adult Religious Education for the Hispanic Community.* The National Conference of Diocesan Directors of Religious Education, 1984.

_____. *LASER: Creating Unity in Diversity.* The National Conference for Interracial Justice, 1985.

_____. "Popular Religiosity and Liturgical Education." *Liturgy* 5, no. 1 (1985).

_____. "Religion and Culture in the Hispanic Community as a Context for Religious Education: Impact of Popular Religiosity on U.S. Hispanics." *The Living Light* 21, no. 2 (January 1985).

_____. "Mary of Nazareth in Cross-Cultural Perspective." *PACE* (May 1986).

_____. "Towards Multicultural Youth Ministry." *Readings in Youth Ministry*, vol. 1. National Federation of Catholic Youth Ministry, 1986.

_____. "La devoción mariana en Latinoamérica y en la América del Norte." *Nuevo Amanecer* (August 1, 1987) Brooklyn.

_____. "Theoretical Foundations for Multicultural Catechesis." *Faith and Culture: A Multicultural Catechetical Resource.* Department of Education, United States Catholic Conference, 1987.

_____. "Providence and Histories: One Hispanic's View." The Catholic Theology Society of America, *Proceedings of the Forty-Fourth Annual Convention* 44 (1989) 7–11.

_____. "Catechetical Needs of Hispanics." *Alive in Jesus Manuel.* Boston: Daughters of St. Paul, 1989–90.

_____. "Catechetical Strategies for a Multicultural Church." *Alive in Jesus Manuel.* Boston: Daughters of St. Paul, 1989–90.

_____. "The Context and Development of Hispanic Ecclesial Leadership." *Hispanic Catholic Culture in the U.S.: Issues and Concerns.* Ed. J. P. Dolan and Allan Figueroa Deck, 166–205. Notre Dame, Ind.: Univ. of Notre Dame Press, 1994.

_____, and Elly Murphy. "The Religious Nature of Dance." *Focus on Dance X: Religion and Dance.* Ed. Dennis J. Fallon and Mary Jane Wolbers. Reston, Va. The American Alliance for Health, Physical Education, Recreation, and Dance, 1982.

_____, Thea Bowman, Martin J. Carter, and Jaime R. Vidal, eds. *Pentecost: A Feast for All Peoples: Celebrating the Multicultural/Multiracial Church.* National Catholic Conference for Interracial Justice, 1988.

_____, and Jaime R. Vidal, "Evangelization: Then and Now(?)." *New Theology Review* 3, no. 4 (November 1990) 6–21.

Hiebert, Paul G. *Anthropological Insights for Missionaries.* Grand Rapids: Baker Book House, 1985.

Hill, William J. "Theology." *The New Dictionary of Theology.* Ed. Joseph A. Komonchak and Mary Collins, 1011–27. Wilmington, Del. 1989.

Hinojosa, Juan Lorenzo. "Ministry in a Multicultural Setting." *Resource* 13 (1985).

_____. "Hispanic Spirituality." *Living Faith* 1 no. 23 (1987).

Holland, Clifton L. *The Religious Dimension in Hispanic Los Angeles: A Protestant Case Study.* South Pasadena, Calif.: William Carey Library, 1974.

Holland, Joe, and Peter Henriot. *Social Analysis: Linking Faith and Justice.* Maryknoll, N.Y.: Orbis Books, 1983.

Hopkins, Dwight N. *Shoes That Fit Our Feet: Sources for a Constructive Black Theology.* Maryknoll, N.Y.: Orbis Books, 1993.

Huitrado-Hizo, Juan José. "Hispanic: Popular Religiosity: The Expression of a People Coming to Life." *New Theology Review* 3, no. 4 (November 1990) 43–55.

Icaza, Rosa María. "The Cross in Mexican Popular Piety." *Liturgy* 1, no. 1 (1980) 27–34.

_____. "Spirituality of the Mexican American People." *Worship* 63 (1989) 232–46.

_____. "Prayer, Worship, and Liturgy in a U.S. Hispanic Key." *Frontiers of Hispanic Theology in the United States.* Ed. Allan Figueroa Deck, 134–53. Maryknoll, N.Y.: Orbis Books, 1992.

_____, Soledad Galerón, and Rosendo Urrabazo, eds. *Prophetic Vision: Pastoral Reflections on the National Pastoral Plan for Hispanic Ministry.* Kansas City, Mo.: Sheed & Ward, 1992.

Isasi-Díaz, Ada María. "Silent Women Will Never Be Heard." *Missiology* 7, no. 3 (July 1979) 295–301.

————. "Women in the Ordained Ministry of the Church and Human Liberation." *Women in Dialogue,* 115–9. Ind.: Catholic Committee on Urban Ministry, 1979.

————. "The People of God on the Move—Chronicle of a History." *Prophets Denied Honor.* Ed. Antonio M. Stevens-Arroyo, 330–3. Maryknoll, N.Y.: Orbis Books, 1980.

————. "La Mujer Hispana: Voz Profetica en la Iglesia de los Estados Unidos." *Pro Mundi Vita* (1982). Brussels.

————. "A Liberationist Perspective on Peace and Social Justice." *Education for Peace and Justice.* Ed. Padraic O'Hare, 223–33. San Francisco: Harper & Row, 1983.

————. "Toward an Understanding of Feminismo Hispano in the USA." *Women's Consciousness, Women's Conscience.* Ed. Barbara Hilkert Andolsen and others, 51–61. Winston Press, 1985.

————. "'Apuntes' for a Hispanic Women's Theology of Liberation." *Apuntes* (fall 1986) 61–71.

————. "A Hispanic Garden in a Foreign Land." *Inheriting Our Mothers' Garden.* Ed. Ada María Isasi-Díaz and others. Westminister Press, 1988.

————. "Mujeristas: A Name of Our Own." *The Christian Century* 106, no. 18 (May 24–31, 1989) 560–2.

————. "Mujeristas: A Name of Our Own." *The Future of Liberation Theology.* Ed. Marc H. Ellis and Otto Maduro, 410–9. Maryknoll, N.Y.: Orbis Books, 1989.

————. "A Platform for Original Voices." *Christianity and Crisis* 49, no. 9 (June 12, 1989) 191–2.

————. "The Bible and Mujerista Theology." *Lift Every Voice: Constructing Christian Theologies from the Underside.* Ed. Susan Brooks Thistlethwaite and Mary Potter Engel, 261–9. San Francisco: Harper & Row, 1990.

————. "Solidarity: Love of Neighbor in the 1980's." *Lift Every Voice: Constructing Christian Theologies from the Underside.* Ed. Susan Brooks Thistlethwaite and Mary Potter Engel, 31–40. San Francisco: Harper & Row, 1990.

————. "Hispanic Women in America: Starting Points." *Christianity and Crisis* 51 (May 13, 1991) 150–2.

————. "Hispanic Women in the Roman Catholic Church." *Women and Church—The Challenge of Ecumenical Solidarity in an Age of Alienation.* Ed. Melanie A. May, 13–7. Grand Rapids: William B. Eerdmans Publishing Co., 1991.

————. "'Apuntes' For a Hispanic Women's Theology of Liberation." *Voces—Voices from the Hispanic Church.* Ed. Justo González, 24–31. Nashville: Abingdon Press, 1992.

_____. "*Mujerista* Theology's Method: A Liberative Praxis, A Way of Life." *Listening* 27, no. 1 (winter 1992) 41–54.

_____. "*Mujeristas:* Who Are We and What Are We About." *The Journal of Feminist Studies in Religion* 8, no. 1 (spring 1992) 105–9.

_____. Defining Our *Projecto Histórico: Mujerista* Strategies for Liberation." *Journal of Feminist Studies in Religion* 9, nos. 1–2 (spring/fall 1993) 17–28.

_____. *En La Lucha—In The Struggle: A Hispanic Women's Liberation Theology.* Minneapolis: Fortress Press, 1993.

_____. "On the Birthing Stool." *Women at Worship: Interpretations of North American Diversity.* Ed. Marjorie Procter-Smith and Janet R. Walton, 191–210. Louisville, Ky.: Westminster/John Knox Press, 1993.

_____. "Praxis: The Heart of *Mujerista* Theology." *Journal of Hispanic/Latino Theology* 1, no. 1 (November 1993) 44–55.

_____. *Mujerista Theology: A Theology for the Twenty-First Century.* Maryknoll, N.Y.: Orbis Books, 1996.

_____, and Yolanda Tarango. *Hispanic Women: Prophetic Voice in the Church.* San Francisco: Harper & Row, 1988.

_____, and others, eds. *The Mudflower Collective.* Pilgrim Press, 1985.

Judd, Stephen. "From Lamentation to Project: The Emergence of an Indigenous Theological Movement in Latin America." *Santo Domingo and Beyond: Documents and Commentaries from the Historic Meeting of the Latin American Bishops' Conference.* Ed. Alfred T. Hennelly, 226–35. Maryknoll, N.Y.: Orbis Books, 1993.

Lafaye, Jacques. *Quetzalcóatl and Guadalupe: the Formation of Mexican National Consciousness: 1531–1813.* Trans. Benjamin Keen. Chicago: Univ. of Chicago Press, 1976.

Lehmann, Nicholas. "The Origins of the Underclass." *Atlantic Monthly* (June 1986) 31–55; (July 1986) 54–68.

Leon-Portilla, Miguel, ed. *The Broken Spears; the Aztec Account of the Conquest of Mexico.* Trans. Lysander Kemp. Boston: Beacon Press, 1966.

Lewis, Oscar. *The Children of Sánchez: Autobiography of a Mexican Family.* New York: Random House, 1961.

Loya, Gloria Inés. "The Hispanic Woman: *Pasionaria* and *Pastora* of the Hispanic Community." *Frontiers of Hispanic Theology in the United States.* Ed. Allan Figueroa Deck, 124–33. Maryknoll, N.Y.: Orbis, 1992.

_____. "Hispanic Faith and Culture—and U.S.A. Religious." *Review for Religious* 53, no. 3 (May/June 1994) 460–6.

Luzbetak, Louis J. *The Church and Cultures: New Perspectives in Missiological Anthropology.* Maryknoll, N.Y.: Orbis Books, 1988.

Maduro, Otto. "U.S. Latinos and Religion: An Interview with Otto Maduro." *America* (August 14, 1993) 16–9.

Maldonado, David, Jr., ed. *Protestantes/Protestants: Hispanic Christianity Within Mainline Traditions.* Nashville: Abingdon Press, 1999.

Maldonado, Luis. *Introducción a la religiosidad popular.* Santandar: Sal Terrae, 1985.

Martínez, Dolorita. "Basic Christian Communities: A New Model of Church with the United States Hispanic Community." *New Theology Review* 3, no. 4 (November 1990) 35–42.

Martínez, Germán. "Hispanic Culture and Worship: The Process of Inculturation." *U.S. Catholic Historian* 11, no. 2 (spring 1993) 79–91.

Matovina, Timothy M. "Liturgy and Popular Expressions of Faith: A Look at the Works of Virgil Elizondo." *Worship* 65, no. 5 (1991) 436–44.

McFague, Sallie. *Metaphorical Theology: Models of God in Religious Language.* Philadelphia: Fortress Press, 1982.

Mead, L. M. "The New Politics of the New Poverty." *The Public Interest* 103 (1991) 3–21.

Mexican American Cultural Center. *Faith Expressions of Hispanics in the Southwest: Workshops on Hispanic Liturgy and Popular Piety.* San Antonio, Texas: MACC, 1977.

Miranda, Rosemary, and Chad Richardson. "Magic Valley/Tragic Valley: Mission on the United States-Mexico Border." *International Review of Mission* 78 (April 1989) 202–9.

Montalvo, Hilda S. "Spiritual Direction." *Spirituality Today* 40, no. 2 (1988).

_____. "Through Mary." *Review for Religious* 48, no. 3 (1989).

Moore, Joan, and Raquel Pinderhughes. *In the Barrios.* New York: Russell Sage Foundation, 1993.

Nida, Eugene A., and William D. Reyburn, *Meaning Across Cultures.* Maryknoll, N.Y.: Orbis Books, 1981.

Nilson, J., "Doing Theology by Heart: John S. Dunne's Theological Method." *Theological Studies* 48 (1987) 65–86.

Pedraja, Luis. *Jesus Is My Uncle: Christology from a Hispanic Perspective.* Nashville: Abingdon Press, 1999.

Pérez, Arturo J. "Baptism in the Hispanic Community." *Emmanuel Magazine* 87, no. 2 (February 1981) 77–86.

_____. "Lent: Conversion Liturgy." *Hosana* 1, no. 1 (spring 1983).

_____. *Popular Catholicism.* Washington, D.C.: Pastoral Press, 1988.

_____. "Signs of the Times: Toward a Hispanic Rite, 'Quizás.'" *New Theology Review* 3, no. 4 (November 1990) 80–8.

Pineda, Ana María. "Hispanic Identity." *Church Magazine* 4, no. 4 (winter 1988) 51–5.

_____. "The Hispanic Presence: Hope and Challenge for Catholicity." *New Theology Review* 2, no. 3 (August 1989) 30–6.

_____. "Pastoral de Conjunto." *New Theology Review* 3, no. 4 (November 1990) 28–34.

_____. "Evangelization of the 'New World': A New World Perspective." *Missiology* 20, no. 2 (April 1992) 151–61.

_____. "The Challenge of Hispanic Pluralism in a Hispanic Context." *Missiology* 21 (October 1993) 437–42.

Podles, Leon J., and Mary Elizabeth Podles. "Saint Makers in the Desert." *America* (November 7, 1992) 348–61.

Pomerville, Paul A. *The Third Force in Missions: A Pentecostal Contribution to Contemporary Mission Theology.* Peabody, Mass.: Hendrickson Publishers, 1985.

Privett, Stephen A. *The U.S. Catholic Church and Its Hispanic Members: The Pastoral Vision of Archbishop Robert E. Lucey.* San Antonio: Trinity Univ. Press, 1988.

Prophets of Hope Editorial Team. *Hispanic Young People and the Church's Pastoral Response.* Prophets of Hope. Vol. 1. Winona, Minn.: Saint Mary's Press, 1994.

_____. *Evangelization of Hispanic Young People.* Prophets of Hope. Vol. 2. Winona, Minn.: Saint Mary's Press, 1994.

Radford Ruether, Rosemary. "Ecumenism in Central America." *Christianity and Crisis* 49, no. 10 (July 10, 1989) 208–12.

Rahner, Karl. "Towards a Fundamental Interpretation of Vatican II." *African Ecclesial Review* 22, no. 6 (1980) 323–34.

Ramírez, Ricardo. *Fiesta, Worship, and Family: Essays on Mexican American Perception on Liturgy and Family Life.* San Antonio: Mexican American Cultural Center, 1981.

Recinos, Harold. *Hear the Cry! A Latino Pastor Challenges the Church.* Louisville, Ky.: Westminster/John Knox Press, 1989.

_____. *Jesus Weeps: Global Encounters on Our Doorstep.* Nashville: Abingdon Press, 1992.

_____. *Who Comes in the Name of the Lord? Jesus at the Margins.* Nashville: Abingdon Press, 1997.

Ricard, Robert. *The Spiritual Conquest of Mexico: An Essay on the Apostolate and the Evangelizing Methods of the Mendicant Orders in New Spain: 1523–1572.* Trans. Lesley Byrd Simpson. Berkeley: Univ. of California Press, 1988.

Riebe-Estrella, Gary. "'Underneath' Hispanic Vocations." *New Theology Review* 3, no. 4 (November 1990) 72–9.

_____. "La Formación Sacerdotal de los Hispanos en Los Estados Unidos: Estudio de los seminarios mayores norteamericanos del oeste y suroeste en los años 1965–1990." S.T.D. diss., Universidad Pontifícia de Salamanca, 1992.

Rodríguez, José David, and Loida I. Martell-Otero, eds. *Teología en Conjunto: A Collaborative Hispanic Protestant Theology.* Louisville, Ky.: Westminster/John Knox Press, 1997.

Rodríguez, Edmundo. "Realities for Hispanics." *Company* 6 (Chicago 1988) 8–10.

_____. "The Hispanic Community and Church Movements: Schools of Leadership." *Hispanic Catholic Culture in the U.S.: Issues and Concerns.* Ed. Jay P. Dolan and Allan Figueroa Deck, 206–39. Notre Dame, Ind.: Univ. of Notre Dame Press, 1994.

Rodríguez, Jeanette. *Our Lady of Guadalupe: Faith and Empowerment among Mexican-American Women.* Austin: Univ. of Texas Press, 1994.

_____. *Stories We Live, Cuentos Que Vivimos: Hispanic Women's Spirituality.* New York and Mahwah, N.J.: Paulist Press, 1996.

_____. "U.S. Hispanic/Latino Theology: Context and Challenge." *Journal of Hispanic/Latino Theology* 5, no. 3 (February 1998) 6–15.

Roest Crollius, Arij. "Seeking Community: The Common Search of Various Faiths, Cultures, and Ideologies." *Towards a Dialogue of Life: Ecumenism in the Asian Context.* Ed. P.S. de Achutegui, 51–61. Manila: Card. Bea Institute, 1976.

_____. "What Is So New About Inculturation?" *Gregorianum* 59 (1978) 721–38.

_____. "Inculturation and the Meaning of Culture." *Gregorianum* 61 (1980) 253–74.

_____. "Jacques Maritain e le culture mediterranee." *Jacques Maritain protagonista del XX secolo,* 183–9. Milano: Massimo, 1984.

_____. "Inculturation: from Babel to Pentecost." *Creative Inculturation and the Unity of Faith (Inculturation IX)* 1–7. Rome: PUG, 1986.

_____. "Societies, Cultures, and Values." *Nouvelles-CICIAMS* 2–3 (1990) 78–92.

_____, and Theoneste Nkéramihigo. *What Is So New About Inculturation?* Rome: Editrice PUG, 1991.

Romero, C. Gilbert. "Teología de las raices de un Pueblo: 'Los Penitentes de Nuevo México.'" *Servir* 15. Mexico. (1979) 609–30.

_____. "On Choosing a Symbol System for a Hispanic Theology." *Apuntes* 1, no. 4 (1981) 16–20.

_____. "Self-Affirmation of the Hispanic Church." *The Ecumenist* 23, no. 3 (March/April 1985) 39–42.

_____. *Hispanic Devotional Piety: Tracing the Biblical Roots.* Maryknoll, N.Y.: Orbis Books, 1991.

_____. "Tradition and Symbol as Biblical Keys for a U.S. Hispanic Theology." *Frontiers of Hispanic Theology in the United States.* Ed. Allan Figueroa Deck, 41–61. Maryknoll, N.Y.: Orbis Books, 1992.

Ruiz, Jean-Pierre. "Beginning to Read the Bible in Spanish: An Initial Assessment." *Journal of Hispanic/Latino Theology* 1, no. 2 (February 1994) 28–50.

Sandidge, Jerry L. "Contextualizing Roman Catholicism." *Evangelical Review of Theology* 13, no. 2 (April 1989) 157–66.

_____. "El Campesino hispano y las iglesias en los Estados Unidos." *Cristianismo y Sociedad* 96 (1988) 7–19.

_____. *On the Move: A History of the Hispanic Church in the United States.* Maryknoll, N.Y.: Orbis Books, 1990.

Sandoval, Moises, ed. *Fronteras: A History of the Latin American Church in the USA since 1513.* San Antonio: MACC, 1983.

Sanks, T. Howland. "David Tracy's Theological Project: An Overview and Some Implications." *Theological Studies* 54, no. 4 (1993) 698–727.

Saranyana, Josep Ignasi. *El Quinto Centenario en clave teológica (1493–1993).* Pamplona: Ediciones EUNATE, 1993.

Scherer, James A., and Stephen B. Bevans, eds. *New Directions in Mission and Evangelization 1, Basic Statements, 1974–1991.* Maryknoll, N.Y.: Orbis Books, 1992.

Schick, Frank L., and Renee Schick, eds. *Statistical Handbook on U.S. Hispanics.* Phoenix: Oryx Press, 1991.

Schineller, Peter. *A Handbook of Inculturation.* New York: Paulist Press, 1990.

Schreiter, Robert J. *Constructing Local Theologies.* Maryknoll, N.Y.: Orbis Books, 1985.

_____. The New Catholicity: *Theology Between the Global and the Global.* Maryknoll, N.Y.: Orbis Books, 1997.

Segovia, Fernando F. "A New Manifest Destiny: The Emerging Theological Voice of Hispanic Americans." *Religious Studies Review* 17 no. 2 (April 1991) 102–9.

_____. "Reading the Bible as Hispanic Americans." *The New Interpreter's Bible.* Vol. 1. Ed. Leander F. Keck and others, 167–73. Nashville: Abingdon Press, 1994.

Segundo, Juan Luis. *The Liberation of Theology.* Maryknoll, N.Y.: Orbis Books, 1976.

Shea, John. "Reflections on Ethnic Consciousness and Religious Language." *Ethnicity.* Ed. Andrew M. Greeley and Gregory Baum, 85–90. New York: Seabury Press, 1977.

Shorter, Aylward. *Toward a Theology of Inculturation.* Maryknoll, N.Y.: Orbis Books, 1988.

Simpson, John. "Ethnic Groups and American Church Attendance in the United States and Canada." *Ethnicity.* Ed. Andrew M. Greeley and Gregory Baum, 57–9. New York: Seabury Press, 1977.

Smith, Huston. *The World's Religions.* San Francisco: HarperCollins, 1991.

Solivan, Samuel. *The Spirit, Pathos, and Liberation.* Sheffield, Eng.: Sheffield Academic Press, 1998.

Spittler, Russell P. "Implicit Values in Pentecostal Missions." *Misssiology: An International Review* 16 no. 4 (October 1988) 409–24.

Starkloff, Carl F. "Inculturation and Cultural Systems—Part 1." *Theological Studies* 55, no. 1 (1994) 66–81.

_____. "Inculturation and Cultural Systems—Part 2." *Theological Studies* 55, no. 2 (1994) 274–94.

Stevens-Arroyo, Antonio M., ed. *Prophets Denied Honor: An Anthology of the Hispano Church of the United States.* Maryknoll, N.Y.: Orbis Books, 1980.

_____, and Ana María Díaz-Stevens, eds. *An Enduring Flame: Studies on Latino Popular Religiosity.* New York: Bildner Center for Western Hemisphere Studies, 1994.

Stravinska, Peter, "Proselytism Among Today's Immigrants: A Preliminary Report." Washington, D.C.: Bishops' Committee on Migration, February 1987.

Swidler, Leonard. *After the Absolute: The Dialogical Future of Religious Reflection.* Minneapolis: Fortress Press, 1990.

Tarango, Yolanda. "The Church Struggling to Be Universal: A Mexican American Perspective." *International Review of Mission* 78 (April 1989) 167–73.

_____. "The Hispanic Woman and Her Role in the Church." *New Theology Review* 3, no. 4 (November 1990) 56–61.

Timmons, W. H. *El Paso: A Borderlands History.* El Paso: Texas Western Press, 1990.

Tracy, David. *The Achievement of Bernard Lonergan.* New York: Herder & Herder, 1970.

_____. "Ethnic Pluralism and Systematic Theology: Reflections." *Ethnicity.* Ed. Andrew M. Greeley and Gregory Baum, 91–9. New York: Seabury Press, 1977.

_____. *The Analogical Imagination: Christian Theology and the Culture of Pluralism.* New York: Crossroad, 1981.

_____. "The Uneasy Alliance Reconceived: Catholic Theological Method, Modernity, and Postmodernity." *Theological Studies* 50 (1989) 548–70.

Traverzo Galarza, David. "The Emergence of a Latino Social Ethic in the Work and Thought of Orlando E. Costas: An Ethico-Theological Discourse from the Underside of History," Ph.D. diss., Drew Univ., May 1992.

_____. "Sin: A Hispanic Perspective," *Teologia en Conjunto.* Ed. José David Rodríguez and Loida I. Martell-Otero, 112–24. Louisville, Ky.: Westminster/John Knox Press, 1997.

Treutlein, Theodore Edward. "Non-Spanish Jesuits in Spain's American Colonies." *Greater America: Essays in Honor of Herbert Eugene Bolton.* Ed. Adele Hogden and Engel Sluiter, 219–42. Berkeley: Univ. of California Press, 1945.

Turner, Frederick W. *Beyond Geography: The Western Spirit Against Wilderness.* New York: Viking Press, 1980.

Urrabazo, Rosendo. *Machismo: Mexican American Male Self-Concept.* San Antonio: Mexican American Cultural Center, 1986.

U.S. Census Bureau. *The Hispanic Population in the United States: March 1991.* Washington, D.C.: U.S. Department of Commerce, 1991.

Valentin, Benjamin. "Nuevos Odres para el Vino: A Critical Contribution to Latino/a Theological Construction," *Journal of Hispanic/Latino Theology* 5, no. 4 (May 1998) 30–47.

Vidal, Jaime R. "Popular Religion in the Lands of the Origin of New York's Hispanic Population." *Hispanics in New York: Religious, Cultural, and Social Experiences* 2, 1–48. New York: Office of Pastoral Research of the Archdiocese of New York, 1982.

_____. "Popular Religion Among the Hispanics in the General Area of the Archdiocese of Newark." *Presencia Nueva: A Study of Hispanics in the Archdiocese of Newark.* 235–352. Newark, N.J.: Office of Research and Planning, 1988.

_____. "The American Church and the Puerto Rican People." *U.S. Catholic Historian* 9, nos. 1 and 2 (winter/spring 1990) 119–35.

_____. "Towards an Understanding of Synthesis in Iberian Hispanic American Popular Religiosity." *An Enduring Flame: Studies on Latino Popular Religiosity.* Ed. A. M. Isasi-Díaz and A. M. Stevens-Arroyo, 69–95. New York: Bildner Center for Western Hemisphere Studies, 1994.

_____. "Hispanic Catholics in America." *Encyclopedia of American Catholic History.* Ed. Michael Glazier and Thomas J. Shelley, 635–42. Collegeville: The Liturgical Press, 1998.

_____, and J. Dolan, eds., *Puerto Rican and Cuban Catholics in the U.S., 1900–1965.* Notre Dame, Ind.: Univ. of Notre Dame Press, 1994.

Villafañe, Eldin. *The Liberating Spirit: Toward an Hispanic American Pentecostal Ethic.* Grand Rapids: William B. Eerdmans Publishing Co., 1993.

Weber, David J. *Myth and the History of the Hispanic Southwest.* Albuquerque: Univ. of New Mexico Press, 1988.

Zapata, Dominga M. "Ministries Among Hispanics in the United States: Development and Challenges." *New Theology Review* 3, no. 1 (November 1990) 62–71.

Index

201